Lifestyle Choices

Luke Pomery

Lifestyle Choices

Author's Note

This memoir is my version of some of my life. There are parts of my story which have been left out. The lifestyle choices I made as a young adult were to some extent the result of my upbringing. There was no reason or explanation for some of the things I experienced, and I never got a chance to say a word in defence of myself because I was always wrong.

Some of the situations I had to face along the way were tough; some of them may be hard to believe. Many times throughout my life when times were tough, I was sure that I would wake up to discover that everything was just a dream. My past is unforgettable, and this has made me the person I am today.

Lifestyle Choices
ISBN 978 1 76109 579 5
Copyright © text Luke Pomery 2023

First published 2023 by
GINNINDERRA PRESS
PO Box 3461 Port Adelaide 5015
www.ginninderrapress.com.au

Contents

Prologue	7
1 Recollections	11
2 Monarto South	24
3 Numbulwar Life	33
4 Western Australia	39
5 First Light	49
6 Mustering Time	61
7 Boarding School	72
8 Showers	79
9 Thirty-three and a Third	90
10 Christmas Holidays	104
11 Drought	124
12 Flat Battery	140
13 Bidjid	145
14 Roper Bar	152
15 Solo Trek	165
16 Thoughtless Act	172
17 Bryce Returns	181
18 Father's Place	198
19 Geraldton	204
20 Squatters	217
21 Bob	226
22 Bush Humpy	232
23 Rod's Jobs	243
24 Stormy Night	247
25 Take Two	257

26 River Rat	263
27 Bibbulmun Track	266
28 Lost Campsite	277
29 Adelaide	284
Epilogue	288
About the Author	295

Prologue

Morning sunshine pours through the visor of my helmet, gently warming my face as I ride east along the South Eastern Freeway in the Adelaide Hills of South Australia. A few minutes later, I am heading into a valley, past old familiar landmarks, places from my childhood nearly forty years earlier, when I was seven years old.

I glance down to where the Dawesley Creek flows through the valley of Aclare, at the farm we once owned. On the property there is an abandoned mineshaft cut into the hill and there stands a smelter stack, which was built sometime around the turn of the last century, along with the remains of some ruins and a few mounds of refined soil. The old smelter stack still towers over everything surrounding it apart from the hillside in the background. I try to catch a glimpse of the entrance of the crumbling mineshaft, but it is too far from the freeway to make heads or tails of anything. Travelling at 110 kilometres an hour on a motorbike doesn't help either.

I remember how much I enjoyed myself, white-water rafting over the slimy rocks in the creek on a big chunk of styrofoam with Bryce and Bidjid, my two older siblings.

Another thought flashed in front of me quickly, of the old wooden dinghy father got. It leaked like a sieve and we had to rapidly bucket water out of it just to stay afloat. The only time I can recall it ever making its way into the water, it nearly capsized as the gallons of water that it was taking on inside the hull swayed from one side to the other when we all frantically tried climbing in it all at the same time, as a red-bellied black snake came swimming towards us. I remember looking over my shoulder while I clung to the side of the boat (because I couldn't really confidently swim far) and the snake gracefully glided along the top effortlessly. Bryce and Bidjid raced to the side and Mum, who was in the boat already, came to my aid.

Several minutes later, the turn-off to Monarto comes into view and images of the farm we used to own there at the same time as the Aclare property mix together with the ones already in my mind. I have been dying to revisit these properties for more than forty years.

On my way home from Murray Bridge, with plenty of time still up my sleeve, I approach the Monarto exit once again. This time, though, I decide to pull off the freeway onto Ferries McDonald Road to head over to our old farm. I make my way over to the intersection of the Old Princes Highway and turn right onto the highway before shortly turning left at the next intersection onto Schenscher Road. Now sealed, it was just a dirt road back in the 1980s and I take in that and all the changes around me.

Marg's old farm now looks like a run-down ruin and, directly across the road from her place, there is the old sporting complex that my father used to maintain when we lived out here. When we were kids, we used the barbecues there to cook chops and sausages, using washers as the payment token. Shortly afterwards, I approach our old farm and a sign on the gate catches my eye. It is written in Adnyamathanha, the language from the Flinders Ranges: *Wildu Mandawi*, meaning Eagle's Foot.

I try to take in as much as I can without slowing down, before continuing for about a kilometre further to make a U-turn at the spot where I used to catch the bus to school with Bryce and Bidjid. As I idle past the old church and cemetery, I think about how we sometimes used to hang around here after school. It was always peaceful reading the names on the tombstones of the people long gone but not entirely forgotten.

After a few seconds, I hit the accelerator and head back towards the farm, where I pull over on the side of the road a short distance from the house, so as not to be intrusive to the current owners. Switching off the engine, I gaze across the paddocks, a beautiful unchanged landscape of dry tea tree scrub scattered among a loose limestone surface.

I turn my head and focus on the exact spot where we used to light open fires. This is where I ate shingleback and blue-tongue lizards with Bryce and Bidjid. I drift off, lost in the memories.

There is still the same small thicket of trees along the fence line, and a few rocks and fallen trees where we often played in the trees. Sometimes they were guarded by spitfire caterpillars and I can see the three of us, all armed with long sticks, poking them – their goop, a thick yellowish mustard, would be regurgitated from their mouths and we'd be laughing, trying not to get any of it on us.

'Dinner's ready!'

A hollering voice breaks my concentration. It is coming from the direction of the farmhouse and sounds just like Mum calling out to us. I turn around quickly and catch a glimpse of a couple of kids racing through the flat. They are roughly the same ages as we were when we lived here, about six to eight years old. The smell of Mum's spaghetti bolognese fills the air. Whenever Mum made it, the whole house would fill with the smell of tomatoes, browned onions and spicy mince. I inhale deeply, recalling her placing the steaming bowls of pasta on the kitchen table in front of us.

'There's plenty more if you want seconds,' Mum would often say with a loving smile on her face.

A movement near the old chook shed, nestled among a dense patch of prickly pear, catches my attention. Someone is picking mulberries from the same bush we used to get them from as kids. They look up, and I raise my hand and wave. Warily, they wave back. I lower my hand, make a clenched fist and give them the thumbs up. But the person just scratches their head, puzzled as to who I am and to what I'm doing.

I continue to lower my hand onto the handlebars. It is time to head home. I push the start button and give a couple of short revs of the engine. Checking over my left shoulder, I look back at the house once more before zooming off.

As I ride on, more memories flood to the surface. Some have been locked away for decades; so many things I had completely forgotten about. Half an hour later, I pull into my garage and, without a moment's thought, I race inside and start jotting them down.

This is my story.

1

Recollections

Midsummer, 1993. It is another scorching hot day, roughly forty-five degrees Celsius. It is like this at this time of the year up in the Gascoyne region of Western Australia. There is not a cloud in the sky, even though on the news the night before, the weather reporter said, 'Thunderstorms are to be expected around midday in the upper Gascoyne and lower Pilbara regions tomorrow. This should bring relief to those pastoralists struggling with this hot weather in those area at the moment.' Something we heard way too often and rarely did the forecasts eventuate.

Father, Bryce, Dansan, Loui and I are near a windmill called Cement Tank in the northern part of the station. It is about forty kilometres north of the Moolapool homestead. We are working on a broken fence line that has been destroyed by feral goats. Dansan and Loui help my father while Bryce and I are putting a few figure eights into the broken wires a little further up the fence.

'Here, Dansan,' Father instructs, passing Dansan his cigarette lighter. 'You and Loui go and gather some firewood from over there and light a fire. Oh, and whack the billy on while you're at it. We'll all stop for lunch once it's boiled.'

They both race off towards a few dry mulga branches and drag them towards a shady tree not far from the Hilux.

Dansan soon has a fire lit and the billy is on. 'Billy's boiled,' he yells out several minutes later.

We put the pliers, post-splitting hammers and wire strainers under the shade of a couple of dense turpentine bushes and make our way over to the Hilux for lunch.

'Grab those chops out of the esky and fry them up on the shovel,' Father instructs Bryce as he reaches into the Hilux and turns up the radio to listen to the midday news, before sitting down in the shade.

Dansan grabs himself a cup and fills it with billy tea then goes to sit down in the shade, but before he gets half a chance, Father asks him to pour him a cup of tea too. Dansan places his cup down in the shade where he intends to sit when he returns and goes in search of another cup for Father.

Meanwhile, Loui flops down and while getting himself comfortable, he knocks Dansan's tea over. He quickly manages to save a quarter of his cup for him but Dansan is not impressed when he returns. He kicks dirt up into Loui's cup. Dansan sits down and they both jab each other in the ribs and it's getting a little rough so Father cuts them off.

'Dansan! That's enough,' he growls.

Everyone sits in silence for the next couple of minutes finishing off their lunch while listening to the radio.

'Is there any more tea in the billy?' Father asks.

'No, there isn't. That's why I was angry with Loui for, for knocking over my cup,' Dansan whinges.

'Arrrr, I see,' Father replies.

After lunch, something on the radio starts Father talking about who of us was the first to walk. He praises Loui for taking his first steps when he was just seven months old. But I was another story.

Father begins, 'We were living at Stonefield at the time. That was well and truly before you two little boys,' Father adds as he smiles warmly at Dansan and Loui.

'You were just too lazy to walk by yourself until you were well over eighteen months old. Whenever you wanted to go anywhere, you would scream your bloody head off and throw your arms high above your head, so your useless mother' (as he always referred to our mum) 'would pick you up and carry you around everywhere.'

Everyone laughs except for Father, who glares at me. 'Eventually, when I was thoroughly fed up with you carrying on,' he continued, 'I thought to myself, I got to do something about you, so this is how I managed to get you to walk. I stood behind you and got you to stand up in front of me. Then I told you to start walking. I would have my hands ready on either side of your head in case you wanted to plop back down on your arse. Then I'd quickly grab you and pull you back up to your feet by your ears. Finally, you got the message and started to walk by yourself.'

'So that's why you always have a thing about our ears?' I ask.

'Yeah, more than likely. Though I never thought about it until you mentioned it. What else do you and Bryce remember about Stonefield?' Father then asks us.

'Ummm, a few things,' I say.

'We had an old Stout ute, didn't we?' Bryce asks.

'Yeah, it was green, wasn't it?' I add.

'That's right. Anything else?'

'There were a couple of underground stone water tanks. The corrugated-iron cover on one of them had collapsed into the tank because the logs across the top had rotted away,' Bryce and I say at the same time, practically word for word.

Father nods a few times and produces a flat smile. 'There was a pigsty across the driveway not far away from the house where we found Bidjid one night, after she slipped away from the rest of us, to spend time with the pigs as she often did. And a big shed right next to the house, and the time you made a dam out in one of the paddocks.'

I look into the distance, trying to recall more, while Bryce shares more of what he remembers. Father scratches the side of his chin with his left hand and nods slowly as we continue recounting our memories of Stonefield.

'Shit, you boys have a good memory, things are coming back to me now,' Father says. 'Not long after I finished making that dam, it rained solidly for about a week. It drove your mother and I bonkers with you three kids stuck inside and climbing the walls with boredom. When it finally cleared up, you, Bryce, Bidjid and I went out to see how full the dam was.'

'Yeah, I remember. Water was still trickling in from the little valley and overflowing out the other side,' Bryce responds.

'It's like it was yesterday,' Father says. 'What gets me is how lucky we all were that day. If we had still been in the dam when it lost all its water down that sinkhole, we'd have died for sure.'

And we were indeed lucky.

Early December 1979. I am four and a half years old and it has been raining hard for days. Bryce, Bidjid and I are standing on the front porch of the property with Father, watching the sun finally breaking through the mid-morning clouds.

'Who wants to come out to look at the dam with me?' Father asks as he walks out into the alluring sunshine.

'Can we please come with you please, Dad?' we all reply in unison.*

'Yeah all right, come on.'

We race behind him, making our way out to the old green Stout ute. We climb up onto the wooden tray and hang onto the timber railing behind the cab as Mum comes out the front to see us off.

'You kids listen to your father,' she yells from the front door.

'Argh, they'll be all right, you really got to stop being overprotective,' Father replies as he starts the engine.

A few minutes later, we are pulling up at the dam and, to our delight, it is full to the brim. We climb down from the back of the tray and follow Father. He then takes off his shirt and throws it down on the bank before wading out into the water. I follow Bryce and Bidjid into the water until it is too deep for us to continue, and Bryce turns around suddenly and splashes water up at us.

---

* Why we chose 'Father' over 'Dad': during the early 1980s Bryce, Bidjid and I are sitting in the lounge room at Monarto. We are worried about Father because things are going pear-shaped between Mum and him and the thought of losing him worries us. He is our hero. We decide to call him 'Father' because 'Dad' sounds too much like 'dead' – he's been Father ever since, well, for me at least, even though the others now call him Dad.

'Don't!' we yell at him angrily and splash back.

'Wow, it's deeper than I expected,' Father yells back above the noise of our splashing.

We can see Father is thoroughly impressed with his achievement now standing with water coming up to his shoulders. He is about 1.88 metres tall, so the water must have been around 1.6 metres deep.

We splash around for a while, making the most of it.

After a while, Father gets out and stands on the edge of the dam to watch us. 'Come on, kids,' he says after a few minutes. 'Uncle Dan should be arriving any minute. We can come back out with him later.'

A couple of hours later, just before midday, Uncle Dan, who's Father's brother, pulls up out the front of our house and we all go out to greet him.

'G'day, Dan. You found the place all right then?' Father asks.

'Yeah. Neil. I missed the turn-off a couple of times,' Dan says.'The number out the front of your property is impossible to see, so I ended up asking a farmer working on his boundary fence just down the road if he knew you lot, and he pointed me in the right direction.'

Father and Uncle Dan shake hands as Uncle turns to Mum, giving her a big hug and looking over her shoulder at us kids.

'Wow, look at you three! You've sprouted up since the last time I seen you all. It's really great to see you again,' Uncle exclaims while patting us on the back of our shoulders.

'You want a cuppa tea, Dan?' Mum asks.

'I'd love one, thanks, Shirl.'

Uncle Dan reaches into the car and opens the centre console and pulls out a block of Cadbury's Snack chocolate and hands it to Bryce.

'Share this up between you three, okay, mate?'

'Thank you, Uncle Dan,' we say as we retreat inside to the lounge room.

Father and Uncle Dan follow us, find a spot at the kitchen table, and wait for Mum, who grabs the teapot from the wood stove and pours them both a cup each.

'Sugar or milk?' she asks Uncle Dan.

'No sugar, just a splash of milk thanks, Shirl.'

Father and Uncle Dan have a good chat, catching up on what everyone else is doing in their family.

'Right then!' Father says as he stands.

'Thanks for the tea, Shirl. That was the best cuppa I've had in donkey's years,' Uncle Dan smiles as he also rises from his chair.

'You're welcome, Dan,' Mum quickly replies.

Mum scoops up their cups from the table and places them on the kitchen counter as we rejoin them before following everyone outside.

Some pigs grunting over in the pigsty catch Dan's attention and he turns to face us. 'You get many piglets this year?' he asks.

'Yeah, there are a few sows over there that have had a few sets of piglets and one sow recently gave birth to seven. Bidjid spends quite a lot of time playing with them – whenever she can. I'm sure she'd rather be a pig herself,' Father chuffs as he scruffs her hair around. 'Come and check out the dam I built, Dan. The rain we've had over the past week has topped it right up.'

'I'll make some sandwiches for lunch and wrap them up to keep them fresh for when you guys return,' Mum says.

We all head over to the Stout, apart from Mum, who sees us off as us kids clamber back onto the tray. But out at the dam again we soon realise that things don't look quite the same as they did a couple of hours earlier.

'What the hell's happened here? One of the banks must have blown out or something,' Father hollers as we pull up alongside the dam.

The dam has already started drying up. Already there are mud plates forming as the sun continues drying the silt left in the bottom.

'I thought you said it was full of water, Neil?' Uncle looks quizzically at Father. 'Looks to me like it's been empty for quite some time.'

Father massages the back of his neck. 'It was full just a couple of hours ago, I swear, wasn't it, kids?'

'Yeah, it was,' we all agree enthusiastically.

'Hang on. What's that over there?' Father says. He points to the middle of the dam.

Just off to the centre is a hole big enough to fit a small car. I climb down from the Stout and follow the others to what earlier was the edge of the water. Puzzled, I gaze across to the dry hole in front of me. I am still confused when I follow Bryce and Bidjid out to take a proper look.

'Hey, you three, you better not go too close. Gee, it's bloody lucky this never happened when we were all swimming around in here earlier,' Father says.

'What happened to all the water, Dad?' Bryce asks.

Father explains that it has drained down into the sinkhole. He turns towards Uncle Dan and they shake their heads back and forth. They both have wry smiles on their faces.

'What do you reckon it could be, Neil? An underground creek perhaps? Who knows where you all would have ended up or if you'd ever have been seen again.' Uncle Dan shoots Father a concerned look.

'Oh well, that's the end of that then, I guess. C'arn, kids, there's nothing much more to see here, we may as well get going home for some lunch,' Father says.

When we get back to the farmhouse, Mum rushes out the door, concerned that something bad has happened to one of us. She always babies us, even though by now we are between the ages of four and six. 'Is everything okay? I wasn't expecting you back so soon,' she says with a look of concern.

Father tells her about the dam. 'It's completely emptied out – bone dry. There's not a drop of water left in there,' he says, exasperated. He turns to Uncle Dan for confirmation.

'It's true. They're extremely lucky that it never drained out while they were swimming in it,' Dan says.

Mum gives us kids a big hug, almost squashing the air out of our lungs, and showers us with kisses. Back inside, we tuck into the sandwiches she has already started preparing.

In the later part of the afternoon, after Uncle Dan has left, we go out into the back room to play. We are rolling a tennis ball back and forth when a large brown snake slithers in and hides beneath the fridge. We are not too bothered about this visitor and continue rolling the ball back and forth until it rolls under the fridge.

'Maaarm…Marm,' Bryce yells.

'What's all this yelling going on in here?' Mum asks.

'Ball, ball.'

We point towards the bottom of the fridge.

'You can get it out yourself,' Mum huffs. She turns round to go back to what she was doing.

'Nooooo, nake in derr!' we all shout before she gets a chance to leave.

That is when Mum notices the tail of the snake slithering further under the fridge. She freezes. 'Neil, come quickly! There's a snake under the fridge. Quickly, you three, come out of there.' Mum's hysterical as she escorts us from the room.

Meanwhile, Father turns up with a broom. There are a few loud thumps, then silence.

A couple of minutes later, he comes out, looking all heroic. 'It's been taken care of. Iit's all safe in there now. Just remember to keep the back door shut from now on,' he instructs.

'What did you do with the nake, Dad?' Bryce asks.

'It's pronounced ss..nnn..ake, snake, Bryce, not nake. Snake! Once I realised it was just a harmless carpet python, I threw a towel over its head and took it outside to the rainwater tanks,' Father explained. After all, they're not venomous. Carpet pythons are only looking for mice and rats to eat. They won't hurt you. Shirl, can you take those vegetable scraps out to the pigs? Give plenty to that sow who recently had a litter,' Father instructs, before he heads back to his chores.

'Who wants to help me feed the pigs?' Mum asks.

We do. Mum picks up the bucket of scraps and we follow her out the door. Bidjid is fascinated by the piglets and within seconds she is in the yard, pushing the piglets around in the mud and acting as if she's a piglet herself.

The following evening, just on dusk, Mum can't find Bidjid anywhere. She asks Father if he has seen her.

'Isn't she playing with the boys?' Father answers, looking over at Bryce and me playing in the bedroom.

'Bryce, is Bidjid in there with you and Luke?'

'No, Dad. I don't know where she is,' Bryce replies.

Father stands up, comes over to the doorway and issues our orders. 'Shirl, you check the pigsty. She's been over there quite a bit lately. I'll check the underground tanks. Come on, Bryce, you're coming with me. Luke, you go with your mother.'

'Bidjid! Bidjid,' Mum yells.

'Bid jeed, Bid jeed,' I yell at the top of my toddler lungs as I follow behind Mum, who is carrying the kerosene lamp to light the way.

We search all around the pigsty while calling out her name, but there is no reply. All we can hear is the pigs grunting. In the distance, Father and Bryce are calling out behind the house near the underground tanks. Mum and I are walking past the front of the pigsty one final time when Mum suddenly stops and starts counting the piglets out loud. She holds her hand up to block out the glare coming from the lamp so she can get a better look into the sty. She counts the piglets curled up with their mum once again.

Suddenly she is frantic and calls Father over. 'Neil, Neil, come here quickly,' she calls.

Father and Bryce come rushing over from behind the house.

'Don't we have seven piglets in this pen? I count eight in here, though. Take a look at that one there, third from the end there, all tucked up,' Mum says, pointing. 'Could that be Bidjid?'

Father focuses on the darkness in the pigsty. 'Ha ha, yeah, that's her all right,' he says, relieved. Passing his lamp to Mum, he climbs quietly over the fence so as not to disturb the sow. Gently he pulls Bidjid out.

She is still sucking on the sow's teat, so Father sticks his finger into her mouth to release the suction. Eventually, she lets go.

Everyone is relieved and we all go back to the house, where Bidjid earns herself a serious bath to wash off the mud and pig shit.

Towards the end of 1979, we move from Stonefield to the city of Adelaide. Our place is at Birkenhead, near Port Adelaide. By this stage, Father is in the police force and he has been assigned to a suburban police station. He also plays a brief role in one of South Australia's budget movies. It is the first attempt to bring Aboriginal music into the modern world.

The movie opens with a scene at the Port Adelaide Hall where Aboriginal bands are performing. There is commotion inside and Father's character is sent in to break it up. Later, there is another clip of him speeding off in a police vehicle to pull over a small furniture truck that has just left the concert. He asks the driver to open the back of the truck to inspect the cargo. And that there is my father's fifteen seconds of fame.

We stay for a few months in Birkenhead while Father organises to have another house built in the neighbouring suburb, Exeter, in which he also partakes in laying a few bricks.

Living in the city is very different to how our days were back out at the farm. The most amazing thing is how the road over the Port River's Gawler Reach at the Birkenhead Bridge crossing rises to allow ships with taller masts through.

Father sells off the Stout and buys a Morris 1100. He takes us kids for a spin around the suburbs of Port Adelaide. I am sitting in the back seat with Bidjid, Bryce is in the front passenger seat and Father's driving.

When we approach the Birkenhead Bridge, it is in the raised position, so we pull up and wait for it to lower back down.

'Looks like they didn't quite give this one enough time to pass through. What do you think, kids?' Father asks, turning to Bryce, then looking over his shoulder at Bidjid and then into the rear-vision mirror at me.

I shuffle a little to the centre of the seat to get a glimpse of what Father is talking about. All I can see is the tip of the mast of a sailboat passing through the opening of the bridge and it looks like the bridge is going to clamp onto it. Bidjid undoes the buckle on her seatbelt and hugs onto the back of Bryce's seat so she can get a clearer view.

'Gee, it's pretty close, Dad,' Bryce says as he cringes back into his seat a little as if that was going to help the mast slip through. But the mast of the boat sails past easily enough, and we all reposition ourselves in our seats and wait for the bridge to fully lower back down.

We are soon setting off again, Father not realising that Bidjid has failed to buckle herself back up. When he takes the next right turn, her car door swings open because she is hanging onto the handle. She clings onto it for dear life. Luckily, when Father straightens the vehicle up, she comes swinging back inside the vehicle and plops onto her seat.

Father slams on the brakes and gives her a good talking to. He tells her to put her seatbelt back on and not to hang onto the door handle ever again.

The house Father builds for us is on a street loosely surfaced with bluestone pebbles. Bryce and I often find iron pyrites, fool's gold, along the edges, especially after the road's been resurfaced.

A month short of my fifth birthday, just before Easter 1980. We move into our newly built house at Exeter. Bryce, Bidjid and I are determined to catch the Easter Bunny delivering chocolate eggs so we can ask for a few extras. On Easter Sunday, we all get up extra early, go out into the corner of the yard and hide out of sight from the Easter Bunny. We listen for sounds of the Easter Bunny hopping over people's fences. When our parents wake up, Mum notices us out in the backyard and calls for us to come back inside, but we crouch quietly in the corner until she comes out to see what we are doing.

'What's going on out here?' she asks.

'Shhh, go away, Marm,' Bryce snaps back. 'We're waiting for the Easter Bunny. We don't want to miss out on seeing him and we all got up extra early for this.'

'The Easter Bunny is not going to come if he knows you're all out here. Anyway, you're going to miss out on breakfast soon,' Mum replies.

She goes back into the house and looks out the window to see if we are coming, but we aren't.

Around mid-morning, we give up. That year, our parents would have enjoyed all the sugary treats themselves. We all realise it is our own fault that we missed out on our share of Easter eggs and never ever again get up early for special events – not for Easter, Christmas, not even for birthdays.

In 1981, the year I turn six, I join Bryce and Bidjid at LeFevre Peninsula Primary School at Birkenhead, near Port Adelaide. I love school and make friends easily. At recess and lunchtime, I share my half-crushed boiled eggs, carrots and steamed chops with Chow, a Chinese kid from my class. His lunchbox is always packed with chocolates, chips, triangle-shaped sandwiches with their crusts cut off and fruit, all individually cling-wrapped and neatly arranged. He shares it with me every day.

After lunch one afternoon, I sit with Bryce watching cartoons on TV in the lounge room, while Bidjid and Mum wash the midday dishes. Father goes outside and we hear digging but think nothing of it.

'Bryce, Bidjid, Luke! Come out the back here,' Father yells from the backyard.

We all head out the back and Father is standing next to a small mound of upturned earth.

'I have some sad news for you about you guys' dog. I had to put it down because it hurt its back leg. I just buried it.' Father sadly informs us as we all start to sob. He cannot contain himself and starts laughing. 'You better carefully dig him up to say goodbye to him then,' he continues.

Straight away we start digging and then one of us hears breathing coming out of the pipe.

'He's alive, quick…dig faster,' Bryce frantically blurts out.

Soon we have reached the bath and we all grab a corner, as the bath slowly rises out squeezes the dog and happily to greet us.

'Aww, there he is,' Bidjid shrieks in excitement.

Tears roll freely down our cheeks, and we all cuddle him at the same time.

Months pass until one day, Father says, 'Come on, we're going to meet a fella up in the Adelaide Hills.'

Father and Mum get into the front of the car while Bryce, Bidjid and I get into the back. By then, I think we had the old Valiant sedan that Mum's brother gave her. Father drives through the city and we head out into the Adelaide Hills. When we get to the designated meeting point near Monarto, there is a guy waiting on the side of the road for us. Father and the guy speak briefly through open car windows before we follow the man to a farm, the farm that Father ends up buying.

Early the next year, in January 1982, we move out of the city, to Monarto. Around the same time, Father buys another block of land not far away from Monarto at Aclare, about ten kilometres down the South Eastern Freeway towards Adelaide. It is surrounded by hills and has an abandoned mine on it. A stretch of Dawesley Creek winds back and forth through the centre of the block, and it has water all year round.

2

Monarto South

Bryce, Bidjid and I start school at Murray Bridge North. Sometimes Mum drops us off but mostly, we just catch the school bus from down the road at the Monarto-Schenscher Road intersection near the Lutheran Church, which is near a small cemetery. We live roughly twenty kilometres from school and the journey takes about thirty minutes because the bus stops and picks up other kids along the way.

Sometimes we ride our bikes down to the bus stop and hide them in the long grass along the side of the road. When we get off the bus after school, we ride them back home. Most times we just walk, though, because we are always getting punctures from the three-corner jacks out on the farm. Walking is better anyhow because Bryce and I usually pick a rock each to soccer along to see who can keep theirs on the road the longest without kicking it off.

When we get home after school, we say a quick hello to Mum, throw down our school bags and shoot out the door again to go hunting for lizards. We search around the obvious spots like under logs and sheets of iron, and we turn over rocks. Sometimes it is all in vain, but other times we find a nice juicy lizard to eat. As soon as we find one, we knock it on the head with whatever is convenient at the time. Then whoever's turn it was next to remove the intestines would get to work with these preparations. We always rotate the task between us as it is only fair. Bryce realises one day after slicing his leg open on the barbed-wire fence while climbing through the fence that we can use the barbs for slicing open the lizards. Then we just reach in and remove what intestines can be seen.

While this is being done, the others prepare a fire; then the lizard is thrown onto the coals. Watching lizards sizzling away in an open fire is always mesmerising. Their little claws curl up and turn black and their skin starts to split open, exposing the meat beneath. As the lizard cooks, Bryce, Bidjid and I squat around the fire, watching and listening to the distinctive whistling noise that comes from them.

Quite often if we failed to remove all the intestines, we would get covered in boiling hot masticated grot as they exploded. This was sometimes the best part, though, I thought, seeing Bryce or Bidjid getting splattered in this filth and the faces they pulled was priceless. Not as much fun when it happened to me, though, although it always provided a great laugh at my expense for my siblings.

The smell of those poor defenceless lizards as they cook on the hot coals has charred the insides of my airways for life. Also, the experiences I shared with my older siblings are indelible to this day.

If I were given the choice of eating those lizards again or dying of starvation, I would have to strongly consider dying of starvation.

In 1982, just before my seventh birthday, we meet Sam and Bert from the neighbouring farm. These two were not having the wool pulled over their eyes and we were going to soon find out.

'The sheep are due for shearing and will need mustering over the weekend – Mr Gregson across the road from us said we can bring them over to his place to get them shorn,' Father tells us excitedly. 'What I'll need from all you three is to help me get them there safely. Mrs Gregson makes her own Easter eggs and has told me she's made a few extras this year for you kids.'

'That's nice of her, isn't it, kids?' Mum asks.

'Mmmm, yes,' we agree.

That weekend, we help Father muster the sheep. We take them over to the neighbour's place and put them in his holding yard at his shearing shed.

'Watch out for those two rams in that yard there, Neil! That's Sam and Bert. They're very protective of their flock and they'll headbutt you if they get the opportunity, so keep your eyes on them at all times, especially your kids,' Mr Gregson informs us.

Sam and Bert manoeuvre their way to the head of the flock. One of the rams snorts loudly and stomps his hoof into the fine dirt, which produces a small mushroom cloud of dust which curls upwards until it disappears.

'You'll need to move my sheep out of that yard to bring your ones through for shearing. Just stick mine into that yard over there.' Mr Gregson points to a smaller yard on the other side of his flock.

'Go on, Bryce. You take Luke with you and go and open that gate over there, so we can push these sheep through. Bidjid, you can help me here,' Father instructs.

Bryce and I climb into the yard and the flock turns round. Sam and Bert also turn but by the time we get halfway across the yard, they are facing us and one of them snorts loudly again.

'You better get a move on, boys,' Father warns with a laugh in his voice.

Looking over our shoulders, we fix our sights on the two rams before picking up our pace a little more. Before we know it, we are running at top speed in fear for our lives with Sam and Bert right on our heels breathing down our necks. We reach the gate and scale it in an instant. Standing like nervous wrecks, we slowly catch our breath.

'That was really, really close,' Bryce exclaims.

I nod in agreement. My eyes are still bulging wide and I am struggling to breathe.

'Open it up now, boys, and step aside. Keep an eye on those rams. They have it in for you two now. You were lucky to escape them once but maybe next time, you won't be so lucky,' Father says.

Bryce opens the gate and we quickly run to the nearby fence and climb over it. Father and Bidjid chase the sheep through, and Father quickly shuts the gate behind them.

'Yeah, bring yours through, Neil,' Mr Gregson says, motioning to Father with his hand.

Once the sheep are all in his shearing shed, Mr Gregson takes us over to his house and Mrs Gregson invites us in. On the table are all sorts of chocolates she has prepared. She sits down to make a few more before the chocolate in the pan sets.

'I've put a few Easter eggs on the table here for you children. Please take them all,' Mrs Gregson insists.

We share them between us and once Mrs Gregson finishes pouring the rest of the chocolate into the moulds, she puts a few more Easter eggs in a bag and passes them to Father.

'These, Neil, are for you and your lovely wife, Shirl.'

'Why, thank you very much, Mrs Gregson. You shouldn't have gone to too much trouble on our account.'

After the shearing is done and the sheep are back on our farm, Father gives each of us some pocket money for helping him with the sheep and Bryce decides to buy himself a second-hand, ten-speed racing bike. When we get home, he pumps up the half-deflated tyres and takes it for a pedal out to the front gate. But as he is turning round, there is a loud bang that sounds like someone has just fired a rifle at him. (This is a familiar sound that we have heard many times before. It was around this time that father had bought an air rifle for Bryce to practise shooting small prey like pigeons.)

He drops the bike and sprints back to where we are all standing out in the flat watching him. His eyes are bulging wide, as he tells us someone has just tried to shoot him. Father goes to investigate. He is standing out at the front gate and scours around looking for the perpetrator, when he notices that one of Bryce's bike's tyres has blown out.

Father pulls the bike upright and wheels it back with him. 'That bang wasn't a rifle, Bryce. It was your tyre bursting. You must have put too much air into it, causing it pop.' Father laughs and so do the rest of us in relief.

Over the course of a few months, things start changing between our parents. At first, we think the tensions in the house will just pass but they only become worse over time. Their arguments get worse and go on longer, and they all seem to be about money. I am only seven at the time, Bidjid is eight and Bryce is nine, us three kids having all been born a year apart. Money and bills mean nothing to us. If you need money, I think, you just get it from the bank.

Much later, when we were able to comprehend, Father told us that he had been giving Mum money to pay the bills, but she was giving it away to her family. Father only discovered it when he would receive final notices, or the power had been turned off. He paid for all our essential living expenses and schoolbooks. Mum didn't have a paid job and was only receiving payments from her welfare cheques.

One day, I'm jumping on the trampoline with Bryce and Bidjid in the rain when, breaking our hysterical laughter, Father calls out loudly from inside the house.

'Bryce, Bidjid, Luke, would you three come inside, please? Your mother and I need to talk to you all.'

We race each other inside and make our way into the kitchen, where our parents are sitting at either end of the table, well away from each other.

'Sit down. We have something very important to tell you all,' Father begins.

Mum and Father both have very concerned looks on their faces. For a moment, I think I have done something wrong at school and look around to see if the report from my teacher is nearby. Or maybe something even more drastic has happened, like someone close to us has died.

'Do you want to tell them, Shirl, or shall I?' Father asks.

'No, you can tell them, Neil,' Mum replies with a sad tone in her voice.

'Your mother and I are going to get a divorce,' Father says matter-of-factly. 'We've tried really hard to make things work out as a family over the past few months, but I'm sure you'll all agree it's just not working. We don't have feelings for each other any more,' Father goes on, looking around the table at each of us. He then fixes his gaze on Mum and waits for her to say something. He nods to encourage her to speak up.

'Yes, we'll both always love the three of you, no matter what. And I agree with your father, we have tried very hard to make this work, but it's true, we no longer love each other.'

Our faces drop and we all start to cry. Mum extends her arms onto the table with her palms up and we grip tightly onto her hands.

'That's basically it, kids. I'll stay over at Aclare from now on. But I'll be checking in on you all to make sure you're behaving,' Father explains.

Father has now been stocking it with sheep over the course of the year and we would drop over there on weekends to see him and to gather field mushrooms or splash about in Dawesley Creek, which flowed through it year round.

We surround him, our arms flung around his neck. We don't want him to leave. I'm crying, and Bryce and Bidjid are crying. Even Mum is crying. It is hard on us all.

Since moving to Monarto, Father traded in the Morris 1100 for a G60 Nissan Patrol four-wheel drive. Father goes to pack his clothes and put a few things into the Nissan. We give him some space and plead with Mum to get him to change his mind, but she knows he is determined to move on, and she just sits there crying.

'Okay, I'll see you in a couple of days. Be good, all right?' Father says.

We give him another cuddle before he sets off down the driveway.

Because there is no house at Aclare, Father buys a caravan the evening he leaves for Aclare and puts it on the property, so he has somewhere to sleep. As Aclare is just short of drive away from us back at Monarto, Father drops in regularly to see how we are all coping, and to shower and do his laundry.

A few months later, he walks in and places his bag down on the floor in the kitchen. 'Luke, can you please put my bag away.'

I grab the bag by the handle and start dragging it through the kitchen. I turn to go up the passage towards the main bedroom, thinking my parents have worked things out.

'No, Luke, I'll sleep in your room with you tonight, okay, mate?'

'Oh, okay, Father,' I say and proudly drag his bag into my room, a big smile on my face, because I really loved being close to Father.

He stays with us for a few days and then heads back to Aclare. And a couple of weeks later when he returns, he brings a lady called Vonn with him and introduces her to us all as his new partner.

Vonn has a young daughter Zoann. Zoann is nearly five years old but is still very dependent on her mother. At first, she doesn't mingle with us much at all, but after a few weeks pass, she too becomes a part of the family.

Vonn is a very placid person and loving towards us all, but she isn't very talkative, and she always speaks softly to Father. She comes from a tiny community called Numbulwar, in Arnhem Land, on the east coast of the Northern Territory. She had moved to South Australia with her husband, but they also divorced. When Father meets her, she is also pregnant. Over the next couple of years, Father and Vonn have two children themselves, Lillie and Loui.

I am asked to move into Bryce's room for a while, and Father and Vonn move into my room, because Vonn is due any day. And shortly after, she gives birth to Dansan.

From the first day Vonn visits, Mum and her instantly hit it off and become great friends. Confusing as this is to us, everyone is happy. And to see Father happy is all that matters. I'm sure Mum is relieved that Father has finally moved on, one way or another.

Soon, Mum moves on as well. She meets Clark and brings him home to meet everybody. To us kids, it appears now that we are one big happy family again. Life sails along smoothly with all of us living under the one roof.

One afternoon, I am standing out in the paddock with Bryce and Bidjid cooking a blue-tongue on the fire when Clark comes tearing down the gravel road and hits a set of corrugations just before our gate. Next thing, he's lost control of the vehicle. It rolls over a few times and eventually settles on its rooftop.

Clark crawls out through the shattered windscreen and staggers up onto his feet as Father briskly approaches him from the direction of the house.

At first, we think Father is going to see if he needs any help. But when he reaches Clark, no words are exchanged. Father just raises both his fists like he is stepping into a boxing ring and punches Clark square in the nose, knocking him onto his arse. He gets back up onto his feet and stumbles against the car for support. Blood runs out his nose, messing up the front of his shirt.

Father is fuming and growls around while Clark remains frozen in fear, cowering, not daring to answer back. Shortly afterwards, a patrol car arrives. Clark tests positive in a blood alcohol reading and is instantly disqualified from driving for six months. It turns out he is pissed out of his mind and has only himself to blame for what has happened. For us kids, though, the best thing about the accident is that Clark has lost a few dollars in the rollover. We scab through the wreck and keep what we find.

Mum isn't too pleased with Clark because the car he has wrecked is the one her brother had given her. Mum demands Clark's licence from him and later that evening, she cuts it in half with a pair of scissors.

When Vonn heads off to the hospital to give birth, Father, Bryce, Bidjid, Zoann and I are all waiting at our place. We are watching the midday movie, *Tarzan, the Ape Man*, on television when the phone rings.

Father answers. 'Hello, Neil speaking. How may I help you?'

There is a short pause while he listens into the receiver.

'Oh, that's wonderful news. How are they both?'

There is another pause…

'Pass on our love from the rest of the family. Thanks for the call.'

He puts down the phone and comes over to us. 'Vonn has just given birth to a healthy little boy. What do you think we should call him?' He has a loving smile on his face, something I haven't seen in a long time.

'Ummm,' we all reply and turn back to the TV.

'How about we call him Tarzan?' Father says with a smile.

'Yes, that's a really good name,' we all reply together.

We are disappointed when we find out they decide against Tarzan, but we often call him Tarzan anyway.

Soon after she is discharged from hospital, Vonn asks Father if he wants to drive her, Zoann and baby Dansan up to Numbulwar, three thousand kilometres away, to meet her family and see her homeland. He agrees and asks Bryce if he wants to go with them. Bryce jumps at the opportunity to get out of school and travel.

A couple of weeks later, he returns on the plane by himself. At first, it's hard to recognise him when he enters the terminal at Adelaide airport because in that short time, he's shot up a few inches. We question him in detail about Numbulwar and he excitedly tells us all about it.

3

Numbulwar Life

During the Christmas holidays in 1982, Father takes Bryce, Bidjid and me along with Vonn, Zoann nd baby Dansan up to Numbulwar. Mum stays back in South Australia to look after the two properties. Before we all return to Monarto, a position for a store manager becomes vacant at the Numbulwar shop, and the community encourages Father to apply.

A few weeks later, at the start of 1983, he is offered the position and we all move up there with him before school starts, apart from Mum, who happily stays back home at Monarto to look after the two farms and be with Clark.

It is fun living in the Numbulwar community, apart from breakfast time. Due to a shortage of cutlery and utensils back then, every morning, Vonn makes a huge serving of Weetbix in a roasting dish. Using the only spoon on hand at the time, we are fed one spoonful at a time. This isn't so bad because I'm always hungry, but seeing the spoon come out of someone else's mouth and their saliva springing back onto it makes me feel sick in the stomach. But even if I didn't want to eat, there was no getting out of it.

I'm able to pick up the Numbulwar community language, Nunggubuyu, a bit more easily than Bryce and Bidjid – though not before I find out what 'juggle' means.

'You, big juggle,' I say to Bryce, laughing.

'No, you're a big juggle,' Bryce replies.

'Hey, you boys, come in here for a second. Do you know what "juggle" means?' Father asks.

'When you juggle things around like a clown?' Bryce answers.

'No, it means "dick" in this language up here, so just be careful saying that around here, all right.' Father laughs.

Many types of edible fruits grow out at Numbulwar. There are mangoes, coconuts, bananas, cashews and wild grapes, called moongoongs. They are dark purple and grow in the sand dunes along the coast. It's like paradise, just as Bryce described it when he came back to Adelaide.

Except when we must 'fly to Fiji'.

Father has come up with an unusual punishment in this paradise. Whenever we are naughty, we must do what he calls 'Flying to Fiji'. This involves getting on our knees, with our backs straight, and not sitting on our feet, with arms extended to the sides.

I hate Fiji, even though I have never been there. When we must fly to Fiji, it goes on for what seems like an hour, although it was possibly only five minutes. By then, my arms feel like they are about to fall off. But if I let them drop, I get more time added onto my journey.

A few months after my eighth birthday, in 1983, Vonn is due to give birth again. Dansan is a toddler by now, and when Vonn comes home from the hospital, it is soon apparent baby Lillie is not coping. The humid weather is affecting her respiratory system.

Many times over the course of the year, Mum promises to come up to see us. The only way she can contact us is by calling the office at Numbulwar, and someone from the community passes on the message for us to be at the office in fifteen minutes to speak with her. Many times, we walk the five-kilometre round journey to the airstrip and back to greet her, hoping she will be on a plane. But any plans Mum has always fall through.

When Lillie is born, Mum finally comes up to Numbulwar to see us and meet the new baby. The day she arrives, it is as though the Queen of Sheba has come to visit. She is dressed very neatly and is sitting tall in the back of someone's Land Cruiser as they pass by. She is so happy to see the three of us and showers us with hugs and kisses. But as soon as she sees Lillie, tears roll down her face.

The tropical conditions are affecting Lillie's respiratory system, so Mum offers to take her back to Adelaide with her to be closer to hospitals where she can get medical treatment. Vonn and Father agree. Bryce, Bidjid and I have been so happy to see Mum, and we don't want her to go, but we are grateful that Lillie is going to be in her good hands back in South Australia.

At the end of 1983, we all return from the NT. Bryce, Bidjid and I move back home with Mum, Lillie and Clark to Monarto South. We are all re-enrolled at Murray Bridge North Primary Shool for the following year. Father, Vonn, Zoann and Dansan spend most of their time at Aclare, living in the caravan, and we spend most weekends out there with them. During the winter, field mushrooms the size of dinner plates are collected from the hills.

Another time, Father cuts the head off a red-bellied black snake basking in the sun using his shovel, then he lights a fire, cooks it up and shares it out between us.

Sometimes, Zoann goes to live with her dad for a couple of weeks. And other times, they all return to Numbulwar, leaving the rest of us to look after the two properties.

During their comings and goings, Father hires a small tip truck and starts collecting moss rocks from the Aclare property. The rocks are used to build farmhouses and he delivers them to a quarry in the Adelaide Hills. I go with him once or twice and, from what I can recall, I'm sure it is the Carey Gully sandstone quarry, between Uraidla and Balhannah. Thirty-plus years later, I unexpectedly stumble across the quarry and remember the two of us, Father and I, pulling up together in the red tip truck full of rocks. For me, it was a very special shared time.

Soon, Father decides to expand his business dealings and starts looking into buying a sheep station in Western Australia. One afternoon, on one of his visits with Vonn, Zoann and Dansan, he calls us into the kitchen for a family meeting. He opens the *Elders Weekly*, a farmers' newspaper, spreads it out on the table so we can all see and excitedly starts reading out loud. 'What do you all think about this place here?' Father points to the ad in the paper at Moolapool station. It is 450,000 acres of prime sheep and cattle country, just south of the Great Sandy Desert in WA. 'It has over twenty-five windmills, mostly pumping fresh drinking water, a four-stand shearing shed …'

Father continues reading as we all sit, listening to him intensely. It sounds like the best place on earth to live. There's even a couple of photos of the station. I stare at the ad and imagine living there.

'Well, what do you all think?' Father asks, looking around at us all with a huge grin. 'It's a really big place. Imagine telling all your friends how much land we have.'

'Yeah, it sounds really great,' we all reply.

Even Mum is happy with the idea.

'We'll be mustering the sheep on motorbikes. You'll all get your own motorbikes,' Father says.

We sit in amazed silence until Bryce says, 'That'll be really good, yeah. When can we go?'

'Well, you three older kids better finish off your year of schooling at Murray Bridge first, while I push for the sale of the properties here,' Father says. But I think I can get some money from the bank right now to put down a deposit, so we don't lose it in case someone else goes for it.' Father's face gleams with excitement.

Vonn is due to have another baby around August 1984 and she ends up giving birth to Loui at Gove District Hospital in the Northern Territory on one of their journeys to Numbulwar. Loui is a healthy, strong little boy. Vonn and Father are so happy with him, just like the rest of us are. We are thrilled to have another brother in our family.

Father's bank loan is approved, so he packs as much stuff as he can into the Nissan and onto the trailer. Even the trampoline we got for Christmas 1982 is packed.

'We'll get things set up over on the station and send for you towards the end of the year, once you three kids have finished off the last term of school,' he says. 'Also, Vonn and I have agreed that we would like it if Lillie can stay with you, Shirl, for the time being, for her to become strong enough to cope out there on the station. But it's entirely up to you.'

'Oh yes, she's more than welcome. I'll take good care of Lillie and raise her up as my own, as I have done so far,' Mum replies, nodding eagerly.

When it is time for them to leave, Father comes over to Bryce, Bidjid and me, and one by one gives each of us a hug and tells us he loves us.

By now, Lillie has become Mum's adopted daughter. She is such a happy, much-loved little girl. Mum has adored her from the day she first set eyes on her up at Numbulwar twelve months earlier.

We exchange hugs with everyone else before Father, Vonn, Zoann, Dansan, Loui and Father's sheepdog, Streak, all get in the Nissan. We stand back and sadly watch them leave.

'Be good for your mother now, okay? I'll send for you at the end of the year, all right?' Father calls out as they drive away.

'Yes, Father, we'll be good. We love you,' we yell as he drives off, waving his arm out the window.

We're all excited about heading to Moolapool in Western Australia and can't wait to be making our own way over there.

Just before the farm sells, a shiny black Ford LTD with chrome rims drives slowly up the road. The driver spots us kids playing in the front yard and pulls over. Inside the car are three adults, two men and a lady, all smartly dressed. The driver asks if we can tell him where the nearest deli is.

We try explaining how to get there, which is to continue straight along the track. It is just on the right, about two kilometres away, we tell them. But they act all confused, mumbling among themselves. Then the man in the back opens the door and asks if we can show them where the deli is, bribing us with the idea of getting us lollies for our effort. Bidjid and I are about to get into the car when Bryce senses something odd about the situation and calls for Mum to come out the front. Suddenly the car speeds off, and Bidjid and I are almost run over by one of the back tyres.

Whether they were people from the welfare coming to take us away, as they still do to this day, or just people looking to kidnap children, we will never know, and I am glad we never found out either.

After the property sells, we move in with Marg, a lady Mum got to know who lived just down the road from our farm. She has a few horses on her place and people come out to the riding classes that she offers. She has three boys, two of them roughly the same age as Bryce and me; the third lives away mostly, with his father, so we rarely see him.

I learn to ride my first motorbike on Marg's farm, and what a thrill it is to be in control of a powerful engine. It was so much fun, and I will never forget the hours and hours I rode around. They are memories to last a lifetime, along with the ones of refuelling the tank. The fumes filled my lungs with a kind of everlasting vapour. It wasn't anything like a normal petrol station smell.

Most days, I want to take off by myself and ride around the farm on my own, but I must share the pleasures of this motorbike with the others. I imagine having my own bike, out on the station in WA, one that I won't have to share. The days till the end of the year can't come quick enough for me. I so badly want to get to that station.

While we are living with Marg, for a reason unknown to us, some spiteful person attacks Marg by slaughtering a few of her horses. It is a brutal death for some of them. A few have their throats cut while others are poisoned. Marg tries to save the poisoned ones by flushing them out. The vet tries to save the others. Overall, Marg loses several horses in one day. I can't imagine who would stoop to that level, harming defenceless animals to get back at someone, but I guess there are people out there who just don't care.

4

Western Australia

When I am nine and a half years old, and as soon as school finishes at the end of 1984, Father informs us that he has set up things for us on the station and paid for our bus tickets to come to WA. We pack our clothing into a few small suitcases and garbage bags and go to the Adelaide bus depot to catch the bus with Mum. It's a long journey and the summer heat doesn't help.

Over a thousand times, I ask Mum, 'Are we there yet?'

'No, baby, we still have a very long way to go,' Mum answers, growing more and more impatient with me every time.

As I look out the window at the barren land, I think the water covering it must be boiling hot. It looks so strange.

'What's all that hot water out there for, Mum?' I ask.

'No, darling. That is just a mirage, not water,'

'What's a marrarsh, Mum?'

'A mirage, Luke, is just a heatwave that looks like water but it's not.'

I'm still confused but I let it go. I can't wait to finally get to the station to be with Father. I miss him so much. He is my hero, and I haven't seen him for six months.

Around Yalata in South Australia, between Adelaide and Perth, the driver takes all us passengers on the bus to a lookout to see the Great Australian Bight. We get off the bus with the rest of the passengers and stretch our legs, but it is windy, and I am worried that one of us will get blown off the cliff into the sea sixty metres below, to our death. I'm happy when we get back on the bus.

From there, it takes another eighteen hours to get to Perth, where we stay the night with an older cousin of ours, Yukka Mary. Yukka means 'big sister' in Adnyamathanha language. Mary had been taken away from her mother, Mum's sister, when she was a small child and grew up with her foster family on the other side of the country.

Perth looks nice, even though we are only in the outer suburbs. And it's good to catch up with family after being crammed in the bus for the past couple of days. The air in Western Australia is a lot drier than we are used to in the Adelaide Hills, a totally new experience for us.

The following day, we thank Yukka Mary and her foster parents, say our farewells and make our way to the Perth depot to catch the two p.m. bus to Meekatharra. We are all excited that there are only 780 kilometres to go before we see Father and the others again. This part of the journey takes the rest of the day and into the early part of the evening.

Mum wakes us up as we pull into the service station. 'We're here, kids. There's your father over there, standing next to the Nissan with the others,' Mum announces excitedly.

The Swagman Roadhouse, which overlooks the town of Meekatharra, is covered in fine red dust that has been stirred up by all the semi-trailers as they pull off the single-lane highway into the loose dirt near the fuel bowsers.

As we get off the bus, Father greets us all with a huge hug. 'Gee, you kids have shot up in the past several months,' he exclaims. 'You're almost taller than me now, Bryce. What has your mother been feeding you?'

'Everything. Mum makes lovely spaghetti,' Bryce reminds him.

'That explains it then – you are what you eat and you're a strand of spaghetti,' Father laughs. 'Let's get your belongings and hit the road. It's getting late.'

We make our way over to the bus driver, who is standing by the luggage compartment.

'Now, which of this is your luggage, madam?' the driver asks Mum kindly.

'That one there, those two next to it and that,' Mum says, pointing with her index finger.

'Is that everything?'

'Yes, thank you,' Mum says, nodding.

Father grabs the bulk of our things; Bryce gathers the rest, and we head over to where he has parked. Vonn opens the back of the Nissan and Father carefully puts our things in the back alongside Loui.

'Try not to wake up your little brother,' Father says, sighing deeply. 'He's been teething and having a cunt of a night's sleep for the past few weeks.'

Vonn can't wait to be holding her little girl Lillie once again and, even though it is summer, she wraps her snugly into her blanket, leaving only her beautiful little face exposed.

'Look how big you've grown, my little girl,' Vonn coos. 'You look so much like Dansan and Loui, your two brothers.' Vonn wipes tears away from the side of her face with the back of her hand.

She kisses Lillie over and over until she wakes her up. Lillie starts twisting about in Vonn's arms, trying to see where Mum is.

'She's forgotten you and she's a little startled from being woken up,' Mum says reassuringly. 'Give her time and she'll remember you again, Vonn.'

'If anyone needs to go to the toilet, I suggest you go now,' Father says. 'It's another hour's drive out to the station from here and there's no toilet stops along the way, okay?'

'Yeah, I need to go quickly. Come on, kids,' Mum says as she heads off.

Bidjid skips a little to catch up to her. Bryce and I follow along not far behind until Mum and Bidjid veer off into the girls' toilets while we continue a little further on to the boys'. When we walk through the doorway, we see the entire floor is covered with stink beetles, over half of them crushed. The toilet smells awful. We manoeuvre our way through a partially clear space, trying not to step on any more, but it is unavoidable. Then we both freeze. We are in the centre of the toilet, with stink beetles on every side. And some are crawling towards us. The urinal trough behind a partition wall is almost full of stink beetles as well. They're slipping and sliding over each another, trying to make their way to the top, to freedom. We walk over and quickly take a piss, then turn back to wash our hands at the basin.

'It sounds like we're walking on eggshells, doesn't it?' Bryce laughs.

'Yeah, and they're slippery too.'

As I reach for the hand basin, one of my legs slides out from under me.

'Gee, that was lucky. You nearly ended up on your back,' Bryce laughs.

'Yuck! Look at that one there. Its insides are hanging out. And it's stuck to the floor, walking around in circles trying to free itself,' Bryce says in a disgusted tone, clamping his teeth together then tilting his head sideways so his teeth show.

We crab-walk past it and it stops to look at us, then it sets off again on its pointless journey. Bryce and I can't wait to get out of there. We meet up with Mum and Bidjid on our way back to the Nissan.

'Were there beetles in the girls' toilet?' I ask.

Mum looks down at me and nods as Bidjid jumps in. 'Yeah, it was horrible, and it really smelt stinky from the dead ones that had been crushed all over the floor.'

Bryce tells her it was the same in the boys' toilet and how sad it was seeing the one still alive but stuck to the floor.

'Rightio then, let's get going,' Father says, cutting off our chatter. 'It's after ten now and getting later.'

'You don't mind if I have a cigarette do you, Neil?' Mum asks. She reaches into her handbag and pulls out a packet of cigarettes.

'No, not at all – as long as you light one up for me and pass it over.'

Mum, Vonn, who is still nursing Lillie, and Father are all in the front while the rest of us are in the back sitting on our bags because there isn't any seating in the back of the Nissan.

Loui is still fast asleep.

'Can I have one of those, Shirl?' Vonn asks, looking at Mum who is holding her cigarette up to the partly open window.

'Oh yes, Vonn. I'm so sorry, I forgot you smoked.'

The two of them are like old classmates, and life could not be any better. Mum takes another cigarette from her packet and hands it along with her lighter to her. Vonn puts the cigarette in her mouth, lights up, then passes the lighter back to Mum. The Nissan quickly fills up with cigarette smoke, but we don't really notice because we are talking Father's ear off.

'Where's Streak, Father?' Bryce asks.

'Oh, he's guarding the homestead tonight,' he says. 'He's turned out to be a bloody good sheepdog. You'll see him in the morning, kids.'

'Are there many animals out on the station, Father?' I ask.

'Yes, Luke. There are loads of kangaroos, emus, goats, birds and even some camels.'

'Gee, I can't wait to see them. Is there a school for us out there, Father?' Bidjid asks.

'No, there's no school but there is a room set up for your schooling. Your schoolwork will be sent out from Perth. Maybe we can look at getting you a governess.'

'What's that?' we ask.

'A teacher, of course. Now sit back and enjoy the ride, kids. We'll be there soon enough.'

It takes just under an hour to get to the station.

Father swings past the shearing shed and living quarters on the way in to show them to us. 'What do you guys think of the shearing shed – pretty good, hey?'

'Yeah, it's bigger than Mr Gregson's shearing shed, the one we took our sheep to at Monarto where they had those two crazy rams, Sam and Bert,' Bryce says.

'Yeah, it certainly is – the shearers even have their own living quarters out here,' Father tells us.

'Where are the shearers now?' Mum asks.

'They only come out when it's shearing time of course. We just finished shearing the stragglers a few weeks back. The big one will be around Easter time, after we've mustered up all the sheep. Mustering starts in late February.'

Father pulls away from the shearers' quarters and heads along another, much narrower dirt track towards the homestead.

'Do we have our own motorbikes, Father?' Bryce asks.

'No, there are a few, but they're too big for most of you kids. You'll be all right, though, Bryce. The homestead's just a stone's throw away now,' he adds.

Sure enough, it suddenly appears in front of us like a shipwreck, towering above the scrubland and mulga trees. As we pull up, a kangaroo by the front gate is startled in the beam of the headlights.

'Shhh, be quiet,' Father whispers, as he quietly gets out from the Nissan. He creeps over to a branch about the size of a pick handle and crouches down to pick it up. Fortunately for the kangaroo, it takes off when it senses Father's presence.

When Father returns, he switches off the engine and headlights. It is pitch dark. We get out and stand huddled in a group, waiting for some lights to come on somewhere. But it is just complete darkness all around us, as if we are blindfolded. Apart from the sound of our feet stumbling about on the gravel, silence fills the night. I have never experienced anything like this before, living back in South Australia or the Northern Territory. My heart pounds and it's difficult to hear above its rhythm pulsating in my ears. I am scared out there in this total darkness. It feels like a demon is waiting to pounce. But I know Father will save us, so I let the thought go.

'Listen to that, would you,' Father says. 'It's the sound of silence. Not a single sound of an engine or any other person is to be heard all the way out here, hey?'

We all stand stock-still, breathing shallowly and just listen.

'Rightio then,' Father booms after a few seconds.

I just about die of fright.

'This way, everyone. Just grab a hold of the hand of the person beside you and follow along behind me.'

We all feel around to find the person beside us and closely follow along behind Father, trying not to lose him in the darkness. We cling onto each other's hands for dear life and walk in a single file. When we get to what I guess is the doorway, Father breaks his hand free from Bryce. He puts his hand on Bryce's chest and we all stop.

'Just wait here a moment,' he says.

We all stand in the darkness, waiting for him. He fumbles around, pulls his cigarette lighter out of his pocket and lights up his way inside to find the kerosene lamp. The lamp, we soon find out, is the only source of lighting on the station. It produces a dull yellow glow.

Father brings the lamp out to where we are all standing on the veranda, waiting for him to light up the darkness surrounding us. 'Rightio, come inside, everyone, and grab yourselves a seat,' Father instructs.

We all follow along behind him as he leads the way into the kitchen. He places the lamp on the centre of the table, and we all sit down. It's so exciting to finally be at Moolapool after the long journey over from SA, and we long for the sun to rise tomorrow so we can get a good look at everything. But I wish there were more lights and not just this dull kerosene lamp.

'So, tell me about the journey? Did you stop at the Bight on your way across the Nullarbor?' Father asks.

'The Nullarbor? Oh yes, we did,' Mum replies. 'You kids remember, where we pulled over at that cliff, where we could see the ocean?'

'Yeah, I thought we were going to get blown over the edge,' Bryce answers.

'So did I,' Bidjid says. It was really windy.'

'I couldn't see much, because sand was blowing around and some got in my eyes,' I add. 'I wish we could have had a swim, but the water was too far down.'

'Yes, we pulled up at the same spot to have some lunch. I even think that's where Vonn boiled the billy for a cup of tea, right, Vonn?'

'Yes, we did, Neilee,' Vonn answers, nodding and biting the edge of her fingernail.

For about an hour, we talk about the long bus journey and what we have been doing back in South Australia.

'Have you ever seen a marrash, Father?' I ask.

'Oh, you mean a mirage, Luke?'

I nod.

'I most certainly have,' he says. 'You'll see plenty of those here.'

'It's a long way from South Australia. I thought we'd never get here. The bus took forever,' Bryce says.

'Yes, it's a long way indeed. I should have organised a train from Adelaide to Perth for you all,' Father says. 'That way, you could at least have got up and stretched your legs along the way. I do think you see more of the country by road, though.'

By now, it is well after midnight and we are all starting to yawn. The dull yellow light from the lamp attracts lots of moths, beetles and other flying insects that are crashing into the glass lamp like kamikaze bombers. Some are knocked out and fall onto the table. After they have collided, they lie there without moving for a few seconds, before spinning around on their backs until they can get back on their feet. Then they repeat the whole process.

As we sit around the table, I remember the discussion we all had at our family meeting several months earlier. Before leaving South Australia, the station idea sounded great and the thought of missing home never once crossed my mind. I had thought about how I could tell my friends how much land we now owned, and how I would have a motorbike of my own, and how envious they would be. Now it dawns on me that moving way out here to the isolated west means I'll lose those friends forever; probably never see them again. And I haven't.

We haven't been here long, just an hour or so, but already the station is nothing like what I had expected. But it is too early to tell. Maybe tomorrow my mind will change.

I cross my arms on the table, rest my head on them and look up at Father. It is so good to see him again. He has a full beard and looks like a proper bushman now, not that I knew what a bushman looked like back then. I try to remember what he looked like without the beard, but I am too tired. I think about the hug he gave me when I got off the bus and how his clothes now smell of campfire smoke. Back in SA they smelled of fresh lemons. I think about how a person can change so much in such a short time and close my eyes for a couple of seconds. When I reopen them, Father is looking at me and smiling.

I look over at Mum and she smiles back at me. Bryce and Bidjid are still sitting there half asleep but the others have gone to bed. The clock on the wall indicates it is just after two a.m., I must have drifted off.

'Why don't you three get your things from the Nissan? I'll show you to your rooms when you get back. You're not scared of the dark, are you?' Father says, with a warm smile.

'No, we aren't scared,' Bryce replies.

I look at Bryce and am about to say that I'm scared but I want to be brave too.

'Here, take my lighter but don't waste all the gas. Just use it sparingly, okay?' Father slides it across the table to Bryce.

'Okay,' Bryce replies as the three of us stand up and make our way out the door into the darkness.

Every couple of seconds, Bryce strikes the lighter and we stumble along the path in the direction we had come earlier. We manage to find the Nissan and bring all our things inside.

Father is still sitting at the kitchen table talking to Mum, but he gets up to show us to our rooms. 'Why don't you give your mother a kiss goodnight,' he says softly.

We each give her a kiss on her cheek, and she gives all of us a cuddle, one after the other.

'Goodnight, I love you,' we say one by one.

'Goodnight, I love you too,' Mum replies.

'Just wait there a minute, Shirl,' Father says to Mum as he picks up the lamp.

Mum takes out another cigarette and lights up.

'Okey dokey, then. Come on, you three, you must be thoroughly exhausted.'

'Yes, we are,' we say together, as he leads us outside to our living quarters. I'm a little worried that we can't sleep inside the house, though.

'You two boys can sleep in this room,' Father says.

He stands there for a couple of seconds while Bryce and I choose our beds. I am so glad to be sharing a room with him because I have never slept outside the main house before, and I am feeling a bit anxious about it.

Then Father turns to Bidjid. 'Right, your room is over here. You can sleep with Zoann.'

'Okay, I was worried I was going to have to sleep alone.'

Father waits long enough for Bidjid to get into her bed before he heads back towards the kitchen. Zoann has been asleep for a while but wakes up and starts talking quietly to Bidjid.

'Goodnight, kids,' Father calls, raising his voice a little so he can be heard above our chattering and shuffling about in our bed as we get comfortable.

'Goodnight, Father,' we all yell back.

And the darkness engulfs the faint glow of the lamp as he disappears back into the house.

5

First Light

Just before sunrise, Bryce and I wake to the sound of Father's voice at our doorway.

'It's time to get up now, boys. Vonn has cooked you a lovely breakfast.'

Bryce and I sit up in our beds and rub our eyes.

'What time is it, Father?' Bryce asks.

Father looks at his watch. 'Just after five. This is the best part of the day and you're going to miss out on it by sleeping in.'

He heads out the door and, before long, we can hear him telling Bidjid and Zoann to get up also. We drag ourselves out of bed and into the kitchen.

'What's for breakfast?' I ask Vonn, who is standing by the wood stove, stirring a wooden spoon back and forth in a saucepan.

'It's porridge,' she replies, still sleepy herself, as we sit down around the table.

'Mmm, yummm, I love porridge.'

We all lick our lips and inhale the delicious smell of the oats cooking. Vonn dishes up and we go over to the counter to grab our bowls.

'Is there any milk?' I ask, looking around the kitchen for the fridge.

'If you want milk, you'll need to make some up for yourselves.' Vonn pushes an open packet of powdered milk in my direction.

'How do you make it?' I ask her, puzzled.

'Just mix some up in a cup. Use one spoonful of powder in a cup of water, okay.'

I grab a cup from the dish rack and mix up the milk according to

Vonn's instructions. It is very watery and doesn't taste anything like milk from a bottle, which was what I was used to back in SA, but I quickly eat my porridge because I want to explore around the house.

After breakfast, we go out and look around the house. There are a few large palm trees on the front lawn, about fifteen to twenty metres tall, and a couple of large pencil pines about the same height. They tower over the trees in the house yard as well as over the mulga trees out in the paddocks that surround the house.

On the veranda, I come across an old kerosene fridge. When I open the door to see what's inside, it is mainly meat. The fridge, as I soon learn, needs refuelling with kerosene every week. And the freezer compartment, roughly twenty by twenty by thirty centimetres is always frozen over. This ice, though, doesn't put any chill into the fridge whatsoever.

It is about six a.m. when Bryce and I venture over to the workshop, where we find a few motorbikes. We climb on them to see if our feet can touch the ground. Being taller than me, it is no problem for Bryce, but I am still too short for them.

I start searching around for Streak but can't find him anywhere around the house. Eventually, I go back to ask Father where Streak is.

I find Father in the lounge room with Vonn, Mum and Loui, having a cup of tea and a cigarette. The adults are talking quietly among themselves. I stand there for a few moments, waiting for my opportunity to speak.

'Yes, Luke?' Father finally says. 'What seems to be the matter?"

'Um, sorry, Father, where's Streak? I've looked all around the house but can't find him anywhere.'

'Oh, he's tied up down at the tank kennel. Get Zoann to show you where it is. I just seen her heading off to the bathroom not long ago, in that direction,' he indicates with his hand.

I find Zoann brushing her teeth.

'Where's the tank kennel?' I ask. 'Father said Streak's tied up there and he told me to get you to show me where it is.'

'Yeah, hold on. I'll show you in a sec, okay.' Zoann spits out the toothpaste and rinses out her toothbrush and puts it away in the cupboard. 'Come on.'

I am so happy to see Streak. He jumps all over me, licking me like mad as I scruff him about.

'Luke... Luke, let Streak off the chain now, would you,' Father yells out from the veranda.

'Come on, Streak,' I say and we both race towards the house, leaving Zoann far behind us.

'Luke,' Bryce yells as Streak and I speed through the small orchard of citrus trees.

Bryce is jumping on the trampoline we got for Christmas back in Monarto that Father had taken over with him on the trailer several months earlier.

'Oh gee, I've really missed our trampoline,' I say, climbing up.

'Be careful, Luke. It has a hole in it there.'

But before I can avoid the spot Bryce points to, my foot slips into the hole, tearing it further apart. The trampoline is useless now.

Only one person will be able to jump on it at a time now and they will have to avoid the hole, which is getting larger with every bounce.

'What happened to our trampoline?' I ask Father later.

'The handle on Dansan's bike rubbed up against it on the trip over here from SA and it ended up wearing a hole in it, I'm afraid, mate. I have an old tarp we can use to sew a patch on it,' Father explains, shaking his head slowly from side to side and giving us a compassionate smile.

'Let's stich it up now, Luke.' Bryce suggests, looking at me.

I nod, thinking about when Father had loaded the trailer back in SA and wondering about how Dansan's bike could have caused such damage. I just want to cry angrily and not look at anyone.

After Father finishes his cup of tea, he hooks up a trailer to the Nissan and tells us kids to get in, sit down and hold on. We set off on a windmill run.

'How many windmills will we be seeing today, Father?' Bryce asks as he is getting down from the back at the first gate Father calls out for him to open.

'Um… roughly a dozen or more up north,' Father responds as he drives pass Bryce holding open the gate.

It wasn't long before we reached our first windmill and father pulled up alongside it and switched the Land Rover off.

'This is Pannikin. It's one of my most favourite windmills on the whole station. The water from this mill is like natural spring water,' Father cheerfully says.

'Mmmmm, I can't wait to give it a try,' Bryce replies as he grabs a cup from the esky. 'Wow, it's so fresh tasting. You should try some, Luke,' Bryce says, passing me the cup he was using.

There's still half a cup of water left in it, which I down to quench my thirst.

'Arrr, that's much better,' I respond, while using the back of my hand to wipe the water off my lips.

Father shows us how he'd like us to clean the troughs and soon we are setting off again.

'What is this windmill called, Father?' I ask as it comes into view.

'This one is called Fork,' Father replies, switching the engine off while letting the Land Rover come to a stop naturally.

'There's some emus over there,' Bryce quietly says, pointing in their direction.

They appear to be a family and soon dash away gracefully. The only thing remaining is the now disappearing cloud of orange/red dust as it settles back down to earth.

'We won't be stopping here until on the way back home later this afternoon, so don't bother about getting off. This one's yours, Luke. Bryce, you may need to help Luke with this one, because these can be a little awkward the first couple of times you open and close them,' Father instructs as we pull up at the next gate.

We both get down from the back of the Land Rover and I stand alongside Bryce as he figures out how to open the gate. This was not any ordinary swinging gate. It was made of wire and is often used as a cheaper solution known as a Cocky Gate. After a couple of minutes, we manage to get through the awkward gate and close it again.

'This windmill is called Eight Mile. It's called Eight Mile because it's eight miles from the homestead. There are a couple of windmills named after the distance from the homestead – there's Four Mile and Six Mile as well. We'll check them out another day.'

'How do you remember all their names?' Bryce asked.

'You'll get to know them all soon enough. Off the top of my head, there's Pannikin, Fork, Eight Mile, Centre Pool, Donald's, Limestone, Naracoota, Mount Leak, Joe and Harry's, Cement Tank, Dead Horse, Crater, Judareena, Gidgee, Salt Bush Johnnie's, Carols, Four Mile, Brownies, Number One, Number Two, Number Three, Glengarry, and Six Mile, Father responds.

Because it is so hot, Streak often jumps straight into the troughs we stop to clean. He lies on his tummy, his back entirely under the water, then jumps out as we get near to him and has a big shake, covering us in water also.

'Streak! Look what you've done now,' I yell as he runs off.

Everyone laughs.

On the way home, Father pulls off the road and tells us to jump out and load up the trailer with wood. As he drives along, he points out logs he thinks are ideal and we throw them on.

'Rightio, that'll do, guys. Jump into the Nissan now and we'll get going back home,' he yells out the window. 'If we throw any more on, it'll just fall off.'

The trailer's stacked as high as a pyramid. We all squeeze in beside each other in the back of the Nissan and I cling onto Streak around his neck.

The wood we have collected is for the wood stove, our only means of cooking meals, and the hot water boiler also known as the donkey, which is used for heating our hot water.

When we get home, Bryce and I unload the trailer, and we are immediately put on wood-chopping duties and fill the wood box for the stove inside the kitchen.

Vonn tends to Lillie during the evening, while Mum makes dinner using the meat from a freshly slaughtered sheep and the supplies in the pantry that Father got from Meekatharra. He does a shopping run every couple of weeks because Vonn still does not have a driver's licence.

As soon as the sun goes down, it is pitch-dark once again and the mosquitoes come out in droves. They have one mission in their short lives, which is to seek out our blood. These things are the size of micro-bats and they are extremely fierce throughout the night. Though I guess I can thank them for all the free karate lessons I get fighting with them.

One thing for sure, I grow tougher shins over the following few weeks, walking blindly through the darkness, night after night, into chairs and other obstacles. At times, I miss the comforts of our home in South Australia, but it is better to be on the station with Father.

Not long after this, Bryce finds an old lighter which has run out of gas and strikes it at night so he can see where he's going. This works well, so the next day he and I walk over to the small rubbish dump and scout around for more lighters that have been thrown out. We get lucky and take quite a few back to our room.

Living in darkness still isn't really for me, and nor are a few other things. I really miss my favourite TV shows, like *Astro Boy*, *Roger Ramjet*, *The Goodies*, *Doctor Who*, *Loony Tunes* and *Danger Mouse*, but those memories quickly fade, and I slowly forget about TV shows and the life we used to have.

I am surprised a couple of weeks later when Father connects a battery up to a diesel generator. It supplies 240-volt power to the washing machine as well as power to every room in the house. The generator has been designed to come on whenever power is being used in the house, and because we are all still used to living with the comforts of electricity, we are switching on lights even in the daytime and every time the generator starts up.

Father very soon gets sick of hearing the generator starting up and removes the automatic starter. After we stuff that up, he decides to manually turn the generator on and off for power. It is now only used sparingly, and the rest of the time we are back to the kerosene lamp for lighting.

As the end of January 1985 comes around, Father heads into Meekatharra to pick up some extra supplies, but mainly to pick up the mail. Our schoolwork arrives by post, sent from the Distance Education Centre in Perth to kids living in the remote outback. There are textbooks for each subject and we either write our answers in the books and send them back for marking or write the answers into an exercise book and send that. It is hard to get used to, especially now that we are always helping Father on the station. But he makes time in the evenings for us to catch up with our lessons.

The weeks roll on, and we start to get into the rhythm of the station and the jobs that must be done to maintain our new way of life. There is a constant heatwave and Father instructs Mum, Bidjid and Lillie to stay back at the homestead while the rest of us set off on a windmill run.

We leave early, just after breakfast. Bryce, Zoann, Dansan and I are on the back of the Land Rover while Vonn, Loui and Father are inside. As we approach the windmill called Fork, Father slows down to go through the dry creek bed.

'This will be running by the time we come back through here this afternoon,' he says, pointing to a small pool of water over the fence.

He knows this because he has seen it happen in the past when there have been storms to the far east of us during the night. I find it hard to believe but I don't say anything.

After being out just about all day, we are back at Fork when Father pulls up at the gate. We are still over a hundred metres away from the creek he mentioned earlier in the day, the one that he said would be running.

'This is your one, Luke,' Father yells out the window.

I climb down and walk up to the gate, unable to get over how many crows are perched in the mulga trees alongside the fence right next to the gate. They seem to be looking straight through me, as if someone I can't see is strolling along beside me. And they are squawking raucously.

As I open the gate, the crows don't budge from the nearby mulga branches; some are within reach of my fingertips. They are still squawking, with their beaks open wide. When I look at them, they stare back at me with piercing, glassy red eyes. I get a shiver down my spine and the hairs on the back of my neck stand on end.

Father drives through the gate and pulls up about fifteen metres away from where he left me. He switches off the engine and gets out to check the tank to see how much water is in it.

'Bryce, clean out that trough over there, would ya,' Father orders.

I shut the gate and make my way over to help Bryce. As I crouch over, I look back towards the mulga trees. The crows by the gate are still squawking but now they are even louder than before.

In the faint distance, we hear the screaming of an engine approaching. Bryce and I stand up to see if we can see anything.

As we look towards the sound, we freeze for a few seconds. The high-pitched whining noise is even louder and clearer now, rising above the squawking crows, soon drowned out by the sound of wailing, and shortly afterwards we can see the Nissan erratically tearing through the creek. We realise the wailing is coming from Mum and she is screaming at the top of her lungs. As soon as Mum sees us, her screams multiply. They are louder and along with her cries we also hear Bidjid's.

Father takes a few steps towards the Nissan and peers inside. His head droops forward, and he shakes it so slowly, it is as though he has moved into slow motion.

When he looks back towards us, his eyes have narrowed under heavy brows. His face is all worry. 'We've lost Lillie,' he says evenly. 'She's gone.'

Everything around me goes foggy. I can't hear a single sound. As the words sink in, I slip into shock. Lillie and I used to spend loads of time together back in Monarto. All those little snippets of Lillie – her loving smile and little bursts of laughter, her hair, and the cheeky eyes she made when she clung onto Streak and made him yip in defence – bubble up in my mind. Tears pool in my eyes and roll down my cheeks.

'She had a seizure and stopped breathing,' Mum wails at the top of her lungs as she rolls to a stop.

Father flings the passenger door open. Lying there motionless on Bidjid's lap is Lillie's little body.

'Oh, no, did you try the Flying Doctors on the two-way radio?' Father concernedly asks Mum as he gently takes Lillie from Bidjid.

'Yes, I held onto the red button. I tried, Neil,' Mum weeps. 'I don't know why but no one responded. I tried several times, but nothing.'

We all gather around Father and look at Lillie. She looks like she is just peacefully sleeping.

Vonn goes into shock and clenches onto Loui, not able to bear the thought of losing him as well. Everyone is hit hard, and Father tries his best to remain cool and prevent any heated disputes erupting.

'Bryce, you take the Land Rover back to the homestead. We'll be right behind you, okay?'

Bryce goes over to the Land Rover and gets into the driver's seat.

'Go on, we'll be right behind you,' Father says again.

Bryce drives away while the rest of us get into the Nissan. We follow several metres behind him. As we pass back through the creek Father said would be running, I look out the window at a tiny stream of water. We are roughly ten kilometres from the homestead when suddenly the Nissan veers off the dirt track and into a channel alongside the road, which has been cut out by the grader to drain water away from it during the wetter months. The Nissan comes to a sudden stop but, completely unaware, Bryce continues driving. Before too long, he has disappeared out of sight.

'Lillie wants to spend more time with us by the look of it,' Father says, as he frantically tries to free the Nissan. He reverses but the Nissan just sinks deeper into the mud.

I cannot begin to imagine the heartbreak he would have been feeling.

'You four better get out and try and push us free. Vonn can nurse Lillie and you little boys, you both stay in the back.' Father looks over to Mum, then back at Bidjid, Zoann and me.

We all climb out and push as hard as we can, but the Nissan only sinks deeper. Eventually, its chassis is sitting on top of the mud and all four wheels are spinning. We're not going anywhere.

Father gets out and looks underneath. 'Luke, you better see if you can catch up with Bryce. Tell him to come back and pick us all up please. You know how to get home from here, don't you? Just stay on this track. It leads straight home.'

'Okay, Father,' I say with a worried look on my face, hoping that maybe he will send Bidjid instead of me.

I set off anyhow, looking over my shoulder every now and then to see if I'm being followed. I run like the wind, crying to myself most of the way, and nearly make it back to the homestead when Bryce appears in the distance, coming towards me in the Land Rover.

'What happened, where's Father?' he asks, pulling up.

I climb into the vehicle, panting and sweating like a racehorse. 'We got bogged not far away from Fork, in a small puddle of water,' I puff, trying to regain my breath.

'Whereabouts did you get bogged?' Bryce queries. 'I never saw any water, apart from that little stream in the creek bed that Father pointed out to us in the morning when we went through, the one he said would be flowing by this afternoon.'

Bryce slowly releases the clutch and we set off.

'Yeah, just past that creek, there was some water in one of those trenches that drain the water away from the road.'

Bryce frowns and says nothing; his eyes are still glassy and there are dry crystalised tear marks on his face. We don't talk for most of the journey until Bryce finally breaks the silence.

'How did Father get bogged out there? I don't understand.'

At long last, we see the Nissan in the distance.

'Yeah, me neither. All Father said was that Lillie wanted to spend more time with us.'

As we pull up, Father is very glad to see us. Bryce and I jump out of the Land Rover.

'Thanks for coming back for us, Bryce,' he says. 'Come on everyone, jump on the back of the Land Rover, you kids. We'll leave the Nissan here.'

Father, Vonn, Loui and Mum, still cradling little Lillie, all squeeze into the front while the rest of us clamber onto the back.

When we get back to the homestead, Father carries Lillie inside and carefully places her on her bed. Mum and Vonn sit with her while Father calls the Royal Flying Doctor Service to notify them of Lillie's passing. It takes a couple of minutes before he eventually gets through on the VHF radio.

After he has made the call, Father asks us to come in one by one to say our goodbyes to Lillie before she is taken away.

As the last bit of daylight is consumed by darkness, a vehicle with red and blue lights on the top approaches the homestead and pulls up.

The local police sergeant from Meekatharra gets out. 'Mr Pomery, my deepest sympathies to you and your family. I'm Sergeant Todd Wilson,' the policeman says. 'I'm extremely sorry we couldn't respond to your call earlier this afternoon. The message was unclear, and we never heard back from the distressed caller, so we didn't know who made the call.'

'Hello, sergeant. I'm sorry we couldn't meet under more pleasant circumstances,' Father responds.

The sergeant shakes Father's hand and places his free hand on Father's shoulder.

'It was unexpected. We never. I mean…' Father chokes back the sorrow in his voice. 'I never showed Shirl how to use the emergency button on the radio properly.'

'We've responded to many life-threatening emergencies over the years, some with tragic endings due to VHF radios, Neil,' Sergeant Wilson says. 'So let's not go blaming anyone now. I'm sure Shirl is feeling bad enough as it is.'

'Follow me please, sergeant,' Father says, straightening his stance. 'Lillie is in the house.'

A few minutes later, the sergeant follows Father back out of the house. Father is carrying Lillie's body wrapped up in her bed sheet. He passes her to the sergeant, who places her carefully across the back seat of the police car. Everyone is crying, more than ever as the sergeant gets back into his vehicle and starts the engine.

'Be strong for the rest of your family, Neil. You all need to be strong for each other, okay?'

'Yes, we will,' Father says, and we all silently agree.

The sergeant pulls away slowly and does a U-turn, then drives past us all extra slowly as he takes Lillie away.

The following morning, Father picks a spot not far away from the house and starts digging a grave for Lillie. It takes him the best part of the day, using nothing more than a shovel and crowbar.

A couple of weeks pass, and it is the day of Lillie's funeral. A shiny black hearse arrives. In the back is a tiny little white velvet coffin with chrome handles along the side and I think of our dearest departed Lillie inside.

After the funeral, Mum only stays for another week and when Father says he is going into Meekatharra to get more supplies and check the mail, she packs up her stuff, says goodbye to us and goes into town with him and heads back to South Australia.

I feel like my heart has been torn in half and she doesn't love me any more.

6

Mustering Time

The blistering heat from the long summer days, when the temperatures reach above forty-five degrees C on a cool day, is now being replaced with much cooler weather. The end of March is approaching. Winter is less than eight weeks away. When we get up at four in the morning, it seems like it is still the middle of the night. But according to Father, it is the best time to be out in the paddocks mustering sheep.

The days start getting shorter but for us, our working days are becoming much longer. We are out in the paddock by five a.m., followed by eight to ten hours of mustering. When we get home, it's late, just enough time to have a shower, eat dinner, wash the dishes and do some correspondence schooling, then back to bed.

'Time to get up, you two. Vonn has made porridge for breakfast,' Father says every morning at four on the dot, before going to wake up Bidjid and Zoann.

I stick on a pair of socks, slide my feet into my oversized boots, then I stagger out the door. In the kitchen, Father is at the table with a cup of tea, waiting to go over the day's plan with us. He waits until we are all sitting down.

'Right, this morning we're heading out to Mount Leak to start mustering the spinifex paddock,' Father announces. 'Bryce, you take Luke with you and head along the northern fence line to the windmills on the eastern side, checking around Dead Horse. Then weave your way south towards Crater. Once you get there, then chase them west towards Granite, where you should meet up with Bidjid and me. Make sure you don't allow any to double back behind you. Bryce, leave Luke with the sheep, while you scout around for more. Bidjid and I will take the eastern side and weave back and forth from the north and we'll meet you there. Then all we need to do is chase them over to the Judareena laneway for holding.'

We all nod and quickly eat our hot porridge.

Vonn has sliced inch-thick bread that she baked a couple of days ago for our lunches. She spreads a thick layer of Vegemite on one slice before topping it with another.

'Finish up your breakfast quickly. We're losing that crucial start,' Father says impatiently. 'Bryce, you and Luke go and fill up the motorbikes with petrol. Bidjid will bring out your lunch in a minute. Make sure you take a bottle of water with you too.'

Father and Bryce are the only ones who can ride the motorbikes that were left behind on the station as part of the sale. Bidjid and I are their passengers. Once we are out in the paddock, we must get off the back of the motorbikes and walk along behind the sheep. This is referred to as 'the tail' and we walk many kilometres that day. By the end of it, we are absolutely stuffed. I have no trouble falling asleep at bedtime that night, or most nights.

Sometimes, although not very often, Vonn, Zoann, Dansan and Loui meet us out in the paddock to pick up the sheep that are not able to walk very far. It is always good when Vonn comes out because she either boils the billy or brings something with her from home for our lunches and passes it out to us with a cup of tea. This beats drinking lukewarm water and eating a half-squashed, sweaty sandwich, anytime. Most of the paddocks are hard to get vehicles through, and Vonn is not used to manoeuvring her way through the scrub, so she usually stays on the dirt track along the fence lines, and we go to her.

Sulkers, that's what we call the sheep that can't walk far. They just drop to the ground on their stomach and refuse to go any further. So, we throw them over the petrol tank of the motorbike, take them over to Vonn and put them on the back of the Land Rover with their legs tied up, so they can't get away.

Sometimes, we find Vonn hunched over the steering wheel crying and calling out. 'Why did you have to take my little girl Lillie away from us?' she would scream.

In the colder months, the water for showering is icy, unless we light a fire to heat up the boiler. It is known as a 'donkey' – a forty-four-gallon drum lying across a steel frame just above ground level so a fire can be lit underneath.

One of the best things about the cooler weather is lighting the fire in the lounge room, because it provides some additional lighting as well as warmth from the chilly desert air.

Staring into the fire is like watching TV. I gaze at the coals for hours, mesmerised by the many glowing shapes before the burning logs turn to ash. Some nights, I can see faces in the coals, but nothing spooky. Or I imagine the coals to be animals. It's like cloud spotting, but I'm spotting shapes among the embers as the coals burn.

A few months after our arrival at the station, Father orders a couple of extra motorbikes. He gets Bryce a 100cc Suzuki AG bike and a bit smaller Suzuki for me, a little DS 80cc. It is a bit like what is known as a pit bike, and it's a nice little motorbike for me to ride.

I am very grateful to be on my own motorbike, but it is hard to keep up with Father and Bryce, who are on bigger bikes, and I don't care to eat their dust.

Bidjid rides an old scooter which has been left on the station by the previous owners. It has street tyres and whenever it is ridden through sand, it snakes all over the track. Sometimes, you get flung off and wind up with a mouthful of sand, but there is no time to sit around feeling sorry for yourself. You just must get straight back onto your motorbike and catch up with the others before they leave you behind.

In the early days of being on the station, Father started taking in young Aboriginal offenders on prison release. It is something he got into back in South Australia when he was in the police force. He would teach them self-discipline and how to stay out of trouble from the law. It was only for short stays, like a week or two, but it gave him the extra set of hands he needed on the station while Bryce, Bidjid and I were working on a schoolwork at home. Sometimes, they prove to be an asset and do their best, but at other times they are more trouble than they are worth, and are sent back to prison or somewhere else, where they can carry out their remaining parole.

One of the prisoners Father is sent can't cope with the station life and struggles with the isolation. So Father and Vonn decide to take him into Meekatharra. It's around three p.m. when they leave, and Father tells us to take it easy for the rest of the day. Father, Vonn, Loui and the young offender set off, while the rest of us take advantage of having the afternoon free to do what we please.

We listen to Aboriginal songs on the cassette player, turned up as loud as it will play, because we are never allowed to do that while Father is around. We dance around like we are having a celebration, jumping about and being silly, stomping our feet in the dirt, singing along with the songs, and clapping sticks together that we found lying around the yard. But I start to feel a little spooked when the sun goes down, and by the time it gets dark, Bryce, Bidjid, Zoann and Dansan are also becoming a little spooked from some of the songs too.

'I think we should go and look for Father, Vonn and Loui just in case they've broken down somewhere,' Bryce says, sensing our collective panic.

We all jump into the Nissan and head off, and as we are nearing the highway, a good five kilometres away, a light appears in the bush.

That must be Father, we all think with a sense of relief.

But as we continue our way, the light steadily keeps its distance, roughly about two hundred metres from us, just slightly off the dirt road we are travelling along. It is not a blinding light; it does not even look like a car light after a while, more like an old-style motorbike headlight, just the one round beam of light shining directly at us, while the surrounding bush remains pitch-black.

After following this light for several minutes, we make it to the highway. By this stage, the light has crossed over to the other side of the highway, which confuses us even more. We set off towards Meekatharra, driving for another two kilometres with the light still shining at us. After a while, a vehicle approaches from the direction of Meekatharra. As it gets closer, we can see it is Father. We are all excited and as we pull off the road, the light that has been haunting us suddenly disappears.

'That must have been a Min Min light,' Bryce says.

We had heard this mysterious word used in songs sung by Slim Dusty and questioned our mother about it. Mum believed it to be a Kurdaitcha man who travelled over the country as a spirit form and kept an eye on us all. Whether or not that is true or not, a Min Min is a light phenomenon that has often been reported in outback Australia which still has scientists baffled to what they really are to this day.

One thing is for certain: after that night, we never mucked about with Aboriginal songs again by pretending we were in a corroboree.

Just before Christmas of 1985, we all set off in the Nissan down to Perth. It takes us all day, from sunrise to sunset, to get there. Father has given each of us some pocket money to buy something for ourselves and, on top of our spending money, he buys a few extra things for us too. It is clear to me now that Father wasn't always mean and that he did care about us. It is something I only understood as I grew older and saw more of life.

Father did have his preferences, however, and as a kid I always felt as though I was the last one he had any compassion for, even though he said he loved us all. As I saw things, Bryce was Father's pride and joy, Bidjid was just above me, Loui was his golden-haired child and Dansan was just below him. Zoann, being Vonn's daughter, was also above Bidjid and me. Since Mum's returned to South Australia, and now that the other kids are growing older, I often feel left out, or pushed away from my former position, where it felt like Father loved me most of all.

Anyway, because we live in the centre of WA, Father tells us that

Father Christmas can't land his sleigh on the sandy soil out here. By this time in my life, I know that it is all fabricated and Father says it for the benefit of the younger kids. So, each Christmas, Father makes tracks in the sand using a plank of wood. He slides it back and forth a couple of times to create an imprint about two metres long, then does another one about 1.5 metres away and parallel, so it looks like a helicopter has landed. He also wears his gumboots to make it look as if Father Christmas has come during the night.

And every year without fail, in the lead-up to Christmas, Father plays all the old Christmas songs and sings along to them. He really makes our Christmases come to life. Every Christmas Eve, we all go outside and look up at the evening sky to see if we can see Father Christmas's sleigh. The lights we see are satellites most of the time, but one evening we are sure we spot the sleigh. Excitement fills our hearts, and Father tells us all to go to bed because if we don't, and Father Christmas sees any of us awake, he won't come.

Once we are fast asleep, Father puts all our presents under the Christmas tree, which is a cedar on the front lawn. He has spent most of the night wrapping them but is always up first thing on Christmas morning to see our excited faces as we open our presents. Vonn's not involved in any of this. He prefers to leave her quietly tucked up in bed with Loui alongside her, so he doesn't wake any of us up during the night. In the morning, he shows us the tracks in the sand left behind by Father Christmas. He really does go above and beyond to make it a special time for us all.

Mum tries to call us but now that she is back in South Australia, the only way she can do this is via VHF radio, so we tend to hear from her either before or after Christmas Day.

One Christmas, though, when there is a drought, Father Christmas can't come because there is no water or food for his reindeers. We save a lot of sheep that week and eventually, a week after Christmas, Father Christmas arrives with sincere apologies to us all.

Father, Bryce and I are sitting at the kitchen table, Bidjid and Zoann are on laundry duties with Vonn. Dansan plays in the sand under the jacaranda tree with his wheelless toy truck and Loui, well, he's just a growing baby.

'Right. Today, guys, we're going to do some fencing out by Carols. I have everything on the old Ford ute but you'll need to fill up the petrol and while you're at it don't forget to check the water and oil,' Father instructs.

'Okay, Father,' Bryce responds.

Twenty minutes later, we are passing Carols and we head south along the fence dividing the Four Mile and Woolie paddock from the Carols paddock. A straining post rotted out at the base is now over on its side and father pulls the Ford up just before the post.

'Grab the pliers and wire strainers from the back, boys. This post has rotted out and will need to be strained out,' Father says, giving us both warm loving smiles.

Father starts straining up the wires one by one and rejoins the wires using a figure eight; a figure eight is commonly used to join broken wires back together. I stand back, allowing Father to show Bryce how to do this and when he's on the last wire Father turns to me.

'Luke, do you think you're able to bring up the Ford?'

'Yes, Father,' I reply happily.

I have a skip in my step and I jump into the driver's seat and shut the door. Soon, I have the vehicle moving and I'm proud of myself until I'm nearing where Father and Bryce are. I can barely see over the steering wheel and my leg is at full extension. The tip of my shoe just manages to touch the pedals. When I go to stop, I take my foot off the accelerator then go to put it down on the brakes but hit hard on the accelerator. The Ford takes off and I'm unsure why I can't stop. Looking down at the pedals on the floor for a split second, I start to veer off the track straight towards Father and Bryce.

'Watch out, Father!' Bryce warns.

The two of them are thankfully saved by Bryce's quick response.

I tear past them and, as the brakes in my personal opinion were failing, the next best thing I could think of to stop the Ford in its tracks was to turn off the engine, coming to a stop on a small mulga tree. All shaken up, I get out and go back to where Father and Bryce are.

'What happened?' Father asks.

'I went to put my foot on the brakes, but it sped up. The only way I could stop it in the end was by turning the key off,' I nervously reply.

'I thought you initially were trying to kill us both. That's how it looked from where I was standing,' Father answers with a bit of humour in his voice.

'No, I wasn't trying to run you both over,' I laugh.

Not long after Christmas, Vonn starts ordering us around, asking us to do jobs while she just sits around listening to Bruce Springsteen and playing cards.

'You're not our mum,' Bryce, Bidjid and I all snap back.

That makes her blood boil, but she keeps herself contained and waits for Father to get back from a windmill run he has gone on with Dansan.

Our retort doesn't go down too well when Father hears about it. He loses his temper and just jumps into the Holden Kingswood and starts it up. He had traded one of the station vehicles for the Kingswood so he had a family car for us to comfortably get to and fro into Meekatharra.

But now, he is tearing around the flat out the front of the homestead doing doughnuts and he looks like he is having a bloody good time, until he nearly crashes into a mulga tree. Then he jumps out and his eyes are red with anger.

'Right, go and get your things and piss off to the shearing quarters,' he orders. 'You can live out there until you've all learned your lesson and can be more respectful.'

Bryce, Bidjid and I are not even in our teens yet, when we are made to live down there for a couple of weeks until Father kicks us out of there because he thinks we are living the life of Riley too much and haven't learned our lesson yet.

So we shift to the Moolapool pools, where we live off the land, catching lizards and eating birds' eggs. If we're lucky with rock throwing, we sometimes get a top-notch pigeon or a galah to eat.

The station is located at the start of the Murchison and Gascoyne rivers. The average annual rainfall for this area is roughly only 230 millimetres. Once a year, when there's good enough rainfall, the shallow Canning Stock Route pool fills up. It can hold water for several months until the heat of the summer returns and it dries up again. Fortunately for us, 1985 is one of those years where we have good rainfall.

Every now and then, one of us sneaks back to the homestead, over three kilometres away, hoping that no one is home. If we are lucky, Vonn feels sorry for us. Even though she was the one who dobbed us in, she usually gives us some food. After a couple more weeks, we have learned our lesson and we are allowed to return to the homestead, but under strict instructions to maintain a happy home.

As spring of 1986 arrives, Father and Vonn take us to the Meekatharra show in town. There are raffles, a competition to guess how many jelly beans are in a two-kilogram container, pony rides and other events. One contest involves trying to catch a piglet. Whoever catches the piglet gets to keep it. We all stand among the other kids, waiting for the instructor to let us know when we can make our attempt.

'On your marks, get set, go!' the instructor yells through the microphone.

About twenty or thirty of us take off after the piglet. It runs very fast, dodging and weaving through our legs. Then suddenly Bidjid dives onto it out of nowhere and clings to it like a hungry beast. She stands up, clasping the yelping piglet to her chest so it can't break free. She is now the owner of the piglet and we take it back home. Bidjid, being a huge fan of the Muppets, names the piglet Ms Flopsy, and from that day, Ms Flopsy follows Bidjid around everywhere. Father tells us pigs are very smart animals, even smarter than most dogs.

When Father gets our mid-year school reports for 1987, not long after my twelfth birthday, when he made me a stuffed zucchini cake, he notices that I am lagging behind in maths. He tells me to go and get my maths books and we head off on a windmill run; he will go through the maths with me along the way. But before we are even two minutes down the road, he becomes enraged because I can't tell him what fractions and pi r-squared are. He pulls over and punches the living daylights out of me for a few seconds, which to me feels like a couple of minutes. After he has calmed down, his mood towards me changes and he apologises for attacking me. It is unlike him to say sorry for anything, but I must have looked scared shitless for him to feel the need to make me feel better.

When we get out to Spinifex Paddock, where the spinifex grows wild, Father pulls up and grabs a fuel container out from the back. It is a tin with a long metal tube which has a rag on it. Once the rag is lit, it is used to ignite a continuous line of small fires. The spinifex takes off, burning away from us. Father walks along the edge of the track while I drive the ute along behind him. All I am thinking of is running him over so he won't be able to hurt me the way he has done earlier, but I can't bring myself to do it.

For a start, I don't want to be hurtful like him. And besides, deep down, I still love him dearly and can't imagine life without him, even though he tends to be cold at times. Not everything you run over is going to die from the hit anyway, I figure. My guess is it is about 50:50.

Sometimes Father says things that sound odd, like 'What do you do if you accidentally run someone over in a vehicle?' Father would jump in answering his own question, 'Reverse back over them to make sure they're dead.'

It is just his sense of humour, of course, but that day I do really think about it.

'Don't worry, kids,' he sometimes says. 'If anything happens to me, I haven't forgotten about any of you in my will. Bryce, you'll have all the money and my shotgun. Bidjid, you can have my gramophone.

Luke, well, I'll come back to you in a sec. Zoann can have my typewriter. Dansan can have my .22 rifle. Loui can have my car. Oh, and for you, Luke, who thought I would forget about him altogether, I say, "Hello, Luke."' Father always says this with a poker face, looking down his nose at me, like he is holding a hot coal in each of his fists.

7

Boarding School

Late spring, early summer of 1987, not long after we finish the second muster to get in the stragglers we missed in the first muster, Father notices a few of the next-door neighbour's sheep in our flock. We load them onto our trailer and take them over to their station, about fifty kilometres away.

When we get there, Father asks the owner, Phil Holmes, how his boys are going at school. Phil says that his boys attend a boarding school in the wheatbelt between Geraldton and Perth. It is a Christian Brothers Agricultural School (CBAS), and he tells Father they are loving it and his youngest son Winton is just completing his first year.

All the way home from Phil's station, Father talks about the boarding school and how much fun it would be for us to make some friends and learn some new things.

Bryce and I agree. So, as soon as we are back at the homestead, Father jumps on the phone and makes a couple of calls. Eventually, he gets both of us enrolled for the next year in the same school as the Holmes boys.

The past three years of correspondence schooling have had a massively negative impact on my education. In that time, my grades have dropped from the good results I recall from my earlier primary school years to the D grades I have been getting more recently. So I am feeling pretty happy when the end of 1987 comes around and I graduate from Year 7.

I am looking forward to going to boarding school, even though I know I will be away from the station. I'm sick of Father's teaching methods.

By the time we are enrolled in our new school, Bryce is fourteen going on fifteen and over six-foot tall, making him one of the tallest kids at the school.

I am twelve, soon to be thirteen, and under five foot and skinny as a rake, which means I am just about the shortest kid in the place, apart from another student called Bran. It is an all-boys school, 550 kilometres from home and thirty-six kilometres from the northern wheatbelt town of Mullewa.

For me, the reality of boarding school sets in fast, even though the Holmes boys made it sound great. As soon as I see the school buildings appear in the distance on the top of a hill, I instantly feel homesick, even though I'm not actually at the school yet.

Unbeknown to me, station life has been growing on me for the past three years. I have become accustomed to the isolation, the peace and quiet, and our own reserved lifestyle. This boarding school will take me right out of my comfort zone, I know, and I am terrified at the thought of being left there with people I don't know. I want to tell Father to take me straight back home.

The principal of the boarding school, a Christian Brother, greets us when we arrive. He shows us around the school. He is a short old man, around sixty-five years old, only about five-foot tall and wearing rectangular glasses. He is smartly dressed in a crisp, white long-sleeve shirt that has been immaculately ironed, beige slacks, shiny black leather shoes, and a matching belt with a chrome buckle.

'You must be the Pomerys from Moolapool station up past Meekatharra. Did you drive all the way through in one day or stop over somewhere along the way?' he asks cheerily.

Father confirms that we are the Pomerys and tells him we have driven straight through, six hours on the road.

The principal introduces himself as Brother Barry O'Who. 'But that will be Brother O'Who to you two boys,' he says.

O'Who looks back and forth at Bryce and me while reaching his hand out to Father. They briefly shake hands as Father introduces himself and us to Brother O'Who.

'Hello, Bratt, it's nice to meet you,' O'Who says, taking hold of Bryce's right hand.

'No, sorry, it's Bryce, Brother O'Who,' Bryce says.

'Oh, I'm dreadfully sorry, Bryce.' He turns to me. 'And you're Luke, yes?'

'That's right, Brother O'Who.'

'Right,' he says, after I've shaken his hand, ' follow me and I'll show you three around. That is if you are not in a rush to get going, Neil?'

'No, I'm in no rush. I don't mind at all. Actually, I'm interested in looking around the school anyhow,' Father replies.

Bryce and I follow behind Father and O'Who. We meet up with a few of the other Brothers and a couple of the class teachers who are at the school, preparing the classrooms for the new term ahead. One elderly man is hobbling along whistling to himself, dragging the toes of his shoes into the ground.

'Hello, Brother Lentil. I would like you to meet our two newest students. This is Bryce and his younger brother Luke. They will be joining us this year, and this is their dad, Neil Pomery. Brother Lentil is one of our farm managers and he'll be teaching you boys Farm Practice,' O'Who explains.

Lentil shakes our hands, speaks briefly to O'Who, and then hobbles away and continues whistling.

Father turns to us and quietly whispers, 'Isn't this place simply amazing, boys?'

We look around like frightened mice and nod slightly.

'This is the Year 8 room where you, Luke, will be doing most of your studies,' O'Who continues.

I look at the rows of desks and instantly feel claustrophobic. I am finding it hard to breathe and can't wait to get out of there. We continue a little further around the same part of the building.

'This is the Year 9 room, and alongside it is the one where you will be, Bryce, in Year 10.'

'They're nice size classrooms here. How many kids are enrolled in the school?' Father asks.

'This year we have a record number of ninety-three students,' O'Who replies.

We continue the tour, Father trying his hardest to encourage us by way of his facial expressions. From time to time, he looks back over his shoulder and raises his eyebrows or discreetly nods, the hint of a smile on his face.

Bryce and I just tag along, sulkily half-dragging our feet. Once or twice, we catch Father's gaze with our sad puppy-dog eyes, but he pretends not to notice. All the while Father and O'Who are talking, Father seems very intrigued by everything at the school and at one point completely forgets about Bryce and me for a few minutes.

O'Who leads the way up a flight of stairs and into a large room with close to twenty bunk beds in it.

'This is the Year 8 living area and will be your dormitory, Luke,' he tells us all but mainly focusing his gaze on me.

We walk past a pool table and a ping-pong table in the centre of the room. Alongside one wall is a huge fish tank and near the bunks are sets of lockers. One already has my name on it.

'This is your locker, Luke, and you're on the top bunk. I hope you're not scared of heights.'

I tell him that I'm not.

We cut through the Brothers' passage to the Year 10 dormitory, and O'Who shows Bryce to his bed. This dormitory is not as big as mine and is made up of a few smaller rooms with single beds.

I look at the bed beside Bryce's and wish I could have it. I am tempted to ask if anyone is sleeping there, but before I get the opportunity, we've left through another doorway out onto the balcony and are heading down another flight of stairs. The principal takes us through a breezeway and another doorway into a church. He dips his fingertips into a little dish of water that is at the side of the archway and then touches his forehead, his chest, and his left and right shoulders and stands there waiting for us to do the same.

'This is the chapel,' he says gently, as if there is a sleeping baby nearby that he doesn't want to wake. 'Evening mass is every night at seven o'clock for fifteen minutes, other than Tuesday night and Sunday mornings, when we have full services.'

We follow O'Who up to the altar, where he drops on one knee and repeats the sign of the cross. Then he stands back up and motions for us to do the same.

'Well, that's basically it,' he says at the end of our tour. 'You'll become familiar with the rest of the school as time goes by. You two boys look like hungry growing lads in need of a nice lunchtime meal, hey?' he turns to us and says.

Outside the office, the smell of food fills the air.

'Yes, I'm hungry,' Bryce says automatically, looking at me.

Suddenly, everyone is looking at me.

'What about you, Luke?' Father asks, patting me on the shoulder.

'Yes, I'm hungry,' I reply, just to please them.

'Well, that's great. You can join them in the dining room, Neil, if you like. I think it's crumbed lamb chops with mashed potato and steamed vegetables today.'

O'Who has a problem with his eyes. He finishes most sentences by blinking rapidly, batting his eyelids up and down a few times. It looks quite funny, as do his long buck teeth.

In the dining room, O'Who introduces us to the other students. 'Now listen up, boys! This is Bryce and Luke Pomery. Bryce will be attending Year 10 this year and his brother, Luke, is just starting Year 8. I do hope he will be with us for the next three years.'

I look around the room at all the new faces and recognise Winton Holmes, the kids from the station next door to ours sitting amongst the others. He looks at me briefly and smiles.

O'Who is clearly waiting for me to agree but I just look at my shoes.

'So please make them feel welcome,' he concludes.

Some of the kids are lined up, collecting plates from a trolley and making their way to the counter to be served by a couple of kids and what appears to be another Brother. Others are already sitting around tables and eating.

'It's really nice, isn't it, boys?' Father asks, like a kid walking through a candy store. He looks like he wishes he'd had the opportunity to go to a boarding school like this one.

'Mmm, it's okay,' Bryce and I reply together.

'You'll enjoy it here, I know,' O'Who assures us, looking over the rim of his glasses as he nods gently. 'Most boys are sceptical at first, but they soon open up and make the most of it.'

He turns to Father. 'I'm going to the Brothers' dining room now, but I'd like to see you again before you leave, Neil. Let's say in thirty minutes out the front of the office.'

'Will do,' Father replies, quickly looking at his watch. 'How is this lovely lunch, boys?' he exclaims, once O'Who has left and we have our meals.

A few kids from the tables around us look our way and stop chewing for a moment.

'These crumbed chops are really tasty,' Bryce replies.

'And the vegetables are so fresh,' Father adds, looking to me for a response.

The other boys put their heads down quickly and pretend they haven't been eavesdropping. As we finish our lunches, kids start lining up for dessert. Father suggests that I gather up our plates and take them over to the cutlery cart where all the other kids are putting their dirty dishes. When I return, Bryce is standing up looking at the desserts, while Father has his eyes on another table where there is an urn and a tray of cups.

'Why don't you two go and grab some dessert. I'm going to make myself a cuppa tea.'

We join the last of boys lined up to get dessert.

'That looks nice,' Father says when we come back.

By the time I remove my apple pie from its packaging, Bryce is already scraping away at the remains of ice cream and apple pie in his own bowl.

'Finish that off, Luke. Brother O'Who will be waiting for us,' Father urges.

I finish my dessert in a couple of quick scoops.

'Run them over to the trolley, Bryce,' Father instructs.

On our way out, a couple of kids take advantage of Father holding the door open for us.

'Thank you,' one of them says as he goes past. It looks like the blond-headed kid I saw earlier up in my dorm near my bunk bed.

'That's not a problem at all, young man,' Father replies.

Out the front of O'Who's office, Father rolls himself a cigarette and tucks it behind his ear.

'I hope you all enjoyed your lunch,' O'Who says, approaching from the breezeway between the kitchen and office. 'It's one of my favourite meals, that one.' He rubs his hands together like he is trying to warm them up and runs his tongue from one corner of his lips to the other.

'Yes, that was an amazing lunch, thank you,' Father says. 'It was the best meal I've had in quite a while. The boys will have no trouble fitting in with the other kids here with meals like that. It's bound to be the talk of the table, I'm sure. They're both extremely respectful towards others, but if you do have a problem, I give you permission to swiftly deal with them in any way you see fit.'

Father looks at Bryce and me as though we are already breaking the school's rules.

'We'll keep them in line, don't you worry, Neil,' O'Who says. 'They look like well-mannered young men already, so we probably won't have to do much as long as they do what is asked of them.'

Father thanks O'Who once again for taking us on a tour, then turns to give Bryce and me a hug. 'Be good now, boys,' he says. 'I'll see you in the school holidays.'

Our faces grow long, knowing he'll soon be on his way back to the station. Then he jumps into the Nissan, reverses a short distance down the driveway to make his turn to exit and stops to light his cigarette. As he heads off, he waves to us out the window.

8

Showers

For the rest of the afternoon, Bryce and I hang around together until O'Who comes by and tells us to head upstairs and have a shower before dinner.

'Come on, Luke, I'll introduce you to Brother Pedro,' he says.

'Oh, okay, see you back out here after showers, Bryce.'

I follow O'Who upstairs into my dormitory. We walk over to the man who served us lunch earlier.

'Brother Pedro, I'd like you to meet Luke. Brother Pedro is the dorm master up this end of the building,' O'Who explains. 'He also teaches some of your subjects.'

Pedro holds out his hand and I shake it.

'Hello, Luke. It's nice to meet you.'

'Hello, Brother Pedro. It's nice to meet you too,' I reply nervously.

Pedro's holding onto my hand like he isn't going to let it go. His hand feels the size of King Kong's. It is smooth and clammy, and I pull my hand free from his grip and wipe the sweat off on the side of my leg.

Pedro has a room adjoining my dormitory. He is tall and towers over ninety-five per cent of us kids. He is heavily overweight too, with a huge nose that looks like a deformed strawberry.

After O'Who leaves, Pedro tells me I had better get into the shower. Dinner is in another fifteen minutes. As he heads towards the bathroom, I go over to my locker and grab a change of clothes. Some of the other kids are taking off their clothes and going into the bathroom with only their towels wrapped around them. I tuck my towel and clean clothes under my arm and go into the bathroom fully dressed. It is not long before Pedro, who by now is patrolling the showers, comes over.

There are roughly fifteen shower cubicles along one side of a long corridor, with terrazzo partitions between them. They are completely open at the front. Only the toilets down the other end have doors. Along the other wall are handbasins and mirrors where we can comb our hair, brush our teeth and wash our hands. Just standing there makes me think of when Mum used to watch *Prisoner* on TV, back at Monarto in the early 1980s. Pedro is that grumpy old Mrs B!

'Go and get out of your clothes, Luke. Come back with just your towel and by that time a cubicle should be free for you.'

I hesitantly turn around, go back to my locker and take off my clothes using my locker door as a shield. I am as nervous as hell. Until now, at the age of twelve, I've never been naked in front of any other kids before, apart from my siblings.

When I return to the bathroom, my towel wrapped tightly around my waist, I quickly jump into the first free cubicle I come across and face the wall.

Pedro is at the other end of the bathroom, but it takes him less than a few seconds to be outside my cubicle. 'It's okay, Luke. You'll get used to this set up,' he says.

'Ha, you think so?' I mumble under my breath into the shower stream. I feel so humiliated as he stands there looking at my naked arse. I quickly soap myself all over and rinse off so I can get the hell out of there.

As soon as I'm dressed, I race downstairs and meet back up with Bryce on the front lawn near the flagpole.

'How was your shower?' I ask.

'Lovely and hot,' Bryce replies. 'I love the high pressure too.'

'I was nervous getting undressed in front of everyone,' I confess to him. 'And Brother Pedro is creepy. I don't like him.'

I look back towards my dorm. Pedro is making his way down the stairs.

'That's him,' I say, just loud enough for Bryce to hear.

Pedro pauses on the last step and looks over at us for a couple of seconds before disappearing down the breezeway into the Brothers' dining room.

The dinner bell rings, and we head in for our meal. After we have eaten, the time flies by and, before I know it, it is getting close to bedtime. I become even more nervous when the bell rings for us to return to our dorms and Bryce and I are split up again.

I am thinking about Pedro. I don't want him coming anywhere near me but know it is unavoidable.

In the dorm with the rest of the kids, I get ready for bed. Pedro is nowhere to be seen. I feel safe until he comes up the stairs carrying a large saucepan of Milo and a packet of disposable styrofoam cups.

'Who wants a nice hot drink?' he asks as he places the saucepan on a small table next to the concrete balustrade.

The boys form a line, and Pedro ladles Milo into their cups.

'Do you want to grab yourself a cup, Luke, before it's all gone?'

I get a cup and hold it out over the saucepan.

He fills it up for me. 'There you go, Luke, get into that,' he says, trying to sound caring.

I walk over to the balustrade at the edge of the balcony. No one else is there. I look down over the lawns in the direction of the trampolines and drink my Milo quietly in the darkness.

All I can think about is how great it would be being back home on the station with Father. This will be the first night I have ever spent away from home. Even though I know Bryce is not far away in the Year 10 dorm, I still feel terribly alone and homesick.

As the other kids finish their Milo, they start getting ready for bed. Another Brother appears from the Brothers' dormitory.

'Good evening, Willsh. You're just in time to meet most of the Year 8 boys,' Pedro says. 'Everyone, this is Brother Willsh. He will be on dorm patrol during the night on both these two dorms up this end of the building.'

'Hello, boys. Yes, I patrol these dorms all night, so no hoo-has or wandering around aimlessly after lights out, unless you're going straight to the toilet or returning from there,' Willsh says, loud enough to be heard over the group of Year 9 kids who have kept chattering while he's talking.

'Hello, Brother Willsh,' some of the kids say.

I just look at him and say nothing.

Willsh looks around the group and his gaze rest upon me. 'It's time for you all to get into your pyjamas now. Come on now, chop, chop. Off you go.'

Kids head off in all directions and disappear through doorways to get changed. I am still on the balcony, slowly finishing off my Milo. I want to give the other kids a chance to get changed because I know I will feel so uncomfortable seeing them naked.

'I'm going to take this stuff downstairs now, Willsh,' Pedro says. He picks up the empty saucepan with the ladle in it and makes his way downstairs to the kitchen, leaving us with Willsh.

'Yeah, no worries. I got this, Pedro,' Willsh replies.

While I'm still standing on the balcony, I see Pedro take off in the school's station wagon down past the horse yards. As he drives away, I wonder where he could be off to in such a hurry, on his own, at this time of night. I throw my empty cup into the bin and go into the dorm. As I open the door of my locker, I notice a couple of kids nearby so I push a few things around inside, pretending that I can't find my pyjamas even though I see them as soon as I open the door. Some of the other kids from my area have already changed and are heading off to brush their teeth. I quickly pull out my pyjamas and put them on. Then I climb straight up into my bunk and make myself comfortable. I lie there waiting for the lights to go off and think of Father.

Willsh is now over by the doorway and has a cassette that he loads into a tape player. He switches off the lights once everyone is in their beds. 'Good night, lads,' he says in the darkness as he presses 'play'.

Old-style music plays for a couple of seconds before the story starts.

'We now present the very first episode of *Dad and Dave*.'

The episode begins to play through a speaker system in the two dorms. Years later, I will learn this radio series was based on a book by Australian author, Steele Rudd, called *On Our Selection*, and that it played for many years between 1937 and 1953.

Tears roll down my cheeks as I lie on my back staring blankly into the darkness. I let the tears flow, crying quietly for a few minutes. I imagine waking up in the morning back out on the station, with Father poking his head in at the crack of dawn, telling me it is time to get up. But it is all just a silly, pointless thought.

There are around thirty-five kids in my dorm and another thirty or so in the Year 9 dorm right next to us, but I can't hear a single sound except the story of Dad and Dave being played. After about fifteen minutes, Willsh switches the tape to a Dire Straits cassette. When the tape finishes, I am still wide awake. The kid below me starts thrashing about in his bed. He is frantically mumbling to himself. It sounds like he's being picked on by bullies or has become possessed by some evil spirit. I am sure the bed is going to snap in two and I will fall out.

Other kids in the dorm are moving about in their beds and making weird noises too, I realise. Then a torch lights up the darkness. I prop my head up to see what is going on. Willsh shines his torch on one of the kids who is talking in his sleep, taps him on the foot and tells him to roll over.

I duck my head under my pillow to block out all the distractions, but after things have finally quietened down, I hear Pedro mumbling to himself. I prop myself up a little to see what he is doing as he makes his way to his room. It is well after midnight.

Click, click, click, click, click, click, is the first thing I hear next morning.

'Rise and shine. Wakey, wakey, hand off snaky. Come on now, Bran, up you get. Wakey, wakey, hand off snaky, Benjamin. Come on now, everybody. Rise and shine. Come on, Osun, get up! Wakey wakey, hand off snaky, Peter! Wakey, wakey, hand off snaky. Up and at 'em, Luke!'

As Pedro goes past the end of my bed, blurting and making the clicking noise, I sit up and rub my eyes. Everyone else in the dorm is sitting up too, watching as Pedro walks by. In his hand is a wooden ratchet noisemaker which he is spinning around as if it is some sort of air raid alarm.

We all get dressed in our uniforms – grey shirt and shorts; long grey socks, with the school colours, a band of green and yellow at the top, and black shoes – and head downstairs for breakfast.

'How did you sleep?' Bryce asks, when we meet up in the breakfast queue.

'I had a dreadful night,' I tell him. 'The kid below me kept thrashing about and moaning. It kept me awake for hours.'

'Yeah, there was one of those in my dorm too,' Bryce laughs as we get a serve of Rice Bubbles each.

Pedro's standing at the counter listening to everything we say as we approach. 'Bryce, please wait here until I return. Luke, you can follow me.'

I follow Pedro over to a table and he pulls out a chair for me.

'You can eat at this table with these boys from my area of the dormitory,' he instructs.

I sit down with my bowl of cereal and he walks back over to where Bryce is waiting.

'Bryce, you can sit over at this table.' Pedro leads him to the other side of the dining room. 'Now listen up, everyone,' he says loud enough to be heard over the morning talk. 'Please check the noticeboard after breakfast to see what roster you're on and complete your duties after you have made your beds.'

After breakfast, we go back upstairs. I am still feeling quite tired because of the kid in the bunk below me keeping me up during the night. When he goes to brush his teeth, I quickly stick a pair of my dirty socks on top of his pillow, then pull his bed cover back up over them. The kid in the next set of bunk beds over from me starts laughing. He thinks it's even funnier when the kid comes back from the bathroom and almost catches me messing around remaking his bed. The kid soon notices that his bed doesn't look quite the same as it did when he left it. He pulls back the cover, and there are the socks I have just left on his pillow. He picks them up and brings them up close to his nose. Even though he must be able to see they are dirty, he inhales deeply. Then he quickly turns his head away, and his face goes red with anger.

He holds my socks up in front of him with his arm fully extended and tries to pronounce my surname. 'Pom-er-ey, Pumery!' He pauses for a moment.

His nostrils grow wide, as he takes in another deep breath, then exhales quickly through his gritted teeth. He notices me snickering to myself, and turns towards me, enraged. 'So, you're Pumery, hey? Don't put your stinkin' dirty, coon socks in my fucken bed, you dirty, black cunt,' he spits.

His face turns even redder, as he throws them at my face. I manage to duck just in time, and they land on the floor behind me. He grabs his comb and goes back to the bathroom. I pick up my socks as soon as he turns away and put them back under his bedspread on top of his pillow.

'Don't get caught by Pedro, hey,' says the kid from the next bunk, 'I just saw that kid talking to him on the way to the bathroom and he was pointing back at you. You'll get cut.'

'What? How will I get cut from putting my socks on his pillow? Does he have a knife there?' I ask him.

'No, you'll be busted, get in trouble,' he laughs.

'Oh, I thought maybe he had something sharp in his pillowcase or something.'

We both laugh.

'What's your name?' I ask.

'I'm Shain Forth. From Bulla River just out of Geraldton. What about you? Where are you from, Pumery, and what's your first name?'

'Oh, I'm Luke and it's pronounced Pom-ery not Pumery. I'm from Moolapool station, out of Meekatharra.'

We shake hands.

'My cousin Albert Quidreeko has a station out that way, near Wiluna. He's in Year 9 here, but I haven't seen him here yet.'

'Hey, Shain, why was the horse scared of the frog?' I ask, just to throw a little humour into the mix, and to see if we click.

He thinks hard about it for a few seconds and scratches his chin, eventually shaking his head, unable to come up with an answer. 'Err, I haven't a clue, man.'

'Because the frog read' up…reddit…reared up,' I laugh. 'You get it?'

Shain nods and we both start laughing.

'That's pretty funny. I like that. I have to tell my sister that one,' Shain smiles.

'Not many people get it. I guess you got to know a little bit about animals,' I reply.

'I got one for you, Luke. How do you catch a squirrel?'

I stand there in silence, looking at him for some sort of clue, trying to figure it out before he jumps back in with the answer.

'You climb a tree and show it your nuts. Get it? Your nuts!' Shain spreads his thighs, arches his back and cups his groin.

We laugh more at that than the actual joke.

When the other kid comes back, he gives me a dirty look. Shain and I are still laughing when he sees his bed has been tampered with again. He throws the cover back, revealing my dirty socks once more on top of his pillow.

He picks them up and looks at me angrily. 'Fucken do it again, ya black cunt, and I'll flatten ya,' he growls.

He hurls the socks at me, this time making a connection with the side of my head. He laughs, as do a few other kids, who have been watching what is going on.

'Stop tossing around in your bed all fucken night and keeping me up then, like you did last night,' I yell back him.

'Yeah, ya loser,' some of the other kids around the dorm chime in.

'What's your name? And where are you from?' Shain asks the kid.

The kid's staring down his nose at me, as though we are in a staring competition.

Now he looks at Shain. 'I'm Peal Birdlic and I live in Geraldton at Beachlands. How about you?'

'Oh, cool bananas, nice to meet a local Geratalian. I'm Shain. I live on a farm just north of Geraldton, towards Northampton, just past the 440 Roadhouse. Do you know where Bulla River is?'

Shain and Peal shake hands.

'Yeah, I've been out that way fishing once or twice with my older brother, Jeff,' Peal says. 'Hey, I'm heading downstairs now. Do you want to come for a jump on the trampolines?'

'Yeah, let's go,' Shain says. 'You coming, Luke? I'll race you both.'

We all take off, bulldozing our way through the doorway.

'Mr Forth, Mr Birdlic nd Mr Pomery.' Pedro's voice booms and stops us in our tracks. 'There will be no running through the dormitories – or up or down the stairs! Have you three checked the roster yet to see what duties you have this morning?'

'Yes, we're doing that right now, sir,' Shain replies.

Pedro is down the other end of the dorm, where he has been talking to another kid who has all his stuff packed in his suitcase. The kid is crying. Pedro is holding onto his shoulder and trying to calm him down, but he isn't the slightest bit interested in anything Pedro has to say.

As soon as we reach the last step, we are off and running once again. When we get to the trampolines, they are being used by a couple of older kids from Year 9. They are pulling silly faces at each other while they bounce.

After a few minutes, Peal says, 'C'mon, let us have a turn now.'

They stop jumping and walk over to the edge of the mat, as if they are about to get off, but instead they just stop and stare at each other.

After a few seconds, they start laughing. They fall onto their backs and each does a small backflip. They land on their stomachs. They start doing more tricks, bouncing even higher than before.

'They honestly thought we were going to get off,' one of them shouts to the other.

'Are you going to be long? We want a turn before class starts.'

The older boys pretend not to hear Peal's plea. But a teacher on yard duty has overheard his request and makes his way over to the trampolines.

'Hello, boys – I'm Mr Davy and I'll be teaching you Social Studies and PE, Physical Education. What seems to be the problem here?'

'Umm, nothing, Mr Davy,' says the kid on the furthest trampoline before any of us manage to reply.

'We just want to have our turn on the trampolines, Mr Davy. But they won't let us. We've been waiting almost five minutes now,' Peal tells the teacher.

The Year 9 boys look at Peal angrily and mouth their words so Davy can't hear their intentions: 'I'm going to get you, dickhead.' They look like they are about to jump straight down his throat.

'That's enough now, Jarrod and Timothy. It's time you both moved along and let these boys have a turn. They've been waiting around to have a go for far too long.'

They come to a sudden stop and step off.

'Come on, Jarrod, I'll race you to the swings.'

They pick up their shoes and race off.

'Hold on one moment, you two – have you finished your rostered duties?'

Davy's raised his voice, to make sure he is heard. But Jarrod and Timothy continue as if they haven't heard a thing. Soon they are up high on the swings laughing at one another.

I look at Shain and Peal, knowing full well we haven't looked at the noticeboard ourselves. They shake their heads and raise their index fingers up to their lips to indicate 'shhhh'. Shain and Peal quickly jump on, and I watch while they attempt to do front flips, but neither of them is as good as Jarrod or Timothy.

'Let me have a go, Peal,' I demand as I catch his eye.

He looks at his watch and jumps off, and I kick my shoes off and jump up on the tramp quickly. I attempt to do some tricks but nearly break my neck when I land awkwardly. It looked a lot easier watching the others, but it is bloody tricky. I try hard but I'm only making myself look like a fool. Fortunately, I manage to avoid further embarrassment because Shain comes to a stop, and gets off the trampoline, and Peal races across the lawn towards our classroom as a bell rings.

'Get back on the other trampoline, Shain, before someone else gets it,' I yell.

At this early stage of boarding school, I am still unaware of what the bell means. I haven't heard one ringing for quite a few years.

9

Thirty-three and a Third

'We have to go to class now, Luke,' Shain explains, waiting for me to get off the trampoline.

I put my shoes back on and follow him into our classroom with my shoelaces dragging along behind me. The teacher looks at us as though we are holding up the class from starting a crucial exam. He taps his wristwatch and shakes his head from side to side as we make our way to two, vacant desks, next to each other.

'Ello, klas,' he starts. 'Hi'm Kebin Sheety, hi'm yee Math nn Sighence deacher. Yee har ta haddress me az Mr Sheety.'

Mr Sheety looks around at the entire class through his parted mop of hair, before flicking it back over his forehead. Then he stops and gazes at Shain for a couple of seconds. Mr Sheety has a strong Irish accent and I find him difficult to understand. He also has a huge amount of hair that looks quite funny.

'Yes, Mr Sheety,' the rest of the class replies, in chorus.

I just look at Mr Sheety with a smile on my face and say nothing.

Mr Sheety looks back at Shain, and his face turns red with anger, but he stops himself from blowing a fuse. 'Nar'w, lhads, on thee tob of yee desks, yee'll find yee dex'boogs. De's arr fa hall yee subjects. Blease geep thee Math boogs hon yee desks, han blace thee ud'ers insud yee desks blease.'

Mr Sheety holds the Maths book up for the class to see. Then he looks at Shain again. Shain still has his desk open and Mr Sheety can see him imitating himself.

'Do yee one'ta gum up thee front ere, Shun, an dell thee klas wad is sor harmusing?'

Shain quickly puts his desktop down and pretends he hasn't heard the question.

'Blease durn ta egg-sa-s'eyes 1.1 in yee dex boogs, hon bage bo-ordeen,' Mr Sheety says firmly, still looking at Shain and me. Mr Sheety then focuses his gaze on me. 'Looq, gan yee blease weed hout thee per'st egg-sa-s'eyes fa thee klas?'

I am sure he does this to humiliate me because he can see I'm nervous. I look at Shain, feeling confused as I continue shuffling through the textbook until, I find exercise 1.1.

'Umm, w…what, is a, thuther..d of w…one hundred,' I read out nervously, in front of the whole class.

'Wull, Looq, gan yee dell thee klas, wod iz thee han-sar?'

'Is it umm, tw…twenty-f…five?' I guess.

'Nor, idz nodt, Looq. Dus hanybody hells nor thee hanswer? Ouwa bowt yee, Shun, gan yee dell thee klas wod his thee hanswer blease?'

'Ummm, yeah. It's thirty-three, Mr Sheety,' Shain answers cockily.

'No, idz nod, Shun. Iddz tirty-twee and a turd.'

The whole class breaks out into a hysterical laughter, with everyone repeating the answer in Mr Sheety's accent, and he turns bright red in anger.

When class finishes, I breathe a sigh of relief.

'That was bloody hard, wasn't it?' I ask Shain.

'Yeah, it was, but also funny as fuck, though.'

There are only two female teachers at the school. One is the elderly Sister Karma. The other is Mrs Mc'Ker, in her late twenties, who is married to a local farmer. The kids all fancy her.

Sister Karma teaches studies in Christian Doctrine and attends mass with us on Tuesday evenings and Sunday mornings. Sometimes, on special occasions, she cooks a batch of scones and invites the class into her living quarters for a little treat.

Mrs Mc'Ker teaches us Ag Science. Sometimes she supervises after-school sports, and every now and then, she comes on cart with us. I don't know how she isn't driven completely insane. We often drive her to breaking point. Not only the kids from my class, but every kid in the school sniffs around her like filthy, deprived transients.

Over the course of the day, we go from class to class with different teachers. Eventually, the bell rings at three fifteen p.m. and it is the end of school for the day. I'm so excited that classes are finally over and I can get back on the trampoline, but while we are all gathering around to collect fruit for afternoon recess, we are instructed to get into our sports clothes and meet up at the flagpoles. I have been banking on being able do what I want after school finishes for the day, but clearly that isn't the case.

Soon we are all in a group again, standing by the flagpoles on the lawn out the front of the office, awaiting further instructions. Once everyone in the school has gathered, we head over to the basketball courts. My class plays on one court; the Year 9s play on the other, while the Year 10s play cricket in the cricket nets.

Classes are split into two groups and captains are chosen for each. Being one of the smallest kids and not good at making friends, I am one of the last to be picked for a team.

At five thirty p.m., when sports training has finished, we all head back to our dorms to shower before dinner. Pedro is patrolling again when we arrive upstairs. Even on my first day at boarding school, he seems to me like such a perverted old man, the way he hangs around the showers. I don't know why he has been allowed to get away with thitis, but he has, and it makes not only me uncomfortable, but also most of the other kids too.

After we shower, some kids race downstairs to the trampolines while others play on the monkey bars and swing set. The rest of us stay in the dorm, playing pool or ping-pong or watching cartoons on TV until the bell rings for dinner at six.

After dinner, if we remain downstairs until the bell rings for evening mass, we get another short break to do whatever we want. After mass, we go back to our classrooms and do homework until eight thirty. Finally, we get half an hour of free time, to unwind and get ready for bed.

This, I realise, is what every day here is going to be like, day after day, apart from the weekends, when there are movie nights down at the outdoor picture theatre. So, as the first week progresses, the routines take shape. Wake up, breakfast, rostered duties, school, lunch, school, sports, dinner, mass, study, and bed.

As the weeks unfold, Pedro proves to be even creepier and I fear being in his presence. He always finds a way of singling me or Shain out from the other kids, by pretending that he has concerns. One time, he has Shain rubbing his naked body because he says he needs a massage due to aching muscles. We all know which muscle aches the most, and it is the one in his pants.

To this day, I cannot understand why he was allowed to do those things to us.

Shain is very good at sports, especially cricket and football, and is soon nominated as team captain. He first picks a few of the other good players, including Peal, who is great at cricket and a few other sports, and when it gets down to the shittier players, he picks me, to remain loyal to our friendship.

At the end of the school week, after study on Friday night, all the Year 10 boys arm themselves with clubs that they have made during Woodwork with Brother Neddle. They meet up near the flagpole, waiting for Willsh.

'Come on, boys, let's go bunny bashing!' Willsh says eagerly.

The boys get on the back of his ute with Willsh's two Afghan hunting hounds and a spotlight.

'Where are you all going?' I ask Bryce as he climbs onto the tray of the ute.

'We're going hunting for rabbits, foxes and kangaroos. They're destroying the crops,' another Year 10 boy replies.

Bryce nods as Willsh starts the engine.

The schoolyard seems a lot quieter without the older boys around, and the other kids make the most of it, but I just go back upstairs. Every now and then, I hear Willsh's rifle firing a round off. I stand out on the balcony and look and see the kids in the spotlight rushing around after a kangaroo in the distance and the dogs tackling them to the ground in a cloud of dust.

The following morning, we have a big clean-up of the school. After lunch, one of the Year 10s fills an old Chamberlain tractor up with diesel and hooks up two old truck beds, which have been converted into trailers with long bench seats on them. Everyone gets ready for an afternoon outing while Pedro instructs a couple of Year 9s to get a crate of apples from the kitchen for afternoon recess and put it on the cart.

Other kids saddle up horses, and then we all set off. The cart is taken to the four corners of the property. We pull up at the shearing shed, roughly five kilometres from the school, for afternoon recess. There are sheep, cattle, pigs, chooks and turkeys on the farm, and crops of wheat, lupins, barley and oats.

It is nearing five p.m. when we get back and, after showering, we have a barbecue for dinner followed by a movie. Sunday is much the same but instead of cleaning, we spend over an hour in the chapel for morning mass.

After lunch, we're back on the cart and, once again, we don't get back till late. The outing is followed by another barbecue and another movie before bed.

As each new week unfolds, I settle into the school routine a little better and my homesickness starts to disappear.

Instead of meeting up at the flagpole after school, some boys head off on foot to the shearing shed. This is punishment for not paying attention or being disrespectful during class. Soon enough, Shain and I are trekking to the shearing shed. Out there is a workbook and a pen. The kids who are being punished must write down their names as proof that they walked out there.

Over the course of the next three years, whenever we are passing the shearing shed, Shain and I always write our names in the book.

Firstly, this gives us a break from Pedro. Secondly, it means we can just hang out in the bush, wagging sports practice for the afternoon.

The following Friday night after study it's Year 9's turn to go out bunny bashing. Our turn is the Friday after that. We all climb up onto the back of Willsh's ute with the hunting dogs and set off into the dark, armed with the clubs we have made during Woodwork. We don't make it far, when a rabbit gets caught in the beam of the spotlight and we all jump off the ute and stampede the poor thing. Clubs are swinging in all directions, then out of nowhere, the two hunting dogs dive in and take the rabbit.

Eventually, we manage to pry it free from the dogs' jaws and throw it on the back of the ute. After a couple of hours, we have several rabbits and a couple of kangaroos to our tally. We are already claiming the ones we have personally killed. When we get back to the school, we stick them in the chiller.

After we have finished our morning duties, those of us Year 8 boys who have managed to strike it lucky race down to the chiller to skin and salt the skins of whatever we had killed the night before and get them ready for tanning. This process takes a couple of weeks and, when they are ready, we use the skins to make mats or ponchos. The rabbit skins are mainly discarded, the kangaroos being the only decent things we can tan out of the hunt. But every Saturday a selection of 'chosen kids' who volunteered to slaughter a dozen sheep would also keep the skins for tanning.

Shain, Peal and I become close friends over the next few weeks, and whenever something is amiss in our classroom, out in the schoolyard or upstairs in the dormitory, there is always the strong possibility it has something to do with the three of us. It's mainly Shain and me, though. Peal doesn't like to push the boundaries; he is more a follower than a leader, although he is forever getting caught up in our antics.

One afternoon when sports training finishes, Shain and I and a couple of other kids are asked to help put the sports equipment away. This takes us several minutes and, when we have finished, we head up to the dorm to take a shower. As we walk into the dorm, we notice Pedro sitting on a chair by the doorway to his room with Osun Bay, one of the other kids from my dorm, lying across his lap. Osun is facing the floor and has his pants pulled down around his ankles.

Pedro has his hand spread wide over Osun's arse and his big finger is resting between Osun's arse cheeks. He is quietly talking to Osun about why he is in trouble. It all looks horribly wrong to me, and I'm glad it's not me across the Brother's knees. After a couple of minutes, Pedro raises his hand and slaps Osun two or three times hard on his arse. As Osun's body convulses in pain over Pedro's groin area, Pedro sits further upright with his back arched forward, like he is getting off on Osun's suffering. Looking back, I am sure Pedro would have had a boner from doing this because, clearly, he was a sick old man.

This sort of thing happens many times with different kids over the course of my time at boarding school. Everyone talks about how Pedro encroaches upon them. I endure his ways many times myself. I try to stay clear of him as much as possible. He makes it his duty to be in everyone's business, so I find myself doing things away from the others a lot of the time.

I love tinkering and making things but it's hard to do so during the school day. Sometimes, towards the end of a woodwork class, I make sure a window in the workroom is left unlocked, so I can return later to work some more on things I have started making. From time to time, Shain and Peal join me. Every now and then, I bump into other kids who are in there mucking around, making things while trying to avoid Pedro, and we laugh at each other. We must wait for the right time, though, either when the Brothers are showering or watching TV, or are in their dining room, drinking red wine after they have finished their meals.

Neddle is always on yard duty before the dinner bell rings and, once or twice, he nearly catches me out in the woodwork room. Sometimes, as he walks past, he'll hear noises coming from inside. He comes over and peers through the window to check if anyone is inside. A couple of times he even unlocks the door and looks around. He very rarely comes across anyone, though, because we shoot out the back window in a flash before he even makes it inside. The time he spends fumbling his way through a bunch of keys, trying to find the right one, always gives us a good few minutes to make our escape.

One time, I make a vivarium for the spiders that Peal and I catch. We get all types – red-backs, funnel webs, black house spiders, huntsmen, and wolf spiders. Anything we catch that has eight legs is put into this vivarium. It is like a colosseum for spiders; the way they fight each other to the death is mesmerising.

Shain's sister has an influence on him through their shared love of horses. She provides horse rides to the public back on their farm in Geraldton. Sometimes, Shain hangs around with the other riders, while Peal and I have our own interests. Peal is fascinated with insects and isn't afraid of catching just about anything that moves. He loves to lure trapdoor spiders out from their tunnels, using a stick; he holds them up in front of our faces and thinks our fearful reactions are funny, but nowhere near as funny as when we react by flicking them back at him.

In my first term at boarding school, after school finishes each day, we gather around to get some fruit for afternoon recess. One day, Pedro comes out of the Brothers' dining room and tells us that there is no sport practice this afternoon.

'Have the afternoon off, boys. No wandering too far, though, and be back around five thirty for shower time,' Pedro says.

We race upstairs, change out of our school uniforms and take off in all directions. I quickly put on something casual then tear downstairs, frantically trying to find Bryce. I come across a couple of kids from his class that I have seen him talking to earlier and ask if they have seen Bryce anywhere.

'Oh yeah, he went that way with a group of other kids,' one of them says.

'They've gone out to their secret hideaway. You won't be able to find them, though,' he yells as I take off like a racehorse goanna in the direction he's pointed.

Along the way, I come across some more kids and ask them too, just in case I am being led on a wild goose chase.

'Yes, he went that way,' they tell me, indicating the same direction.

I continue running until I am in the bush. I stop and listen. I can hear kids in the distance, talking. I start walking faster towards the sound of their voices, stopping to listen every few seconds until I see some footprints in the dirt. I follow them and walk straight into their secret hideaway.

'Hey, who showed you where our fucken hideaway is?' one of the Year 10s shouts.

'No one! It wasn't that hard to find. I could hear you all yelling around from the road and I just followed your tracks.'

I point to the eroded path that has been created through the bush and the footprints they have left in the dirt. One of the biggest Year 10s storms straight over and grabs me by the front of my shirt, practically lifting me off the ground. He raises a clenched fist in the air. I look past his shoulder, trying to fix my sight on Bryce. I am starting to get worried because I can't see him anywhere. I notice Bran, one of the Year 8s, standing just behind the Year 10 kid who is about to punch me.

Bran's eyes are wide open; he stares at me in shock.

'Hey, let him go now, Deano. I think he's got the message,' one of the kids says.

'That's Bryce's younger brother,' another one chips in, looking towards the cubbyhouse.

But Deano is too busy being a hero and doesn't hear what the other kids have to say. He is about to lay into me when Bryce comes out of the cubbyhouse.

'Hey, Deano! Let go of Luke right now, or else,' Bryce says.

Deano instantly lets go of me and I run over to Bryce and stand alongside him as I regain my nerves.

'Thanks, Bryce,' I quietly whisper. 'He'd have got stuck into me, for sure.'

'Even if I wasn't out here, I'd have sorted him out for you,' Bryce assures No one fucks with you while I'm around, Luke.'

Deano looks at Bryce but never says a word. He just turns and walks away. Bran follows along behind him, like a puppy in love. Deano has taken Bran under his wing, and they often hang around together just because they have similar surnames, even though they are not related.

'He can't stay here, he has to go,' a couple of the other Year 10s now say, trying to side with their top dog, Deano.

Deano stops and looks back at us.

'Don't worry, we're going,' Bryce responds. 'Funny how you so easily tracked us down to this so-called secret cubby house out here, Luke,' Bryce adds out loud, in a mocking tone.

We laugh and Deano shoots me a dirty look.

'Come on, Luke, let's fuck off from this dump.'

Bryce puts his hand on my shoulder, and we head back through the bush towards the school.

'They hated how easily I found their cubby, didn't they? Maybe next time they'll try not to make such a big trail out to their secret hideout, hey? I'm sorry I ruined it for you, Bryce.'

'Nah, Luke, forget about it. I didn't like their cubby house anyway. I've grown out of that type of stuff, so it was perfect timing for you to arrive. But they really were shocked to see you, weren't they?'

'Yeah, they didn't think it was like leaving a trail of candy for me to follow.'

I start to wonder whether I will be able to cope with the bullies in the next couple of years when I'll be at boarding school all by myself and suddenly, I feel worried. 'I'm glad you're here, Bryce. I don't know how I'm going to be able to defend myself when you've gone, hey?'

'Don't worry, Luke, you'll be fine. You've made a couple of friends now and if you all stick together no one will hurt you.'

I continue to work on my friendships, knowing that in the two years ahead, Bryce won't be there to back me up if I get into trouble.

As our first term comes to an end, parents start arriving to pick their children up. Kids race off to the dormitories and collect their belongings. Soon, most of them are on their way, leaving only a handful of us. Some of the other kids leave later that afternoon when Pedro takes them into Mullewa to catch the bus down south to Perth and beyond.

'What about us?' I ask Bryce.

'Father said we're to catch the bus and he'll pick us up from Meekatharra.'

By this time, Bryce and I and a couple of kids from Yalgoo and Mount Magnet are the only ones left at the school. The following morning Pedro takes the rest of us to catch our bus north. Five or so hours later, we arrive in Meekatharra, where Father is waiting at the Swagman Roadhouse to pick us up.

Term two starts and everything goes by quicker than I recall. When the Easter break comes around, I ask Shain if it is all right for me to go to his place. His parents say they are happy to have me stay over and if my father agrees it is okay. I phone Father, unsure of what to say. As I pick up the receiver, I take a long deep breath in and exhale slowly. I dial the number at the station and wait for him to answer.

'Hello, Neil speaking. How may I be of assistance?'

'Umm, hello, it's me, Luke speaking. We must be related somehow,' I reply with a slight chuckle.

'Oh, hello, Luke speaking. Yes, we're definitely related since we have the same last name. How is school going? I hope you're trying to learn as much as you possibly can.'

'Yes, Father, school is going great, I really enjoy it here now.'

'That's good to hear.'

I explain that I have phoned because I want to go to Geraldton for the long weekend with my friend Shain.

'I don't see any harm in that, Luke, as long as you're good. But you better pass on my phone number to them just in case you become too much of a hassle.'

'Thank you, Father. I will be good, I promise. I'll pass you on to Bryce now. Thanks again, Father. Goodbye, I love you.'

'Goodbye, Luke. I love you too, mate.'

As soon as I get off the phone, I tell Shain I have Father's permission.

'Geraldton is a good place,' Shain tells me. 'We live not far away from the roller drome. Do you know how to roller-skate? If not, I'll show you how. You'll absolutely love it.'

I tried roller-skating on the footpaths around the house back on the station, but I never got the hang of it, I tell him.

'But I'm definitely interested in giving it another go in the roller drome though.'

'Cool bananas,' Shain replies.

I notice Pedro standing on the balcony above us and looking our way.

'What are you two up to?' he asks.

We look up at him and pretend we haven't heard his question.

'C'arn, let's go for a bounce on the trampolines. Look, no one's on them,' I say.

'Yeah, okay. I'll race you there. Doesn't Pedro just give you the bloody creeps?' Shain asks, as we kick off our shoes to jump onto the free trampolines.

'Yeah, and guess what? I overheard him talking to the head chef earlier today, and the chef said Pedro would make a great principal. Can you imagine Pedro in charge of the school? That would be my worst nightmare.'

'Yeah, mine too. Fuck that for a joke.'

I have such a great time in Geraldton. We go to see Shain's mum in a stage play called *Fiddler on the Roof* at the Queens Park Theatre. I have never seen a play on stage before and it captures my attention the entire way through. The rest of the time we hang around the wharf, playing arcade games and swimming at the front beach near the Sail Inn Snack Bar, which was owned and operated by Shain's mum back then. Shain's mum gives us lunch from her shop to keep us going during the day, and in return, we do the dishes and restock the fridge with drinks for her. When we get back to school, I tell Bryce all about my holiday in Geraldton.

Towards the end of the first semester, Shain asks if he can come out to the station with me. Father agrees, so when school breaks up, Bryce, Shain and I all jump on the bus and head up to Meekatharra. Father picks us up and I notice he is not as harsh on us while Shain is staying with us.

Shain's good at doing many of the station chores. He and I team up and go out mustering. We fix fences and windmills together. Even back at the shearing shed, he isn't afraid to get in and get his hands dirty, drafting, tailing lambs, branding sheep, or dragging out the ones that die. He is a good worker, and Father really likes having him helping during the holidays.

When we return for the third term that year, Bryce and I rarely see much of each other, except for mealtimes. I start hanging around with Shain and Peal a lot more and prepare myself for the next two years. On the last day of school, there is a graduation ceremony for the Year 10 students, which is held in the church. As the kids are called up to the front of the chapel to receive their certificates, their parents take photos.

After all the names have been called, O'Who once again takes to the altar. 'I would like to personally thank each and every one of you for making this a truly unforgettable event,' O'Who says. 'Also, I'd like you all to give the Year 10 students a great big round of applause.'

Everyone starts clapping extra loudly as O'Who removes his glasses and wipes away some tears.

Everyone heads home except those kids waiting to catch the bus, and the next day we head back to Meekatharra, where Father picks us up and takes us back home to the station.

'So you finally graduated, hey, Bryce? Any ideas what you'll do next?' Father asks.

'Um, I'm not sure yet, Father. I was thinking of helping you on the station.'

'Okay, I think I can sign you up on the books. After all, we've had a bloody good year this year – wool prices are over $35 a kilogram.'

'What about you, Luke? How does it feel to have completed Year 8?'

'It feels good. And guess what, Father, I won the Woodwork award for my class.'

'Good on you, Luke, well done,' Father says proudly. 'You must have inherited my woodworking skills.'

10

Christmas Holidays

It is great to finally be back home and see the rest of the family again.

Dansan and Loui have shot up in the past couple of months, and Bidjid and Zoann have turned into beautiful young women. I haven't seen or heard from Mum for about two years now, but the lack of communication from her has started to feel normal. That first night home, we sit around watching TV and I feel so happy. But that all changes first thing the next morning when it is all hands on deck again.

'Today we got to go on a boundary run and replace all the rotten posts,' Father starts. 'Grab your swags and some supplies because we're going to be out for a few days. Luke, you can fill the water containers up and take everything off the Rodeo and load up the fencing gear. Don't forget the post-splitting hammers and throw the wire wheel on too just in case we need to run some new strands of wire here or there. Bryce, grab a box of bullets for the .22-250 and fill up the Rodeo with diesel. Make sure you check the oil and water. And don't forget to check the spare tyre. I snagged a sharp rock the day before yesterday, and I haven't had a chance to fix it yet.'

Bryce and I head over to the workshop.

'Bryce,' Father yells from the veranda.

'Err, yes, Father.'

We stand silently on the gravel between the house and the workshop, waiting for Father's instructions.

'We better sign you up for employment first, don't you think? Leave that with Luke for the time being.'

Bryce heads back over to the house while I jump into the Rodeo, drive it over to the fuel bowsers and fill up the tank with diesel. Just as I finish topping up the oil and water, Father and Bryce join me and help with loading up a few posts and the other things we need.

'The spare tyre is good,' Bryce says, kicking it a few times.

As the weeks pass, Bryce is happy working for Father now that he is getting paid for it. Father pays him quite well. He can do so because he is in a good financial position at the moment, having received a wool cheque of over a quarter of a million dollars several months earlier.

Towards the end of the summer holidays, we are out fixing a fence line near Meryl, a holding paddock windmill when Ruben Davids from Lime and Bell, the station to the east of us, comes over to see Father.

'G'day, Neil, how's everything going?' Davids asks.

'Yeah, everything's going quite well for us,' Father says confidently. 'With the lovely year we've just had, the lambing season has been extremely good. How's things over at yours?'

'Not too bad at all, Neil, not too bad at all. Who are these young lads you have working for you?'

'This is Bryce, my eldest son, and my second eldest son, Luke.'

'How ya doing, fellas?'

'Yeah, we're good, thanks,' Bryce and I reply.

'Would you like a cup of tea, Ruben? The boys are about to light the fire and chuck the billy on for lunch.'

'Hell yes, I'm parched. I could murder someone for a cup of tea right now. So you better hurry up, lads, I'm not joking.' Davids pulls an angry face and shows his teeth.

'Well, you haven't got time to lose. Get onto it quick smart, you two,' Father laughs.

Father and Davids have a smoke while Bryce and I get the fire going and make a billy of tea. When we sit down, Father turns to Davids.

'Ask Bryce yourself, Ruben.'

'What would you think, Bryce, about spending a couple of weeks over at Lime and Bell helping me muster up?'

'Yeah, that sounds like fun.' Bryce nods eagerly.

Davids looks pleased and starts giving Bryce directions. 'If you stick on the track after you go through the boundary gate and continue along for roughly another twenty-five kilometres, you'll come across the homestead. All right, mate?' He gives Bryce a warm smile.

After lunch, Davids leaves and we continue with the fencing for the rest of the day. We can see Father is deep in thought, but he doesn't say anything until we get home.

'Mr Davids is putting his station on the market,' he says.

'Oh, I wonder who'll buy it,' Bryce muses.

'I'm not sure at this stage,' Father replies.

For the next couple of months, Father keeps his eyes peeled in the *Elders Weekly*, waiting for Lime and Bell to come on the market.

When it is finally up for sale, he calls us in for a family meeting. 'Vonn, Bryce, Bidjid, Luke, Zoann, Dansan and Loui – please come into the kitchen. There's something I want to discuss with you all.'

We all make our way inside and sit down around the kitchen table. Father waits for us to settle into our chairs.

'Vonn and I have been looking at buying Lime and Bell. What do you guys think?' he asks.

We all look around the table at one another.

'I think it would be great. It is a lovely station, Father. When I was over there helping them muster, I saw plenty of nice places to explore,' Bryce says excitedly.

'What about the rest of you?"

'Yeah, buy it, Father,' we all agree.

'Okay, I'll go to the bank and see if I have enough equity on Moolapool to refinance the loan so we can grab it.'

At the time, it seems like a great idea and we are all for it, so without much consideration, Father has soon bought Lime and Bell. It nearly triples our station size from 450,000 acres to 1.2 million.

Father is still going through the final stages of the settlement for Lime and Bell by the time school starts back up in February 1989.

I can't wait to tell everyone that our station is even bigger now. When I get back, I'm a little nervous at first because I'll now be facing life at boarding school alone. But my anxiety soon passes, especially when I notice all the new Year 8 kids looking very teary-eyed when their parents leave.

I soon find which part of the dormitory I'm staying in and I am relieved it's at the other end of the building, away from Pedro's gawking stare. Unfortunately, I can't escape him. He still humiliates me on several occasions throughout the year, making me lie naked across his lap with him caressing my arse. I feel sorry for the new Year 8s being exposed to this but know there is nothing that can be said or done to make things better for any one of us.

Shain soon arrives, and I'm pleased that he's stuck to his word and come back to boarding school. I tell him my news straightaway.

'Really? How big is your station now?' he asks.

'It's 1.2 million acres.'

'Gee, that's bloody massive. It'll take at least two days or more just to drive around checking all the windmills now, won't it?

'That's right,' I reply.

Not long after, Peal walks into the dorm and, just like the three amigos, we are hanging around together again. It is great to see Shain and Peal, and as Bryce said, things aren't going to be so bad if I'm with my friends. And that year, Shain comes out to the station nearly every school holiday, which is bloody good.

We all carry on making the most of school, but when I return after first term holidays, I find that I've been split up from the dorm Shain is in, and I'm now down the other end of the dormitory. This doesn't keep us apart at all, though; if anything, it just makes our relationship stronger.

One evening at dinner Pedro enters the dining room with a man in his early twenties. He speaks quietly with him for a couple of minutes before calling us all to attention. 'Listen up, boys,' Pedro cranes his head around, eyeballing the kids who are still talking.

Silence fills the room.

'This is Father Phyle, our new training priest. I want you all to give him a warm welcome.'

'Hello, Father Phyle,' we chorus.

Phyle looks around the room nervously. 'Hello, everyone, I look forward to getting to know each one of you all personally.'

'Father Phyle will be moving into the vacant room in the east wing dormitory and will also be your dorm master,' Pedro continues.

He turns to Father Phyle. 'Follow me, Peter.'

They cut through the kitchen into the Brothers' dining room. We all wait until they are out of sight, and then the room fills with laughter.

'Did you hear his name? I hope he doesn't come anywhere near me,' one of the Year 10s sitting at Winton's table says.

'Yeah, that's all we need, another Pedro,' Jarrod huffs from another corner of the dining room.

'He didn't seem that bad,' Shain says to me.

'Yeah, I'd prefer him over Pedro any day,' I reply.

That evening during our study period, Phyle moves his stuff into his room, and by the time we get back upstairs, he is patrolling my dorm. When I say hello to him, he asks me what my name is.

'I'm Luke, Father Phyle. Have you set up your room already?' I ask politely.

'Yes, I have and, Luke, please call me Peter. It's a bit late now but tomorrow, you boys are welcome to come and check it out if you like.'

I look around the dorm. A few other kids are standing around nodding.

'Yeah, that'd be awesome,' Osun Bay says.

The following afternoon after we have had our showers, Phyle invites a few kids to his room. I pop in to see what everyone is doing.

There is a huge selection of porn magazines on the coffee table that the kids are flicking through. And a porn movie is playing from the VCR on the TV. I race off to tell Shain and he comes back with me. We go into Phyle's room and start looking at his dirty magazines with the rest of the kids.

Phyle soon takes a shine to Shain and me, and before we know it, he is buying us alcohol and other things we have asked for whenever he is heading into Mullewa. At the time, this does not feel as bad as it actually is, but in retrospect, I think he was trying to figure out which one of us he could have his way with.

Phyle really likes Shain and treats him like he is one of his friends. Sometimes, he visits us in our cubby at night when we are allowed to camp out. One time, he even travels more than a thousand kilometres to spend time with us for just a couple of hours, until Pedro tracks him down and tells him to get back to the school.

When I go back to the station at the end of first semester, Bryce looks exhausted. Since Father purchased Lime and Bell, there is now three times as much work to do.

'How's school going?' Father asks me.

'It's going great, Father.'

'Well,' Father starts, 'I got a call from Brother O'Who. He said you called Brother Neddle an egghead. Is it true?'

I tell him it is.

'What I'd like to know,' Father continues, 'is this Brother Neddle bald?'

'Yes, apart from a little bit of hair just above his ears.'

Father starts laughing. 'Oh well, that explains it.'

'I never thought of it that way,' I nervously reply.

Later, I quietly tell Bryce about the porn and alcohol the priest is supplying us with at school, but it doesn't seem to raise any alarm with him, so I just shrug it off as nothing.

Work on the station is repetitive and relentless but fixing windmills and fences every day of the holidays makes the time goes quickly., Before I know it, I'm getting back on the bus to boarding school for third term.

When I discover that one of Willsh's working dogs has had a litter of pups, I plead with him to let me take one home with me at the end of the term. He finally agrees, so as the next holidays get closer, I find an old cardboard box and poke a few holes in it, ready for the trip. Father does not know I will be bringing the pup home with me, because I figure he would say no if I asked if it was okay, and I cannot bear to be separated from the little kelpie.

Pedro takes me to catch the bus and says it's more than likely I will not be able to take the dog with me. I quietly ask the driver if it is okay to bring the pup with me in the box, but he strictly forbids animals onboard. When he is not looking, I quickly shove the box into the luggage compartment and put my bag in front of it so he cannot see it.

A couple of hours later, when we pull into Mount Magnet for dinner and to let passengers off, the driver hears the pup whining as he opens the luggage compartment. He strides into the service station and tells me off in front of everyone. 'I said you can't take animals on the bus, didn't I? Now go and get rid of it right now.'

While the driver goes to the counter and orders a cup of coffee, I race outside. The box is sitting alongside the bus. I open it up, reach in and pull the pup out.

'I'm sorry, I have to let you go. The driver doesn't want you on the bus,' I say, as I cuddle up to the puppy.

'Why don't you leave the box there and shove the pup down your top?' suggests another passenger, who overheard the conversation with the driver as she was getting on the bus.

'That's a good idea.' I follow her onto the bus.

'Here, pass it to me,' she says. What's its name? I'll hold it because I'm sure the driver will check around your seat for it.'

'I haven't given her one yet and I just call her puppy dog,' I respond as I hand the puppy over and take a seat in front of her. As the other passengers start boarding the bus, the driver walks up the aisle to where I'm sitting.

'Did you get rid of that pup?' he asks, poking around the blankets on my seat, while looking for the puppy dog.

'Yes, it ran off that way,' I tell him, pointing out the window at the empty box.

The driver's just starting to make his way back towards the front of the bus when suddenly the pup starts to whine. He spins around and walks briskly back to my seat.

'Right, where is it? I know you have it here somewhere, I just heard it whining. Come on, stand up out here.'

'I don't have it, see…' I say, as I stand in the aisle.

'We won't be leaving until you get the animal off the bus,' the driver says angrily.

'It's okay, it's here,' I confess.

I take the pup from the passenger in the seat behind me and hold it close as I nudge my way past the driver. I am just about to step off the bus when the driver stops me.

'Wait…if you promise you won't let the pup run up and down the aisle, and clean up after it if it goes to the toilet on here, you can keep it,' he says.

I promise to do all he asks.

I quickly return to my seat and on the rest of the journey I make a few friends with people who want to pat puppy dog. Still, I am very glad to get to Meekatharra and get off that bus.

That year, the final term goes by in the blink of an eye. The Year 10s graduate and once again O'Who becomes teary-eyed. This time, though, what follows comes as a shock.

'Congratulations to all the Year 10 boys. It has been great to see you all mature into intelligent young men and it'll be sad to see you leave,' O'Who starts.

He pauses for a few seconds, looks the Year 10s over one by one and smiles. 'For some years now, I have been thinking about leaving myself,' he resumes. 'I know many of you will be sad to see me go, and others might be quite relieved. Anyway, the Brothers and I have appointed someone you are all familiar with. So now I'd like you all to give another great big round of applause to your new principal who will be starting next year.'

O'Who turns towards Pedro, who is sitting in a pew at the back of the church and extends his arm towards him.

Pedro stands up, manoeuvres his way past Neddle, Sister Karma, Mrs Mc'Ker, Willsh, Sheety, Lentil and Davy, and makes his way to the front of the church.

'Your new principal, Brother Pedro,' O'Who announces once more.

All us kids are in shock, but the parents start clapping immediately. We join in as Pedro scans his eyes over us before raising his hand, and gracefully signalling for us all to be quiet.

'As your new principal, I've decided there will be a few changes next year,' he begins. 'I won't go into too much detail now but those of you who'll be returning will find out next year. But as this year has now come to an end, I wish you all a safe holiday and I will see many of you next year.'

I look at Shain and we slowly shake our heads.

Then I take a step closer towards him. 'What do you think about that? The conversation I overheard a year and a half ago came true.'

'Oh man, that's fucked up, hey,' he says. 'Our worst nightmare has come true.'

We both start laughing. I agree.

'Oh well, anyway, mate, I got to get going, Mum's got to get back to the shop in Gero,' Shain says. 'I'll see you next year if you're coming back.'

'Yeah, I'll be back for sure. This place beats correspondence schooling any day, and besides, you'll be here, won't you?'

'Yes, of course I will. I can't let you have all the fun. I love this place, apart from Pedro of course. Anyway, catch ya up next year.'

When I get back home, the puppy dog has grown a lot and she has really taken to Vonn, who has spent a lot of time with her while I've been at school.

'What's her name?' I ask because she was still just 'puppy dog' when I left.

'We decided to call her Boots because of the white markings on her legs.'

'Yeah, I was thinking Socks, but I like Boots better,' I say.

A couple of weeks into my holiday, Father receives a call from the Holmes family inviting us to have Christmas lunch with them. When we get there, Winton, who only just graduated from school, tells me about a hessian bag full of beer in one of Brother Simon's dams, back at school.

'You should check it out, Luke. It's quite easy to spot if you know what you're looking for.'

I can't help thinking about that beer for the rest of summer, and I long to tell Shain about it as soon as I get back to boarding school.

It's great to see Shain and Peal again, and this time, they've both brought their bikes with them. I can't wait for the first long weekend, so I can pick up a bike for myself in Geraldton with the pocket money that I have earned from years of helping out on the station.

Shain has a nice BMX, nothing flash, while Peal has a BMX Mongoose. He constantly shows off on it by performing daring tricks.

As soon as I get the chance, I tell Shain about the hessian bag full of beer in Brother Simon's dam. 'What do you think? Do you want to check it out?'

'Ah, it's probably just bullshit,' he says.

'Let's check it out anyway,' I insist.

Shain's a little sceptical. He reckons Winton is just sending us on a wild goose chase. 'I bet the Brothers have already found it by now anyway,' he says.

'We have nothing to lose if it turns out there's nothing there,' I argue.

'Yeah, I guess not,' Shain replies, but I can tell he is still full of doubt.

On our next free afternoon, we head down to the dam.

'It's hard to believe that we are now the Year 10s,' I say.

'Yeah, who would have known we'd make it this far,' Shain replies.

We scour around the bank, looking for the hessian bag. We are just about to give up, when I notice something tangled up in the branches of a tree and dangling in the water.

'What's that over there?' I nod towards the branches.

'I think that could be it,' Shain says. He kicks his shoes off and wades into the water. He reaches into the bush, feels around, then pulls up a hessian bag. There must be close to a carton of beer in it. He drags it out, and pulls it behind himself, to the edge of the dam.

We open the bag, grab a couple of cans, and crack them open.

'Here's to Winton! Cheers, mate,' I say.

Shain and I tap our cans together. We each take a gulp and instantly spit the beer out onto the ground.

'Yuck, that's fucking gross,' I say, wiping the froth away from my mouth with my forearm.

I've never been much exposed to beer or beer drinkers, even though Father keeps a carton of cans down at the shearing shed for when the shearers come out. Then he has a beer with them, but always just the one; he doesn't drink the whole carton. In fact, the carton lasts years.

'It's gone off, I'm sure,' Shain replies. He spits a few times, trying to get the taste out of his mouth.

'Nah, fuck this shit! Let's open them all,' I suggest.

We crack all the cans open and tip the beer into the water. We throw the empties back into the hessian bag with a couple of rocks and toss it out as far as we can into the dam.

'They probably went off being out in the sun all summer, is my guess,' Shain says.

'I don't know if it was off. Could be that's what hot beer tastes like,' I laugh.

'Maybe we should have taken a couple of cans back to school and hidden them in the freezer down at the killing shed. Oh well, a bit too late for that now.'

All that remains of our haul is a load of froth along the edge of the water.

Pedro has allowed kids to bring their bikes to school this year, and I yearn for the long weekend to come so I can get a bike myself. When it eventually arrives, I go to Geraldton with Shain and buy my bike. A couple of weeks later, Pedro gives us a free afternoon and I finally get the chance to join Shain and Peal for a pedal. We head beyond the school, towards one of the dams where there is a vegetable garden, because there are some nice steep slopes we can jump over down that way.

'Quick, let's get 'em,' I hear.

I look over my shoulder. A few guys on horses are headed our way. Shain and Peal take off on their bikes towards the thickets to get away from them. I know I have a snowball's chance in hell of escaping, so I just stand my ground and wait to see what is going to happen. One kid's horse comes cantering straight towards me; the others go after Shain and Peal. As the one coming for me gets closer, I notice its rider is Jose Taddon, a cocky little punk from Year 8.

Taddon slows his horse to a trot but keeps coming towards me. The horse stomps its hooves as they get closer because Taddon is pulling hard on the reins and forcing his horse to keep going by digging the heels of his riding boots into its ribs. I don't want to get trampled, so I pull my bike up onto its rear tyre and run at the horse, growling like a wild bear. Then I ring the bicycle bell. This spooks Taddon's horse. It spins around and takes off in a full canter, back through the thickets towards the school.

I jump back on my bike, and continue towards the dam, looking for Shain and Peal. After a while, I see them riding towards me.

'What happened to you?' Peal asks when we are finally reunited.

I fill them in.

'I don't think Taddon will be coming after me again,' I say.

'Yeah, fucken cunts, shouldn't be riding horses if they're only out here to chase us around,' Shain adds.

Later, back at school, I'm heading through the dorm to have a shower, when I run into Taddon. He has a cast on his arm.

'What happened to you?' I ask.

'You, you did it.'

'What do you mean I did it?'

'When you came at me on your bike and spooked my horse, it bolted and went straight under a low branch which knocked me off,' Taddon snaps. 'When I landed, I fell across a fallen branch straight onto my arm. So now it's broken, thanks to you.'

'Oh well, you won't be chasing me again, and if anyone else wants to try, I'll do the exact same thing to them,' I reply, without a hint of guilt.

First term dragged on a little, but it was a whole lot better to be at boarding school than to be stuck on the station being ordered about by father. He really became unbearable and Shain knew just how much of an asshole he can be to me and my siblings.

Pedro tried his hardest to separate Shain and me by placing Shain down the opposite end of the building to me, but we always found a way to hang out and do the crazy stuff we used to get up to.

As the term was nearing the end, once again I found the excitement/fearfulness flicker inside of me from having to go home. I was glad when Shain rang his parents and asked if it was okay for him to come with me back out to the station for the first term holidays. Shain finds Father kind of threatening but he doesn't take offence to it and just laughs it off in front of him and we also have a laugh with me after.

Father, Bryce and Bidjid have been mustering sheep out in the Spinifex paddock and continue do so, while Shain and I are sent south to muster the sheep from the Moolapool paddock into the holding paddock.

For the first day or two, Shain and I spend most of the time chasing each other around on the motorbikes, doing doughnuts and basically flogging the shit out of them. Somehow, Father finds out and he isn't impressed one bit, which we find out at dinner that evening.

'How are you and Shain going with the Moolapool paddock?' Father asks.

I can tell just looking at him that he knows we are just fucking around out there.

'It's getting there. We did put about seventy sheep into the holding paddock but when we came back, we found that someone went through and left the gate open,' I reply.

Shain backs me up on the story I'm spinning by claiming to be the one who shut the gate. I see Father just isn't buying it but feel glad that Shain is here.

'I believe that you're both getting around in the paddock trying to muster the sheep but it's too hard riding a motorbike with one hand while your other one is holding on to each other's cocks,' Father replies humiliatingly.

'We are looking for sheep, though,' I snap back cautiously.

'Tomorrow, you boys can take the Nissan and check the boundary fence over the Glengarry Rangers, I think you'll need to tow start it because the battery isn't good at the moment,' Father instructs.

Bright and early the next morning, Shain and I head over to the workshop. After trying to start the Nissan and the battery power is only enough to make a clicking sound come from the starter motor, I position the Little Truck in front of the Nissan with a tow rope.

'Do you want to jump in the Little Truck and tow me out to the flat so we can tow start it, or do you want to be in the Nissan?' I ask Shain.

'I'll tow you with the Little Truck,' Shain replies as he goes to get in the vehicle.

Soon we are ready and Shain has taken up the slack in the rope with the Little Truck. I wave my hand slowly out the window and Shain releases the clutch too quickly, causing the Little Truck to go into a bunny-hopping stage and start bogging down.

'Shain,' I yell from the Nissan.

Shain stops and looks back at me for further instructions.

'Reverse back and take up another position, Shain,' I order.

Soon we are ready to try again and this time Shain hits the accelerator to the floor before taking up the slack in the rope. I sit and watch as everything unfolds in front of me as the slack is taken up quicker than it should have been. With the aggressive approach he took, it led to the pipework Father had welded onto the Little Truck to snap at the welds and it almost was yanked completely off the vehicle.

'Stop!' I yell, but the damage has already been done.

'Shit, your dad's going to want to kill me. I never meant to jerk it off in the Little Truck,' Shain mumbles.

'Don't worry too much about it, mate. Father can weld it back up again. You might want to choose some better words, though. I'll never let it go that you jerked it off in the Little Truck,' I snigger.

Eventually, we manage to get the Nissan running and we go and check the boundary fence. There are a few wires and a straining post we fix up. The day drags on and we get back to the house just on dusk, thoroughly exhausted.

A week in and still I haven't been over to Lime and Bell and, from what Bryce has told me about the station, it's supposed to be amazing.

'Father, do you think we'll be able to go on the next windmill run over to Lime and Bell with you next time?' I ask curiously.

'Tomorrow, Bryce is going over there if you boys wanted to go with him and have a look,' Father responds.

'Yes, that would be great, thanks,' I reply.

The next day, Bryce, Shain and I head over to Lime and Bell.

'Do you know many of the windmill names over here, Bryce?' I ask.

'Most of them I do. We now have two Four Miles, two Salt Bushes, two Limestones and two Joe and Harry windmills because Lime and Bell also have windmills with those exact names. The other ones off the top of my head are Northmill, Breakaway, Cornermill, Two Mile, Inkies, Meeks, Rainbow, Sampsons, Bob's, Emerald, Windy Tank, Divide, Morries and Desperate,' Bryce answers.

We make the most of it and going with Bryce is like going on a sightseeing adventure. We just drive, talk and laugh most of the way, Bryce is envious of me still at school and warns me that it's hard work on the station and he can't wait to get away when he turns seventeen in a couple of months.

Before we know it, the holidays are over and, Shain and I are on the Greyhound bus heading back to school.

We laugh about all the shit we got up too while on holiday on the station and I tell Shain I can't wait to tell the other kids about him when we get back.

When I return to boarding school, Father hires Edvard Sure and his son Ty, who's a couple of years younger than me, to help him with odd jobs on the station because he knows that Bryce will be hitting the road to start his journey soon. Father has always told all of us kids, even Bidjid and Zoann, that when we reach seventeen and get our driver's licence, we will be sent on our way for a year, to learn how to survive on our own.

By the middle of the year, Bryce has just turned seventeen and not long after that, he gets his driver's licence. He comes to see me in his pride and joy XB Ford. It looks tough and sounds even tougher when he starts it up. The V8 engine rumbles and the sound of the engine is carried around the buildings. Within moments, nearly every kid from school has flocked around in aura. Bryce then kicks down on the accelerator and the sound reverberates around between the buildings. Pedro steps out from the Brothers' lounge room and stands with his neck craning in our direction, his chin held high. In the whole three years of boarding school, Bryce is the only visitor I have had here.

Towards the end of third term, I go catching yabbies down at the dam with Shain and Peal, and one of them is a female with a load of eggs. I dig out the now derelict vivarium Peal and I used to put spiders in to fight each other to death, scrape out the remains and put enough water in it to transport the female yabby back to the station on the bus. As soon as I'm back home for the holidays, I head out to Merly's and put the yabby straight in the dam there.

I am disappointed to discover that while I have been away at school, Father has let Ty use my motorbike. It is broken down and has a flat tyre now, plus it will not start, so now I have to use Dansan's motorbike for mustering. Even though I'm still quite short for my age, Dansan's bike isn't suitable. My knees knock against the handlebars and it is hard to turn, so I ride around with my legs apart. It is not easy riding like that, believe me.

In the first half hour of getting out into the paddock, I get a flat tyre. No one else is around and I cannot mend the puncture. I bounce over rocks most of day, riding back and forth, even though I do not see a single sheep the entire time. Father is driving the blue Nissan that day and cannot really get out in the bush too easily. When I reach the corner of the paddock, I come across him smashing through the mulga trees. He is tearing around back and forth, trying to get some sheep through the gate. Father has set the Nissan up as a cattle mustering vehicle. It has welded roll bars all over it, and a section of railway iron on the front which acts as a bull bar. I swing into the action and after several minutes we eventually get the sheep through.

But Father isn't appreciative. 'Where the hell have you been all day? You useless little cunt,' he yells while making his way over to me.

'I've been zigzagging back and forth through the paddock looking and listening out for sheep and also trying to find someone else who I can grab a pump and patches from, so I can fix this tyre,' I say, gesturing with my hand in the direction of the tyre.

Father continues marching towards me as his nostrils flare out in anger, his two front teeth showing like a savage Rottweiler about to attack. He is still fuming and I feel like any moment now I'll be seeing stars.

'And how long have you been riding around on that flat tyre?' He spots a branch on the ground and swoops down to pick it up.

'I got the flat tyre nearly straightaway after I headed out. I tried looking for someone so I could fix it.'

Father raises the branch and swings it at my head. I hear it connect and then break as I fall to the ground. There is a sudden white glare as I'm knocked out for a couple of seconds.

These fearful moments seemed to become more frequent as I grew older. Father would lose his temper in the blink of an eye. He only ever really saw me as a useless person, especially if he runs out of tobacco and starts hitting the withdrawal stages, which I'm sure he had done that day he knocked me out.

It appeared to my siblings and me that everyone who knew our father feared him in one way or another. That look he saved especially for me for me, though, cut deeper than he could have ever imagined. It was as if I was shit on the bottom of his shoe that he could never get off, no matter how hard he kicked to get it free.

He starts carrying a machete around on his motorbike like he's some crazy sunstruck nomad who has just taken forty days to cross the Great Sandy Desert in search of God. He is ready to tear off after any of us who don't follow his strict mustering plans. In an instant, his left hand at full reach, fist clenching the machete, kind of a hard thing to do while riding through scrub on a motorbike. We must always keep our wits about us and constantly be aware of where he is, even more than knowing where the sheep are when it comes to pushing them through the gates. I quickly get to know his moves. When I sense he is about to come after me in a rage, I race off like a bat out of hell. Fortunately, my motorbike is lower to the ground than his and the handlebars narrower, so I can head for the lower branches and narrow openings of the mulga trees, while he has to circle the thicket a few times. Once or twice, he gets off his bike and races after me on foot. But I can leave him for dust.

When I return home, he is always waiting for me. It is scary not knowing what to expect. Most of the time, he is unpredictable. Sometimes, he just laughs about how I took off and the fear in my eyes. Other times, he punches me in the guts, sending me flying onto my back. I lie there winded, in agony, trying to regain my breath, while he stands over me like a schoolyard bully.

'Get up off the bloody ground,' Father yells.

Even the tone of his voice makes me quiver when he is in a rage, and if I'm not quick enough back on my feet, I cop another blow.

Father and I go out checking the rusty old fence lines to see if there are any repairs that need to be done before mustering, which is due to start in a few weeks' time.

'There's a broken wire there, Luke. You get out here and I'll head up to the straining post and untie it for you. Whack a figure eight in it and quickly catch up to where I'll be. We have a long way to go.'

Father pulls up and I get out, grabbing a pair of pliers off the back of the Rodeo.

'Righto, Luke,' Father yells out.

His deep, booming voice often causes birds to flee from their nesting branches, even if he is more than three hundred metres away.

Whenever we are repairing fences, I put the figure eights in the wire as quickly as I can. Sometimes while I am doing it, Father fires off a round in my direction from his high-powered rifle. Father grew up around rifles on his parents' farm. On the station, we have a few rifles too. We all use them for survival purposes and, like Father, we have become great marksmen ourselves.

Dirt sprays up from the ground within a metre of me and rocks flick up.

'You fucken dickhead,' I mutter.

I know he can't hear me, but it gives me great satisfaction to curse him when he's out of range.

'Okay, Father, I've done it,' I yell to him at the top of my lungs, once I'm done.

If he can't hear me, I wave my arms about as if I'm directing a jumbo jet onto a narrow runway. As soon as he starts straining up the wire, I race to where he is, as fast as an Olympic sprinter, wanting to get back to him before he starts shooting at me again.

'You're a bloody quick runner,' Father says.

I stand exhausted alongside him, trying to catch my breath. 'Yeah, I didn't want to hold you up,' I lie.

Father has an excellent scope on his rifle, and he is very accurate with his shots too. He can drop a kangaroo jumping through the scrub from up to a hundred and fifty metres away. But I absolutely hate it when he lets rounds go at me. Up till now, Father has mostly been loving, someone I aspire to be like when I'm older, but during this time, he's turned out to be awful, a person I despise.

Back at school, I complete the rest of the year. We make our way to the chapel and we're waiting for our graduation certificates. Pedro and Mr Davids are standing up the front of the church and our names are called out one by one.

The church is packed with students, teachers, brothers and parents. Each time someone's name is called out, the student gets a huge round of applause and their parents quickly jump out into the aisle of the church to take a photo of the proud moment. I know that when it's my turn, there will be no cameras clicking for me, just a brief round of applause.

'Luke Pomery,' Mr Davids calls out and passes it to Pedro.

I stand up and make my way up to receive the certificate that Pedro holds in his hand.

'Congratulations, Luke, well done,' Pedro announces.

He hands the certificate over. In that split second of achievement before everyone starts clapping, I hear a familiar sound.

Click!

I turn quickly to see who snapped the photo but see no one standing out in the aisle and wonder to myself who it could have been. To this day, I still have no idea who it was.

11

Drought

With the lead-up of a long dry spell for the last half of 1990, by the time December/January 1991 comes around, a drought hits WA and the station takes a severe hit. There is no pasture for the sheep, and little to no wind to turn the windmills to pump water. We are racing all over the place carting water and loads of lupins out to the windmills to keep the sheep alive. Most of the paddocks around the windmills are starting to look barren. Father orders in a semi-truck load of lupins to feed the sheep but they are dying quicker than we can keep up the feed to them.

The drought is tough on us all, especially since Bryce is still away. And things go even further downhill over the next couple of years. There is no wind, no rain falls, sheep perish everywhere and wool prices plummet. A lot of other station owners nearby just walk away from their properties. Father manages to make a bit of money from the fleeces of dead sheep, but only because he ha saved on petrol and the time spent in mustering them up and shearing costs.

'Time to get up now, Luke. Luke, come on.' Father alerts me from a deep sleep I was having.

'Oh, okay, Father,' I say as I sit up and rub my eyes.

A couple of minutes later, I make my way into the kitchen and grab a pre-filled bowl of porridge from the counter and sit at the table across from Father, who's sitting there with a cup of tea in front of him while he rolls himself a cigarette.

'How was your sleep, Luke? Father asks.

'It was good. You called out to me in my dream, and I thought when I heard you in person that it was just a dream,' I reply.

'I thought you were,' Father responds. 'Right then. Luke, I want you to take the fencing equipment with you on the boundary run today. Take one of the little boys with you for company, Dansan isn't doing anything,' Father instructs.

I finish off my porridge and make a cup of tea and sit back at the table again. Dansan and Vonn enter from the lounge room at the same time I'm about to sit down.

'Dansan, you go with Luke today and help him with the fences and gates, okay, mate.' Father pats him on the shoulder.

'Okay, Father,' Dansan replies in a sluggish tone.

After breakfast, we pack the fencing materials onto the ute and head south to the nearest boundary to begin the check. I spot a broken wire and drop Dansan off to put a figure eight in once I have untied the wire from the straining post just up the fence line. I get out at the strainer and untie the wire and inform Dansan he can now tie of the figure eight. While he is doing that, I notice a rotten post just past the strainer and I grab the post-splitting hammers to knock the post off the fence. A couple of small lizards who were living in the post fell to the ground and one darted under a dead branch while the other disappeared.

A few hours later, there is this twitching muscle on the inner part of my thigh and I dare not to touch it as doing that tends to stop the sensation and I was enjoying the feeling. This went on for about two minutes until I eventually lowered my hand to the area and touched upon the twitch. Hairs instantly stood on their ends when I felt a lump in my pants and it tried to move. Suddenly I flew out of my pants and threw them to the ground. At the same time, the lizard that disappeared from knocking the post off the fence a few hours earlier fell to the ground a little stunned at what was happening and then darted away to the nearest bush, where it froze and looked back over its shoulder at me.

'What the heck are you doing?' Dansan questioned my sudden reaction.

'There was a small lizard in my pants and I didn't know what the fuck it was, so I wasn't going to take any chances and I just ripped my pants off,' I replied, still with a shaky voice as I checked the inside of my pants for more critters. If I was at boarding school, the boys would never let this one down, I thought to myself.

Heaviness consumes me as I start thinking about the friends I made at boarding school and how I could not wait for school to be finished forever while I was still there. Now, I am on the station, hundreds of kilometres away from those now distant memories and I deeply sigh out loud to myself.

By this stage, I am nearly sixteen years old and father isn't as hard on me as he was eighteen months earlier. He even tells me to stand up for myself if I think I am right, and to argue the point.

This is put to the test one day when he walks in on me working on my motorbike. It needs fixing after the last time Ty used it and put dirty fuel into the tank, clogging up the jets in the carburettor with grit.

'What are you doing there, Luke?' Father demands an answer.

'I'm cleaning out the carby on my motorbike,' I reply. 'I'm just replacing the needle back into the jet now. I've already fixed the flat tyre up.'

'Go on, give it here… You don't do it like that,' he snaps, as he tries to take it from me. 'You got to put the float in first.'

'No, this carby isn't like most of the others. You have to do it this way,' I explain, while not allowing him near it.

Father raises his arm and clenches his fist. Suddenly, he slowly drops his arm. I can see he is thinking about what he said to me about standing up for myself and maybe he is feeling proud of me for possibly the first time in my life.

'Where'd Bidjid go?' Father asks, looking back towards the house. 'Oh, here she comes now. What have you been doing, Bidjid?'

'Errr, umm, n…nu..nothing, Father. I'm going to fix the flat tyre on my motorbike,' Bidjid nervously answers. She quickly grabs an old twenty-litre flour drum and wedges it under her bike to hold it up, so she can remove the tyre.

She's been over at the old laundry checking up on her dog, Clamsy. She continues with taking off her tyre but as soon as Father leaves, a couple of minutes later, she prances happily over to me. 'Clamsy's about to have her first litter any day now, Luke. Any day. Would you like to choose one for your own when they're born?' she asks. 'Especially now that Boots seems to be more Vonn's dog than yours.'

'Oh yes, please.'

Clamsy is just under a year old; she is the offspring of Boots, the dog I smuggled from boarding school onto the Greyhound bus at the end of the third term in in 1989.

A few days later, Bidjid calls me into the old laundry to select a pup from the litter of newborns.

I pick one up and hold him close to my chest. 'I'll have this one, I say, snuggling the pup.'

'Yeah, he's very cute,' Bidjid says. 'I like his big white markings. What are you going to call him?'

'Ummm...I'll call him Bob, hey. After the song Mr Bob Dobalina,' I respond.

'Oh, boy, how stupid! You make me sick. Ha ha. It's a line from the song Mr Bob Dobalina,' Bidjid laughs.

It was good that Father bought Lime and Bell but for us remaining behind on the station, besides our Father, we sensed an eerie presence at the homestead.

I'm still not sure where or how we found out, but it was said that the house was constructed from the materials from a demolished church from somewhere in the area. How that mattered was also unclear, but things started happening at Lime and Bell that cannot be explained.

Often, we would hear the shower running but when we went to investigate, no one was in there. The shower was dripping, the bathroom floor was wet and the light was left on. None of us would leave the light on because we all knew the house was on solar and only had one battery. Wasting power was not something we did.

At night, we would see a light beam in the shearing shed roughly a hundred and fifty metres away from the house – but we knew no one was there, and the goose bumps tingled across our skin instantly. Trying to ignore these strange occurrences became harder, and at the same time the mystery was alluring.

With all the dust storms that swept over the airstrip next to the house, the top of the ceilings filled with fine bull dust, like talcum powder. Whenever I went to stay there with anyone, we would check out the house thoroughly by climbing up into the ceiling to see that nothing was up there.

At night, we would hear noises and look up at the ceiling only to see telltale dust falling from the small nail holes in the pressed metal sheeting. In the dark, we had no way of checking what was up there, and it was terrifying.

One night of the many times Bidjid and I camped at the homestead, we decided to barricade ourselves in the kitchen because it was warm and felt safer. We used the kitchen chairs to prop up under the three door handles and balanced empty tins on the handles of each of the doors, so if anyone tried to open the door it would fall and make one hell of a noise, hopefully waking one of us up.

I woke up later that night to the sound of something scraping over the small-profile corrugated iron, known as chicken iron.

Chilled to my bones, I lay there with my head tucked tightly under the blanket trying to recall if the iron was on the inside of the kitchen or on the outside, but I was not going to get up and check in the dark. Shivering with fear, I listened as the sound continued to make its way around the room. I knew it was not my sister because I could hear her faintly snoring beside me.

When the morning light woke me, I sat up and looked around the room. The first thing I looked for was Bidjid, to make sure she was still with me, which she was. When I turned to look at the doors, the one closest to me was half open, the chair stood on all fours and the empty tin was on the ground only inches from my head. I jumped to my feet, as Bidjid stirred alongside me.

'Did you get up already?' I asked, pointing at the open door.

'No, I just woke up,' she replied, looking around at the doors. 'What about you?'

'I only just got up now too, but last night I heard some noises, and I didn't open that door either.' I pointed back at the open door.

Eager to survey the outside of the house, I remove the tin and chair still blocking the way to the back door and open it to go outside. I make my way around to the side of the house to check out the wall. Staring at the clean lines of the flat surface of the fibre sheeting, I stand there tingling as I try to figure out how it was that I had heard the distinct sound of something rubbing on a corrugated surface. Another shiver passes through me and I walk quickly back into the kitchen, where the inside walls are lined with chicken iron.

'Fuck that. Last night the noises I heard were of something rubbing over chicken iron – the iron inside this kitchen.'

'Really? So, whatever it was last night was inside,' Bidjid exclaims. 'They are really messing around with us.'

Another time, Vonn, Dansan, Loui and I were camping here for a few days and Dansan and I were sleeping in the cool shed. The cool shed, like most others on stations, was set up with a few mulga posts to construct a room and a tin roof covered in brush. This was lined with chicken wire both inside and outside of the structure, with dense mulga brush shoved between the wire. There were a few loosely packed spots to allow airflow though and around the top, water would trickle down through the brush cooling the area inside by a few degrees.

On this occasion, Dansan and I had an argument over something petty, and I went to bed in the cool shed, expecting that he would join me later. What I liked about this cool shed was that it could be locked from the inside, and it gave us security from whatever was spooking us.

I had left the door open that night so that Dansan could make his way to bed and lock the door behind him. I slept restlessly, waiting for him to come to bed, so I felt safe once the door was locked. The noise of Dansan's bed creaking alongside mine woke me up and I opened my eyes. A figure hovered about two inches from my face and I felt the warm air being exhaled by whoever it was and I thought it was Dansan mucking around.

'Is that you, Dansan?' I asked, but there was no reply.

I reached for the torch on the table next to me. As I stumbled about, I kept my focus on the figure which now started to rise. The bed creaked much more loudly now because whatever the thing was started to get off the bed. Once it was fully standing on the opposite side of the bed from me, I could see that it was not Dansan because the silhouette was about six-foot tall. It made for the doorway, and by the time I had found the torch and shone it at the figure, it was gone.

One thing for certain, it was not Vonn. She was only about five-foot tall, and Father was over at Moolapool, so it couldn't have been him either.

I turned the torch to Dansan's bed, and it was empty, so I jumped out of bed and raced to the doorway, I shone my torch around in the direction that the mysterious figure went. Whatever it was, was no longer there. Realising that, I quickly shut the door and locked it, knowing there were a few hours left before dawn, I jumped back into my bed and tucked my head tightly under the covers, eventually falling back to sleep as I trembled in fright.

Whenever Dansan and I had to stay at Lime and Bell, we would set up camp back in the cool shed after dinner. I would grab the rifle out of the Rodeo, and as dusk approached, I would let off a few shots around the cool shed to ward off any presence. This action only really put our minds at ease. Sometimes, during the night, we'd hear noises nearby and I would shove the tip of the rifle barrel through the chicken wire and brush and let a couple of rounds off.

Father and Loui return from a windmill run after checking over the entire station. Normally, this is done once a week but as it is now into the hotter months, it must be done every few days.

'Bidjid, Luke, come over here, so I can fill you in on the windmill run,' Father calls out from the front veranda.

We head over to the house and sit down, while Vonn makes us all a cup of tea.

'Loui and I came across two major issues. One is Emerald on Lime and Bell. It has only enough water for another day or two and needs to be fixed. And the fence line between Frog and Six-mile, along the boundary, has a rotten straining post. I didn't have any strainers on me, so I just propped it up with a couple of branches. So, on the next windmill run, make sure you take some strainers with you,' Father says, looking at us both.

Bidjid and I nod.

Two days later, we set off to fix up the well and the rotten strainer. When we get close to Emerald, we see hundreds of sheep standing with their bellies tucked up, waiting for water from the trough. Other animals are also hanging around. We pull up and the smell of death in the hot still air hits us. We go over to the tank and notice a few of the logs that covered the well have been pushed off, creating a gap. The smell is rotten. I get the rear-vision mirror from the Rodeo and use the sun's reflection off it to see what has fallen in. There's a mass of rotting kangaroo corpses floating at the bottom of the seventy-foot well.

'Fuck, look at them.' I turn my head away from the disgusting smell.

'Ewww,' Bidjid replies, quickly stepping back.

I replace the logs so nothing else can fall in. 'What do you want to do?' I ask, but in not any enthusiastic way.

'Umm, I don't know.' She still has a look of horror on her face.

'What if we check the rest of the windmills first and try to fix it on our way back?' I suggest, making my way back to the Rodeo.

Bidjid agrees, so we immediately take off, hoping for some fresh air to sweep the rotten smell out of the Rodeo.

We continue along on the rest of the windmill run, fixing things that we encountered on the way. By the time we get back to the Emerald, it is already early evening and hard to see. We set the winch up and pull up around thirty feet of pipes until a sticky grey sludge starts to appear. At this point, we decide it would be best to finish the rest in the morning when we can see.

We set up our swags, light a fire, have some dinner, and then jump into our swags, ducking our heads well under to get away from the smell. I am so tired that as soon as my head hits the ground, I'm asleep.

Around two a.m., Bidjid wakes me up. 'Luke, Luke,' Bidjid pokes me in the ribs. Can you hear that? It sounds like the Nissan… Father's coming.'

We both sit up and watch as the headlights become more visible through the mulga trees.

'Fuck – let's just tell him we had to fix up Salt Bush and a broken straining post near Joe and Harry's due to a camel knocking it down, and by the time we got back here it was too dark to do anything more on the windmill and we were going to get to it first thing in the morning.'

We jump out of our blankets and brace ourselves.

Within a couple of minutes, Father is flinging open the door and jumping out of the Nissan like he has just been stung by a bee and is now ready to take on a heavyweight boxer.

'Ahh, for fuck's sake, what the fuck have you lazy cunts been doing all day?' he yells.

The Nissan has barely come to a stop.

'What the fuck's going on out here? Why are all these sheep still hanging around dying of fucken thirst…and why the fuck haven't you stupid cunts fixed the fucken windmill yet?'

Still yelling and cursing, Father races over to us like a raging bull. 'I ought to throw you both down the well with a couple of buckets to bring up some water for these poor sheep here.'

'We had to fix up the outlet pipe at Salt Bush,' I say, 'and there was a broken straining post near Joe and Harry's.'

Bidjid picks up our agreed-upon explanation. Father looks back and forth between her and me. Our practised lines are almost too perfect.

Besides, we have already set up the winch and pulled some of the pipes out from the well. Father is fuming. His blue eyes sparkle blood red in the light of the campfire. Enraged, he strides off into the darkness in search of a branch. When he returns a few seconds later, he makes a seat out of it and hooks it up to the winch. Then he lowers me slowly into the well, shining a spotlight down on me.

I'm thinking that I'll surely die if the branch breaks. As it is, I can barely breathe with all the stinking toxic gases down there. But I would rather face death than argue with Father any day. He'd beat me into the dirt in the blink of an eye. I cling onto the pipe and hold on tightly for dear life. The pipe becomes even more covered in fatty grey sludge the further I am lowered. It is like the smelly grease that gets caught in household drains.

When I reach the bottom of the pipe, I dangle beneath the pump, trying to pull out the kangaroo fur which has been pumped up into the clack. But there's a sifter on the base and I can't do much. Father pulls me back up to the surface and we spend the next couple of hours stumbling around, pulling up the pipes, cleaning the fur from the pump and lowering the pipes all back into the well.

'Right, Luke, climb up to the top of the windmill and turn the fan to pump up some water for these thirsty animals,' Father orders.

Without question, I climb the seventy-foot tower and start spinning the fan.

In a few minutes, the trough is filling with water. The sheep come straight up, pushing and shoving each other about to get a drink. Some are being trampled and a couple even fall into the trough.

'Okay, that'll do. Come down now,' Father says.

I could have stayed up there the rest of the night to keep away from him, but I was relieved when he told me to come down. My arms were like jelly by this time.

'We'll just stay here for a bit to make sure no more animals get trodden on or upturned, then we'll get going back home,' Father says.

Early the following morning, Father is at my door and snarling like a barbarian. I suddenly realise why when my ears prick up to the distinct sound in the distance of dogs barking.

'Jump up, Luke! There's a couple of dogs are out there ripping the fuck out of the sheep. I think I can hear Tuffy, but I'm not quite sure if the other one is Boots. You better get out there quick smart! Bring them back here and tie them up to the front fence,' Father orders as he kicks me up the ass for taking too long to put my boots on.

'Okay, Father,' I reply.

I race off to grab some rope with Father right on me like a leech before running off in the direction of the dogs barking out in the paddock. Before long, I see that it is Boots and Tuffy as Father had guessed. They instantly let go of the sheep that they had ganged up on together and it hobbles away in pain dragging one of its half torn-off limbs behind itself like a ragdoll when they sight me appear from the shrubs.

Boots and Tuffy wearily skulked over to me where I to tie the rope around their necks and lead them both back to the house. I'm glad that when I get back to the front yard Father isn't hovering around with the .22 like he normally would be in these cases. Instead, I find him back in the house drinking a cup of tea with a cigarette in his mouth.

'I have them tied up he front now, Father,' I regretfully inform him, knowing too right what is about to happen next.

'Which dogs are they?' father asks.

'It's Boots and Tuffy, Father.'

'Right, as you brought Boots back with you from boarding school, I think it's only fair that you put it down, and while you're at it, you can put Tuffy down as well,' Father instructs.

Dansan and Vonn both go out to see their dogs for the last time. Tears stream down their cheeks and Dansan even pleads with Father to not shoot his dog Tuffy.

'Please, Father, I'll care of my dog more. Please don't shoot him!'

'This is what happens when you don't look after your dog! If you neglect them, love, then they become desperate and turn to entertaining themselves by killing animals,' Father grunts.

After having a quick bite for breakfast, I go and grab the .22 and the two dogs and walk out into the bush. Tears are flowing as I look down at the two dogs tied to the end of the rope. 'Why did you have to go out attacking sheep for?' I ask them. 'Now I have to put you down, this is so hard for me,' I continue.

In the past, I have hunted small game, things such as lizards and birds to eat, and for a few years now I have had to knock orphan lambs or baby joey kangaroos on the head too (so they wouldn't have to suffer starving to death). All that does not compare to having to deal with a family pet. This by far has to have been the hardest thing I have ever had to do in my life.

A couple of small dead mulga trees several metres apart from each other, made a perfect place to tie the two dogs up at one tree and using the other tree as a support to keep the rifle steady.

Looking down the scope of the .22, I pause for a moment watching Boots walking back and forth before she stops and looks over to where I am several metres away and tears pool in my eyes. All of a sudden, I feel like I am in a steamy hot sauna and the walls are closing in on me.

'Sorry, Boots,' I said as I checked one last time that her head was still in the cross of the scope. My finger tightened on the trigger as I shut my eyes and the rifle fired. Suddenly, there was yipping and when I opened my eyes, Boots was running around in pain. She had turned her head just after I closed my eyes and the bullet went through her snout. This is where I had no choice but to calm her back down enough for me to place the barrel on her head and pull the trigger. Tuffy was by now freaking out and trying to break free from the rope he was tied to and when he stopped moving for that split second, I managed to place the barrel on his head and took his life away.

When I returned to the homestead, Father came over to me.

'It takes a whole lot of courage to do what you had to do, Luke. I was around your age when my dad ordered the same deal for me, it was so hard, but I knew that once you have a killer dog, you will always have one. What was that third shot you fired?' Father continued with a concerned face, his hand lowering gently on my shoulder to comfort me from my recent ordeal.

'Oh, I missed the first shot and it went through Boots's nose, then she was yipping in so much pain and I couldn't bare it any more so I went over to her and finished her off,' I reply with a sniffle.

Vonn and Dansan both watch me from the house, partially concealing themselves behind the hibiscus shrubs growing around the veranda. I can't bear to look them in the eye right now and feel more sorry for them than my own feelings of having to had to do that ruthless act.

When the rush to save the station eases as the cooler months of autumn arrive, Father signs Bidjid and me up with the Commonwealth Employment Service, called the CES back then, because he can't afford to pay us both wages due to the crash in the wool market. We love this idea because it involves getting away from the station to attend TAFE in Geraldton for two to three weeks every six months.

The apprenticeship covers fifty per cent of our wages, which means Father basically only has to a pay a minimum wage for one person while two of us work for him. Smart thinking on his behalf, given that Bidjid and I have become the two main station workers since Bryce left, and Edvard and Ty temporarily moved up to Marble Bar. Other kids from over the state are also travelling to Geraldton to do the course, so we get to meet some nice people and make some new friends.

Towards the end of 1991, Bidjid and I are up late one night at the Batavia backpackers' hostel where we are staying while attending TAFE. We are waiting for our turn at the pool table in the common room where there is also a microwave and TV. A couple of guys in their mid-twenties are playing, and Bidjid and I wait patiently for them to finish their game. Eventually, close to midnight, they hand the table over to us. We set up the balls, while the guys sit down on the lounges and start smoking a pipe.

'Do you want a pipe?' asks one of the guys.

'What is it?' I ask, as the smell of smoke fills the air.

'Weed, man. Don't tell me you haven't had weed before?' He looks back and forth between his mate and Bidjid and me.

'No, we haven't,' Bidjid says.

The guy with the pipe walks over to us. 'Here, have a try and see if you like it. It won't kill you."

I am nearly sixteen now, and Bidjid is nearly seventeen. Everything is exciting and new, and we are both eager for a change. The guy passes the pipe to Bidjid and she studies it closely, raises it up to her nose and sniffs it a couple of times before passing it to me.

'What will happen?' I ask, unsure of whether I should smoke it or not.

'Nothing. It'll just make you feel relaxed and mellowed out,' he says.

I put the pipe in my mouth, light it up and inhale deeply. Suddenly I'm choked up and coughing out a lung full of smoke. My head starts to feel cloudy. I cough for about a minute non-stop, while tears pool in my eyes and roll down my cheeks.

Bidjid pats me on the back, trying to help me. 'Gee you should see your eyes,' she says, laughing. 'They're really red.'

'Man, that is really harsh,' I splutter, when I finally stop coughing.

'It's good, isn't it?' says the guy as he packs a pipe for Bidjid.

She puffs away cautiously but halfway through the pipe; she's coughing her lungs up too. By this time, I feel like my legs are no longer holding me up. I just want to lie down.

I make my way halfway up the stairs and sit clinging to a step. Bidjid and one of the guys help me up and into the dormitory, where I collapse on my bed. I feel like I'm spinning around on a record turntable, but I just lie there, gripping my covers, trying not to move, in case I fall out, until I finally pass out.

At TAFE, Bidjid finds herself a nice fella and they start going out, so at the end of our on-campus work, I go back to the station, while Bidjid stays on in Geraldton with her boyfriend. Now it is just me back on the station working with Father, with a bit of help from the little boys.

Dansan becomes my offsider until Bidjid returns a few weeks later. But while she is away, Father, Loui and I go out to Sampson's, one of the windmills on Lime and Bell, to build a trap yard around it. This windmill pumps water into a small dam, which provides the sheep with their drinking water. It is more than seventy kilometres from Moolapool homestead, and about twenty-five kilometres away from the house at Lime and Bell, so we take our rugs to camp out until we finish the job.

We work on the trap yard all day, digging posts into the tough red dirt, but still have a way to go before we will be finished. It is getting late in the afternoon, and Father does not want the sheep coming in to drink overnight because shearing is just around the corner and given the dense bush, the sheep in this paddock can be quite difficult to muster up.

We light fires in three locations around the dam to deter the sheep from coming in. Loui is only seven years old and he sits up listening to Father and me talking into the night. The radio in the vehicle plays in the background. It is getting late and Loui starts yawning. Father tells him to climb into the vehicle, stretch out across the bench seat and have a sleep.

Father and I keep talking and listening to the radio, assuming Loui is asleep by now. Next thing, a dingo howls not far away from us. Loui springs up and turns the radio off, and Father and I stop talking. We all focus our eyes on the direction of the howling. The sheep suddenly take off and are running into the darkness.

We listen intently for any signs of the sheep being attacked, but the night falls silent. Father reaches into the vehicle for his rifle. He loads a round into the chamber and fires it in the direction of the dingo, above the tree line through the night sky. We can hear the bullet travelling for a few seconds, making a sound like a whizzing jet. Then all is quiet again.

'Rightio, Luke, you may as well set up your bed over at that fire,' Father tells me. 'Loui can camp in the vehicle near this fire, and I'll go to that fire over there.'

Father and I set off in different directions towards our allocated campsites. Father takes the rifle with him and tucks it next to his blanket before he falls asleep.

I settle down in my blankets and look over at Father once again, wishing that he had given me the rifle. I close my eyes but wake a few hours later to the sound of branches breaking. I sit up. My fire is almost out but Father's is raging. He is dragging branches across the ground and stoking up the flames.

I get out of my blanket and go in search of some branches for my own fire. It is around three a.m. and the temperature has fallen rapidly. I get my fire cranking when I sense I'm being watched by a dingo. Quickly, I jump back into my blanket and tuck my head in. The daylight can't come soon enough.

By the time I wake up, Father is walking around to check if there are any injured sheep. We finish making the trap yard and set it, before heading back to the homestead.

Once there, Father can't wait to tell the story about the dingo. 'You should have seen Luke,' he chuckles. 'He was shaking like a leaf. He jumped into his bed quick smart and tucked his head under the blanket, too afraid to look out.'

"You should have seen Father, though,' I say. 'He was the most scared out of all of us. He slept with the rifle all night, with his finger on the trigger, didn't he, Loui?'

'Yes,' Loui laughs.

'No, Loui,' Father retorts, 'you should have seen your face when you sprang up in the vehicle. I was as white as a ghost.'

A couple of days later, we go to check the trap yard. All the sheep are now trapped in the yard, so we chase them over to another windmill where there are more sheep in another trap yard.

Not long after, Bidjid rings up from Geraldton to say she will be on her way back next week. It will be good to have her on the station again. It's always easier when so much of the responsibility isn't just on my shoulders.

12

Flat Battery

Early summer of 1991 just before Vonn, Dansan and Loui all head away to Numbulwar for a break. Dansan and I go over to Lime and Bell to fix a windmill that has stopped pumping water. The leather buckets in the pumps often wear out, so replacing them is common when it comes to windmill maintenance.

Dansan ha's just turned seven, nearly ten years younger than me, but he's a great little assistant. He passes me wrenches or knocks the clamp 'dog' off when I need to lower the winch to grab at the pipe in a lower position. He and I are always teaming up and doing jobs together, and on this job, we take a twelve-volt car fridge with us to cool our drinking water down.

I should know better than to leave the fridge plugged in as we pull the pipes out with the electric winch. It is draining power from the battery, but I figure it will be all right. By the time we have just about winched the final pipe from the bore, the winch starts to slow right down.

Oh shit!

'What's wrong?' Dansan asks as I run back to the Rodeo.

'I think we've just flattened the battery,' I tell him.

Even though I have been driving station vehicles around for close to five or six years now, this is the first time I have run a battery flat. I race around to the driver's side of the Rodeo and give the ignition key a turn to try to start the engine. But the starter motor just makes a faint clicking noise. I notice the fridge is still plugged in and I quickly unplug it.

'Fuck,' I yell, annoyed with myself.

I look up at Dansan, who is still halfway up the windmill tower. He has a worried look on his face, as if to say, 'What can we do now?' but he says nothing.

I open the bonnet and look at the battery. 'We'll have to take the battery out,' I tell Dansan. 'It's our only choice. We'll have to take it back to the homestead and charge it up on the solar panel there.'

'It's like a two-mile walk back, isn't it?' Dansan asks. 'Isn't that why the windmill is called Two Mile?'

'Yeah, two miles one way, but what other option have we got? Father will be really wild if he has to come all the way over here to Lime and Bell just because I left the fridge plugged in.'

I remove the battery from the engine bay and place it on the ground. The battery isn't light. It weighs close to fifteen kilograms, but there are two rope handles on the top which make it a little easier to carry. The handles have been designed for easier battery installation but hauling the battery over this distance feels like the rope is going to cut my fingers off.

'You better come and get yourself a big drink before we set off, mate,' I say, trying to sound like I know what I am doing.

It takes just over an hour to get to Lime and Bell homestead, and my arms are killing me by the time I put the battery down and connect the solar panel up to it. It is not like a normal battery charger, and it'll take hours of waiting around before the battery's charged.

I call Vonn at Moolapool and pass on a message for Father over the telephone. I tell Vonn not to worry as we are about to head back out to the windmill and should be okay. But, as I find out later, when Vonn relays my message, Father is not at all impressed with me.

Pottering around the homestead, we find an old pram and a bike with flat tyres. I tie the pram to the bike and put the battery in. Dansan walks along behind the pram but soon starts lagging far behind, so I tell him to get into the pram with the battery. He looks much happier to be getting a free ride, but it is hard going for me, cycling through the sand on flat tyres with him in tow. What's more, one of the pram wheels keeps falling off under the strain of the extra thirty kilograms of Dansan's weight. Every now and then when this happensm it quickly brings me to a halt.

By this time, I am as thirsty as a camel and think only of the water container sitting on the back of the Rodeo.

Before long, I abandon the bike and Dansan and I push the pram along, taking turns. I push for a few hundred metres then Dansan takes over and pushes for as long as he can handle. When we finally get back to the Rodeo, we're so happy. After quenching our thirst, I quickly throw the battery back in and try to start the engine. But the battery barely cranks the engine one revolution before it starts clicking again.

'Ah, for fuck's sake,' I curse. 'I thought we gave it plenty of time on the charge. Now we've got to take it back to Lime and Bell again.' I pull the battery back out and put it back in the pram.

By the time we get back to Lime and Bell, there is only about an hour's worth of sunlight left. We do not want to sleep at the homestead because it is too spooky, so we take off again as soon as there is no more sun. We walk in the darkness until we are well clear of the homestead.

'If Lime and Bell wasn't built from an old church and didn't have that eerie feeling to it, I wouldn't mind staying there, would you?' I ask Dansan.

'No, I wouldn't mind either.'

'Let's have a rest in this creek for a little bit,' I say to him.

It is nice when we first lie down and soon, we fall asleep. I wake around four a.m. and it is really cold. I lie there shivering, wondering if Dansan is cold too. When dawn breaks, we jump up straightaway. I tell Dansan I had thought of waking him up during the night to ask if he wanted to go back to the homestead.

'I was going to ask you the same thing, but I thought, stuff going back there, and just folded my arms and rolled up into a ball on my side and went back to sleep.'

We both laugh.

'I hope the battery starts the Rodeo this time, hey,' I say.

'Me too,' Dansan replies. 'I'm getting tired of walking back and forth pushing this pram with this battery in it.'

We both laugh again.

Around seven a.m., we get back to the Rodeo. Once again, the battery is not charged up enough, so back we go to Lime and Bell. I call home again and this time Father answers the phone.

'We're back here at Lime and Bell because the battery was too flat to start the Rodeo after we charged it yesterday,' I explain. 'This time we're going to leave it on the charge for a few hours, but if we don't have any luck you may need to come and help."

'Oh, good one, Luke,' Father says. 'Thanks for keeping me in the loop, I was just wondering about how you two were getting on. I'll wait to hear back from you then.'

We leave the battery on the charge for a few hours and by the time we get back out to the Rodeo, it is after midday. I put the battery back into the Rodeo and this time we are good. It is such a relief to finally hear the engine start up again.

We leave the engine running while we quench our thirst with a big bottle of milk we made up, and quickly finish fixing the windmill before we set off back home.

'I hope Mum doesn't make us any milk when we get home, hey?' I say as I feel the milk churning inside me. 'I don't think I can drink any more today. Because we haven't eaten anything since yesterday morning before we left home, there'is nothing for the milk to mix with and it feels like claws are scrapping at my ribcage,' I add.

'Yeah, mine too,' says Dansan, rubbing his churning tummy.

When we get home, Father is there to greet us, and we follow him inside.

'I bet you won't ever leave the fridge plugged into the vehicle again while you're fixing a windmill,' Father mocks once he has heard the whole story.

'No, I think we've learned our lesson.'

Vonn comes over to the table with two cups and places them in front of us.

'Arrr, ha ha, it's milk,' I say, looking up at Dansan, and we both shake our heads and start laughing.

'What's wrong?' Father asks curiously.

And once more we fill him in.

13

Bidjid

As soon as Bidjid returns from Geraldton, we set off on a windmill run on Lime and Bell. Before long, we come across a young camel, roughly three months old, tangled up in the fence by Nundhirribala, a solar pump that father had put in. There were a couple of extra watering holes Father had set up – King Oscar and Stonefield – and Father had also put an extra windmill in, between Glengarry and Six Mile which he named Frog.

'Oh look, Bidjid, it's just been left here to die,' I say as we pull up alongside it in the Rodeo. 'Can you see its mum anywhere?'

We sit in silence, listening out as we scour the bush each side of the fence for its mother, but we cannot see her. We look through the back window of the Rodeo.

'Nah, she's not round here,' I say.

'We can't leave it here. It'll get its eyes eaten out by crows,' Bidjid says sorrowfully.

We get out and go up to the calf, which wouldn't be much more than a metre high, if it were standing. It struggles in the fence for a few seconds but cannot free itself. It is stressed and starts calling out at the top of its lungs for its mum. Bidjid and I look back around through the bush once more but there is still no sign of the mother camel.

'Let's take it home with us,' I say. 'I'll reverse the Rodeo up to the fence and we can shove it on the back.'

As I jump back in the Rodeo and reposition it closer to the little camel, Bidjid starts untangling its legs from the fence. No sooner than we have it up on the back of the Rodeo, its mother comes charging through the bush towards us. I quickly jump in the driver's seat while Bidjid hops onto the back and holds onto the calf.

'Quickly, Luke, it's getting closer.'

I look over my shoulder. Bidjid is lying over the baby camel to pin it down and about twenty metres behind us, the mother camel is crashing through the bush, coming straight towards us.

'Fucken hell, hold on tight, Bidjid,' I yell out the window as I plant the accelerator to the floor.

We speed off, leaving clouds of red dust swirling in the air behind us. I swerve in and out of the mulga while the mother camel just keeps crashing straight through branches and over small trees. After countless kilometres, we finally leave it behind in a clearing.

'That was bloody close. I thought it was never going to give up,' I gasp as we pull up at the next windmill.

'Yeah, at one point, it was less than a couple of metres away from us,' Bidjid replies.

The camel is panting on the back of the Rodeo. It stretches its neck up high and tries to get up but Bidjid quickly pins it back down again.

'Here, Luke, just hold onto it for a minute.'

She jumps off the back of the Rodeo and goes over to the trough to fill up the billy to give the camel a drink, but it just spits it out all over her arm.

'Well, don't have a drink then,' she snaps, wiping her arm on the back of the camel's neck and tipping out the water.

'We still better take it home,' I say. 'It'll likely just die out here. We only have to clean out one more trough on the way back anyway.'

'Grab the rope over there so we can tie it up,' Bidjid orders, while the camel once again struggles to break free from her hold.

I race around and tie the camel's legs together. 'There, that should hold it.'

Bidjid twirls her wrist around. 'Bloody thing nearly ripped my hand clean off,' she says. 'For a little camel, it's quite strong."

When we pull up back at the homestead, Dansan and Loui come

running out to meet us, as they often do. We are all excited. Me especially. At sixteen, it's the first encounter I've ever had with a camel. Loui races inside and Father and Vonn both come out to have a look.

'Go and grab a rope, Luke – tie it loosely around its neck, make sure you give it plenty of room, so it won't choke itself,' Father says enthusiastically. 'What do you think we should call it? Is it a boy or girl, do you know?' Father asks, but everyone is still too fascinated to respond.

'It's a boy,' Bidjid finally says, and we all gaze at the camel in silence.

Suddenly I pipe up. 'What about Kamal? Kamal the camel, ha ha.'

Everyone nods and agrees Kamal is a good name.

'Okay then, let's get Kamal off the Rodeo and get him used to the lead,' Father says.

We all crowd around to help.

When Kamal first lives with us, he really knows how to spook the living daylights out of us all.

He is good at playing chicken and if you turn away from him, he breathes right down the back of your neck like he's about to take a huge bite out of it. If you pick up your pace, so does Kamal; even if you run for your life, you know he has you beat. Kamal races as fast as you can sprint, his two front legs moving in a sweeping motion behind you, as if he's trying to trip you over. Kamal is one scary camel and, much as we all love him, none of us can bear the thought of being trampled by him.

Several years later, even Father admits that Kamal made the hairs on the back of his neck stand on end.

Kamal never strayed too far from the house until one day Bidjid's old mare Jessy came into the house paddock to visit us. Jessy often went out bush for a few months and then, out of the blue, she would reappear.

Jessy is not too sure about Kamal, but Kamal is unfazed and follows Jessy around everywhere. Eventually, they become inseparable. Over the next few months, Kamal grows very quickly and is soon the same size as Jessy.

One day, when we return from one of our outings, Kamal is lying out in the paddock. He doesn't get up, so I go over to investigate. His back leg looks broken. I figure that he must have been trying to mate with Jessy and she hasn't wanted a bar of him.

When I tell Father what has happened, he tells me to grab two pieces of poly pipe and some masking tape and put a splint on Kamal's broken leg. Kamal does not put up a fight. He just lies there as I bandage his limb.

After a while, I manage to get him up onto his legs again. He follows me into the chook pen, where he lies down and does not get back up for the next two months.

Eventually, Kamal ventures off by himself and we do not see much of him after that. Every now and then he drops in, but he is always only passing through and is soon on his way again.

'Tomorrow we will be heading out to Granite to take the sheep there in the trap yard to the Judareena laneway. Make sure your motorbikes are fuelled up and ready to leave at five a.m. I'll take the little boys with me,' Father informs Bidjid and me.

'Okay, Father,' we both reply.

'I'm going to fill up now, Luke. You going to get your bike ready too?' Bidjid asks.

'Yes, I'm going to just finish things here first,' I reply. I look over my shoulder at her and scan the kitchen for any dishes before pulling the plug out.

I follow Bidjid and we fuel up the motorbikes and check the oil levels.

'Bidjid, I'll be using the Nissan tomorrow. Will you be kind enough to fill it up for me?' Father asks.

'Yes, Father.'

The following morning, we set off just after five a.m. and about half an hour later, we are heading along the northern boundary fence pass the Cement Tank turn off and heading towards Dead Horse.

Father is just in front of us and he pulls up not far from the Dead Horse turn-off. 'This is were we go our own ways. What I want you two to do is sweep through the paddock once more and make sure to switch off your bikes and listen out for any strays. Me and the boys will be working on Crater because the last time I went by, it was barely pumping up any water. More than likely the leather buckets have worn out in the pump,' Father instructs.

'Where will we meet up with you next? I ask.

'We'll meet you at Granite around midday. I want you, Bidjid, to work your way south zigzagging from east to west and you, Luke, you can work the eastern side of the paddock. Push all sheep in the south westerly direction.'

We soon part ways and I pray that I don't find any sheep until I get closer to Granite. I switch off my motorbike and listen for a moment as the sounds grow quieter with the Nissan and Bidjid's motorbike quietly fading away.

To my left, I hear a couple of sheep baaa and it sounds like there could be quite a few here. I start my motorbike and ride into Dead Horse and roughly thirty sheep scatter into the bush heading northeast. I remain on their trail for a moment and continue driving them further away before turning my motorbike round and made tracks hastily to get well away from them. I head out into the centre of the paddock and switch off my motorbike again and listen. To my southwest I hear Bidjid's motorbike engine and she sounds like she's already over halfway through the paddock. I stay off the main track because I know Father will be counting up how many times I was pointlessly riding up and down, and eventually I find a shady tree to have a quick snooze under.

A couple of hours later, I jump up and know it is nearing midday by the position of the sun in the sky. The sound of Bidjid's motorbike engine starts up and she must have been no more than a kilometre away from where I am. Quickly I start my motorbike and race over to her and I find her sitting behind a small flock of about seventy sheep.

'You got any sheep?' Bidjid asks.

'Na, nothing. I did see about thirty on the other side of Dead Horse but they were just sulking so I left them,' I reply.

'Oh yeah, I was lucky to find these ones here, so I haven't had to do much with them at all. Let's just stay together now and put these sheep with the others at Granite,' Bidjid insists.

'Yeah,' I respond.

Father and the little boys arrive not long after we put the sheep into the trap yard with the others that had been caught already. Father looks disappointed in us but he maintains his cool.

'Right, as soon as we get these sheep into the Judareena laneway, we'll head home. I'll go up to the laneway gate now and put the billy on. We'll have lunch ready for when you get here. Dansan, go and open that gate over there so the sheep can be chased out of the trap yard,' Father instructs.

Soon we are driving about five hundred sheep along the fence line and Bidjid is on the wing keeping the sheep together while I am just bringing up the tail end. We work like a pack of dogs trying to keep the mob together but the dense bush gets the better of us and the sheep split into the scrublands.

'We've lost them,' Bidjid gloomily says.

'Fuck! What's Father going to do?' I ask.

'I don't care what he has to say.' Bidgid replies as she switches off her motorbike and kicks the stand down. She puts her feet on the foot pegs and crossed her arms over the handlebars and lowers her head onto them.

I switch off my motorbike and do the same. We are probably only several hundred metres away from the laneway gate and all we can hear is silence. The sheep have now split and disappeared back into the bush, I close my eyes and wish that when I open them, I will find that the life I thought I had was only just a dream. Thoughts of Geraldton swirl around in my mind and out of the blue a enraged voice breaks the silence.

'What the fuck are you pair of cunts doing? Where are the rest of the sheep?' Father demands an answer as he marches to Bidjid and kicks the side of her motorbike and they both crash to the ground.

Father continues marching until he punches me in the left shoulder. 'You're a pair of useless fucks. Bidjid, you head over that direction while Luke and I will see if we can collect the rest of the flock. Fortunately, ninety per cent of the mob has gone into the laneway already,' Father continued.

Bidjid sets off on foot while Father and I scout around for any of the sheep that got away.

Soon Father gives in and I follow him back to the laneway gate, where we park up the motorbikes.

'Grab yourself a quick bite and a cup of tea,a Luke. Bidjid, grab the jerry can out of the Nissan and fill up the motorbikes. We'll leave them here for the night and come back tomorrow morning,' Father orders.

14

Roper Bar

The heat of January 1992 was a little milder than previous years.

Everyone else is away and I am helping my dad run things on the station. I am still only sixteen years old. My older brother Bryce, who is now living at Numbulwar in the Northern Territory, purchases a small four-wheel drive Suzuki Sierra from Father. As Bryce is now working full-time at the Numbulwar power station over three thousand kilometres away, it is a two-man operation, and he has no way of getting time off work to pick up the Suzuki himself.

Father suggests to Bryce that because Bryce and I look alike and are close in age, I could say I am him and take a short holiday from the station work and deliver the Suzuki to him. I have driven quite a lot on the station but am excited at the prospect of travelling up the highway on my own. The next day I pack a few essentials into the Suzuki and set off on what should be a straightforward journey, expecting to return to Moolapool from Numbulwar on the bus in a couple of weeks.

It takes me a few days to drive from the station to Roper River in the Northern Territory. For a few nights before reaching the river, it rains heavily and by the time I arrive, the crossing is already flowing over the bar at about two to five kilometres an hour. The depth gauge shows the river level to be only 0.4 metres deep and there is a fine layer of slime on top of the concrete already, making the crossing slippery.

Since setting off from the station, this crossing has been my main concern. The crossing is a single lane concrete bridge roughly two metres wide, which is raised out of the river by about 0.5m. This is known as the Roper Bar, which divides the saltwater from the fresh.

When I get to Roper River, the water is flowing over the concrete bar. I see a couple of larger four-wheel drives waiting on my side to cross the river, so I walk over and ask one of the drivers if they think it's safe for me to cross.

'Oh no, I wouldn't if I were you, buddy,' says a man in his late forties, who kind of reminds me of the Bush Tucker Man. Dressed in the same khaki clothing, he has the Akubra to match, which is shaped the same way, and an old long-wheelbase Land Rover, exactly the same as the one the Bush Tucker Man had on the TV show.

'You wouldn't even make it halfway across in that little thing, I can assure you of that. I've seen people who've risked the crossing in these slippery conditions, and they've been washed right off the bar. We're not even game enough to attempt it,' he continues.

'Are you waiting to cross?' I ask, looking him up and down.

'Yeah, I'm heading that way into the communities. I got a load of second-hand clothes I'm taking in,' he says.

I turn back to the Suzuki and decide to take his advice on board. I will just wait it out like they are doing and see what the water level is like in the morning.

Half an hour passes and I am now sitting in the Suzuki thinking about my next move.

Suddenly the Bush Tucker Man lookalike jumps back into his Land Rover. 'I'm going to give it a go, fellas,' he yells from his window as he drives out into the water.

'He won't get far. My guess, all wheels in,' I hear another person say.

'Yeah, but if he does get through, I'll certainly following suit.

His four wheels soon enter the water and by the time it is up to his axles, the whole front of his vehicle starts to slide from the pressure of the river current on the slippery slimy concrete crossing and he quickly shoves it in reverse and manages to get back out onto dry land again. His face is as white as a ghost and he does not bother to stop to say goodbye. He must have felt like a useless fool and just took off like a yipping dog with its tail between its legs.

The wet season in the Northern Territory started a week earlier than usual. Water runs east from the Kakadu National Park into rivers like the Roper River, making river crossings impassable. Kakadu National Park and some other remote areas have already been closed to the public, I learn. This Roper River crossing, from one side of the bank to the other, is roughly a hundred and fifty metres, and the waters are crocodile-infested.

I sleep in the Suzuki and in the morning, I check the depth gauge in the river. The water has risen overnight to 0.6 metres and crossing looks even more dangerous. The other guys with their bigger four-wheel drives have taken off and I'm the only one there. I drive to the Roper Bar store, just a minute back down the road, and ask the owner if there is any other way of getting across.

'There's an ex-army 6 x 6 truck that carts vehicles across for a couple of hundred dollars. Do you want me to line it up for you?' the store owner asks.

I tell him I will think about it and see if the water levels subside over the course of the day.

Back at the river crossing, I'm looking at the depth gauge again when an old Holden Kingswood pulls up with two traditional blackfellas from the area in it. They are walking over towards the river when suddenly they stop and one of them points to the ground.

'Ehh, look out, Garpuli,' one fella says to the other.

'Uy em, Big Charlie Edbouy,' Garpuli replies.

They both have worried-looking faces as they gaze towards some reeds growing alongside the riverbank and further out into the river. I go over too curious to investigate.

'Hi, what is it?' I ask, keen to know what they have seen.

'Thar looq, ue see thum truks jar? Iz Ole Charlie, em a bery big ole croq tharn, han em bin goh that'a wai, uy u savy tharn,' Edbouy tells me, while making slithering motions with his hand.

I look at the tracks, feeling very nervous. I can feel the hairs on my neck standing on end, so I quickly go back and sit in the Suzuki.

The two fellas meanwhile open their car boot. They take out a hand reel, a piece of wire, some pliers and a bread bag. Garpuli sits down and bends the piece of wire up with the pliers, making a fishhook, while Edbouy scours over the ground not far away from me, picking up small pebbles and checking their weight before throwing some of them away and picking up others. When he finds ones the right weight, he puts them into the bread bag and ties a knot. Then he rips off the remaining part of the bag, leaving a few long strands like tassels exposed.

Garpuli finishes making his improvised fishing hook fixed to the fishing line and gets up to his feet. He takes the bread bag with the small pebbles in it from Edbouy and ties it onto the fishing line. All this while they are talking in their traditional language while looking out at the river, trying to decide where to launch the line. Garpuli then passes the fishing line to Edbouy, who must be the better fisherman, and he goes down closer to the river and hurls it out, about thirty metres into the river. Then Edbouy slowly pulls the line back in and it falls alongside him in a heap on the ground.

While he's doing this, Garpuli gathers some wood from the bush nearby. Suddenly, Edbouy yells out to his Garpuli, who races down to his side. Edbouy continues pulling in the line, keeping it taut, until a lovely-sized barramundi appears at the end of the line. It flaps about, trying to break free, but cannot.

Edbouy picks it up and takes it over to the vehicle and quickly sticks a fillet knife into its head, putting it out of its misery. Then he starts to prepare it. Garpuli makes a fire with the wood he has gathered, and they cook up the fish.

Good as it looks, I do not even think about asking them for any of it; I am still living off the food that's in the Suzuki.

Once they have finished their meal, the fellas get back in their car and leave. I have often thought since, how simple it looked for those two to catch such a lovely-sized fish that day. They had no need for electronic fish finders, fancy lures, or expensive bait, and yet they pulled in the catch of the day.

After adding up the money I have left from what Bryce sent to Father to give me for petrol and food for the journey, I decide to pay for the army truck to take me across the Roper River crossing. So, before the store closes, I go back and pay the $200 to be carted across on the back of the 6 x 6 the following day.

Next morning, the 6 x 6 arrives, and I drive the Suzuki up a ramp made of earth and onto the back of the truck. It feels weird to be up that high and the driver suggests I might want to just stand on the back of the truck in case the Suzuki falls off. I think that is a great idea, and quickly jump out and take a firm hold of the pipework at the front of the tray, behind the cab of the truck on the passenger side.

The driver slowly steers the 6 x 6 down to the water. I look over the edge of the truck and watch as the tyres plough into the water, which ripples against the wheel rims. We reach the point of no return, just beyond halfway across. The current is stronger on that side of the river and the truck slides sideways. I think we are goners for sure, and I am convinced my heart has stopped beating, but the driver manages to pull it back.

When we get to the other side, I am so relieved to be off the truck. I stand by the riverbank, a trembling pile of nerves but thankful to be on solid ground once again. I watch as the truck goes back to pick up another vehicle. Once again, the truck slips and starts bouncing at the same spot as before. I cannot stand the watching any more, so I jump into the Suzuki and head to the small community town of Ngukurr.

Once I am there, I call Bryce to let him know I am only a couple of hours away. We are both excited to be finally seeing each other again after a year and a half.

The guy at the service station is keen to know where I have come from and where I a'm heading. When I tell him, he says that there has been plenty of rain and the dirt road to Numbulwar will close soon so I better get going straightaway.

It is several years since 1983 when I'd last been out to Numbulwar. I was only eight years old back then, half my lifetime ago, so I do not really know the track at all. But I do remember that somewhere along that dirt track, someone had placed a water buffalo's skull in the fork of a tree. I recall looking up to where the skull was lodged and noticing that it was practically a termite mound. The tree had been taken over by termites and their mound had encased most of the skull of the buffalo, leaving only the horns exposed.

I drive along for over seventy kilometres, looking for the buffalo skull marker but nothing looks right. I cannot find the turn-off. I start to think I have taken the wrong road because there are plenty of forks in the one, I am on, and they are confusing the hell out of me. I decide to turn back to Ngukurr, call Bryce again and ask if he can fly down and drive the Suzuki to Numbulwar from there because I don't want to get lost.

I manage to find my way back to Ngukurr and Bryce says he will be on the very next flight down. I hang around eating junk food while I wait for the plane and, an hour later, I go out to the airstrip to pick him up when I see a small Cessna circle overhead before coming into land.

It is so good to see Bryce after so long. He has his mate JohnJon with him, and he introduces us. We shake hands. I pass Bryce the keys to his Suzuki and we all jump in.

'Right, let's refuel,' Bryce says. 'We better get going before it gets too late.'

At the servo, we are all hungry, so Bryce gets pies when he goes to pay for the petrol. Within ten minutes, and without giving a second thought about buying any more food, we are on the road to Numbulwar. We drive along the dirt track for a couple of hours. When the going is good, this drive normally takes just over six hours.

'Did you make it this far?' Bryce asks me at one point.

'Yeah, I think so, but it's just a bit hard to say exactly,' I say, looking around, trying to identify something that I may have seen earlier.

We pass through a few creeks, and finally get to the Phelp River, which is running quite fast.

'Did you get through this river?' Bryce asks, looking out the windscreen.

'Yes, I crossed through, but it wasn't up this high before.'

'You would have been over halfway to Numbulwar then. It's a pity you didn't keep going, hey.'

'Gee, I can't believe I was on the right track,' I say.' It's all them forks along the way that confused me.'

'This is the crossing where Father had to use the crank handle of the Nissan that time, do you remember?' Bryce asks. 'The bank was a lot steeper back then.' He points to the bank on the other side of the river.

I do remember. It was dark, and the Nissan moved only about an inch each crank of the handle. How lucky, though, that the Nissan had a crank starter.

We all get out and look at the river. It's roughly a hundred metres wide and we decide to cross it by foot first to see if it is possible to cross in the Suzuki. When we reach halfway, there is a stronger current and the water is flowing through a deeper channel which is easily over 1.5 metres deep. The force washes my feet out from under me, so I end up swimming the rest of that section until I am clear of the undertow. Not once am I in fear for my life, knowing Bryce would be able to save me if I hit a spot of trouble and after all the swimming lessons at boarding school, I am a pretty good swimmer even though I'm still small.

'Gee, that current is really strong,' I exclaim, once I am safely on the other side.

'I don't think we'll be able to cross until it drops down again,' Bryce replies.

We all swim back to the Suzuki. The wet season comes in the summer months, so it is not too bad to be in the river, although I do wonder if there is a crocodile watching and waiting for a quick feed. Bryce says we will have to stay at the outstation, about two minutes' drive back from where we have come.

'That billabong has catfish and barramundi in it,' JohnJon tells us.

It is right next to the outstation, a small shed with a wood stove in it for cooking and two mattresses, one of which JohnJon claims straightaway. I dive onto the other one.

I have a billy and a twenty-litre container of water in the back of the Suzuki and after a while, ask the others if they want a cup of tea.

'Yeah, I'd love a cup of tea,' Bryce replies.

'Me too,' JohnJon says.

While I put the billy on, he looks through the cupboards.

'Yesss, look what I found,' he exclaims, pulling out a fishing reel. 'Barramundi for dinner, mm..mmmm.' He goes out to the Suzuki and starts looking for something to use as bait.

Once the billy is boiled, I make the tea, apologising that I only have teabags. We take our cups outside and sit under the shelter of the small veranda. I'm starting to get hungry now and cannot stop thinking about that barramundi those fellas caught at the Roper River the other day and wonder if JohnJon will have as much luck as they had.

'Hang your teabags in the tree here because we haven't got any more,' I say.

JohnJon gets up and says he is going to see if he can catch anything in the billabong.

'Okay, mate, hopefully you can,' Bryce says. 'I never thought we'd be staying out here tonight, that's why I didn't get any stuff from Ngukurr before we left.'

JohnJon says he has a good feeling about things and disappears out of sight behind some small shrubs in the direction of the billabong.

'I hope he catches something, hey?' I say, as my tummy rumbles loudly.

'Yeah, me too,' Bryce agrees.

I am telling Bryce about how the guys back in Roper River caught the barramundi, when JohnJon reappears.

'Look what I caught, fellas.'

He is carrying a nice big fat catfish, his fingers in its gills.

'Excellent work,' Bryce replies.

'I saw a frying pan in one of those cupboards before. I'll go get it,' JohnJon says, walking past with the fish.

I jump up to gather more wood to throw on the fire I lit earlier to boil the billy. When I get back, JohnJon has already gutted the fish and rinsed out the frying pan.

'Do you want to cook it on the fire out here or are you going to light the stove?' he asks.

'Nah, we might as well cook outside here, hey? It's getting a bit dark in there now to see what we're doing,' I say.

I stir up the coals and throw on some leaves. The embers smoulder away before the fire catches. Then, I put some small dead branches on, just a few at a time, Once the fire is established, I nod in the direction of the fire for JohnJon's benefit. He goes over and places the frying pan over the fire, and then grabs a long stick from the nearby pile of wood to turn the fish over with.

Immediately, the smell of the fish cooking makes my mouth water. I'm like a starving camp dog. I imagine the section of fish I will be eating and guard it with my eyes.

'That looks done to me, what do you reckon?' JohnJon asks, pulling the frying pan off the fire.

'Yeah, that looks right,' Bryce replies.

I peer at it and nod. I do not know if it is because I am so hungry but boy, does that fish taste delicious.

As the night approaches, out come dozens and dozens of mosquitoes. After years of practice, defending myself from the vicious mosquitoes back on the station, I expect to be prepared. But the mozzies there are only amateurs compared with these.

I pull out a bottle of Aerogard and apply the repellent all over. Then I pass it on to Bryce. By the time JohnJon has started using it, the mosquitoes are biting me again as if I had no repellent on at all. I apply some more, and we continue passing the Aerogard around like a bottle of vodka that we're drinking to warm us up on a cold winter's morning.

We tolerate it for a few hours until Bryce says, 'Stuff this,' and he climbs into the Suzuki to get away from them and stretch out to sleep.

I jump onto the mattress I claimed earlier and pull my covers right up and lie listening to the buzzing above me.

In the morning, I get the fire going and we make cups of tea with the teabags we left hanging in the tree. Then we head back to see how things look at the Phelp River crossing.

'Fuck, it looks like it's even higher,' Bryce says in dismay.

'Yes, it is,' JohnJon agrees. 'Look at the way that current's now churning its way through the centre now.'

'We might have to go back to Ngukurr and fly out to Numbulwar,' Bryce suggests, shaking his head.

I get a rock from the side of the road and place it on the waterline as a marker to check whether the water is still rising.

Several minutes past the outstation, though, we're faced with another creek, which has almost turned into a river.

'Shit, it looks like we could be flooded in out here,' Bryce exclaims.

He gets out, disconnects the fan belt, and covers the distributor with a plastic bag so the engine won't stall. We only just manage to get across the creek.

'That was bloody lucky,' Bryce says. 'I thought we'd had it when the water came over the bonnet.'

He reconnects the fan belt and removes the plastic bag from the distributor, and we set out again. After only a couple of minutes, we are faced with another flooded creek. It looks like a billabong in front of us; there is no strong washing current, just a lake.

The only way we can see where the road runs is by the treeless stretch of water, which extends for a few hundred metres and disappears at what is probably a bend.

'Well, we can't get back to Ngukurr along this road any more,' I say.

Bryce and JohnJon both laugh, trying to lighten the gloomy mood.

'Looks like we'll have to wait for the Phelp River now,' Bryce says as he makes a U-turn, and we head back to the outstation.

Before long, we are faced with having to get back across the same river where Bryce took off the fan belt. We are all talking as the Suzuki enters the river, but you could have heard a pin drop once we start washing downstream. Going back and forth has taken a good couple of hours but as we approach the outstation, Bryce decides to continue driving to see what the Phelp River looks like now. We all get out and look at the water rushing in front of us.

'Where's that rock I left on the waterline?' I ask.

Bryce spots it, submerged under the water a couple of metres of water from the now new waterline. I put another rock on the new waterline and we drive back to the outstation.

'There's no more tea,' I say, standing next to the shrub where we'd hung our teabags.

I light a fire and put the billy on anyway. When the water has boiled, I pour some hot water into a cup and throw in one of the already twice-used teabags.

'Cool. it's still working,' I exclaim cheerfully.

Bryce and JohnJon make themselves a cuppa, and when I have finished mine, I take off with the fishing gear to see if I can catch anything. We have not eaten anything since the catfish JohnJon caught the day before. I manage to cast far into the billabong and reel the line in slowly.

Suddenly, I feel something has the hook and run as fast as I can away from the water. When I look over my shoulder, I see that whatever I have caught is big because the water is rippling up around it as I drag it out to the surface.

I keep running until I have landed it. When I look back, it is not moving; it just lies on the ground, motionless. I try to figure out what it is. Suddenly I realise that I have just run like a fool for nothing because the only thing I have caught is a useless old car tube. Maybe JohnJon will have better luck, I think, as I unhook my catch.

Bryce and JohnJon are excited to see me coming back from the billabong but less excited when I tell them about my catch.

'Don't worry. We can stretch it out between us,' Bryce says, and we all laugh.

'I'll have another go,' JohnJon says as he picks up the fishing line.

I put the billy on again and make yet another cup of tea from my teabag. Bryce and I talk for a bit, mostly about how things are back on the station.

'Did you explore many of the breakaways out on Lime and Bell?' he wants to know. 'That windmill to the north of the homestead out there, the one called Breakaway, has some nice big breakaways just south of it. Have you checked them out?'

'Yeah, but I haven't come across any as good as the ones back on Moolapool just north of Dingo in the Floating Rock paddock.'

'Nah, me neither,' Bryce says. 'It's funny when people up here ask me about the station, and I tell them about the floating rocks. They look at me in wonder until I explain about the two big boulders sitting on few small rocks not much bigger than a clenched fist which sit on top of a few larger boulders at rocky outcrop.'

'Kids at school never believed me either but Shain vouched for me and he was always convincing,' I say.

'How's Shain going these days?' Bryce asks. 'What did he do after he left boarding school? Do you know?'

'Yeah, he's got a job in the shopping centre. Apparently, he's the manager of the fruit and vegie section in Coles, or was it Woolworths?' I question myself.

Just then, JohnJon turns up holding a barramundi, a bit smaller than the one the blackfellas caught in the Roper River.

'You were only able to catch that because I attracted it with that tube,' I tease him.

'Nah, I just know how to fish for the real thing,' JohnJon replies as he starts to gut it.

'This is the best fish I've ever eaten,' I exclaim after he's cooked it on the fire.

'Is there any more tea left?' JohnJon asks as he rolls himself a cigarette.

'We might get lucky if we throw all the teabags in and boil them up together,' I reply, filling up the billy and putting it back on the fire.

The water slightly browns as it churns its way around inside the billy. I pour the mix into our cups and pass them around.

'It tastes like a cross between weak tea and campfire smoke,' Bryce says after his first sip.

That night, we fight the mosquitoes once again. We pass around the bottle of insect repellent until it's finished, then we all climb into our swags and hope for some sleep.

15

Solo Trek

Next morning, there's no more billy tea, just hot water. As I am filling up my cup Bryce jumps out of the Suzuki and says he might lie down for a bit on the mattress I have been using. I sit in the Suzuki listening to JohnJon snoring and before a minute has passed, Bryce is snoring along with him. I a'm looking around to see if there is anything to eat, even though I know we have nothing, when I see Bryce's wallet on the dash. I open it up and find two notes, a $50 and a $20. I pull out the $50, climb down from the Suzuki and squat next to Bryce.

'Bryce, Bryce,' I say quietly.

Bryce just moans and rolls over, so I pick up a stick and etch a large arrow into the dirt, pointing towards Ngukurr. I have another drink of water and think about how I do not want any of us to die of starvation out here. Then I set off towards Ngukurr to ask for help. Every now and then, I stop to see if the Suzuki is coming but there is nothing.

I make it to the creek where we nearly got washed away and sit there for five minutes. But there is no sound of a vehicle; all I can hear is rushing water. The creek is now a river. I put the $50 note in my mouth, then take off my thongs and shove them down the back of my shorts. As I wade out into the river, I look over on the other side making sure it is clear of crocodiles, because I definitely do not want to be faced with one of those ancient dinosaurs. Then I leap in and swim like a bat out of hell, facing upstream but focused on where I am heading downstream, where I intend on getting out. The current still manages to carry me a good fifty metres further downstream than I anticipate.

My heart is thumping; blood races through my head, making me feel light-headed. I keep telling myself I am doing the right thing going to get help. I walk back along the edge of the river through the scrub until I am on the road again. Then I stop and look back across the river, hoping Bryce will appear any second, flashing his headlights at me. After a few minutes, there is still nothing but the sound of the river, so I continue on my way.

I swim through a few more fast rivers after that and start to get the hang of judging my exit – most times, anyway. A few hours later, I reach another outstation, the last one I remember seeing on our way in. I go inside, hopeful of finding some food, but the cupboards are empty. Back outside, I come across an old BMX bike with a punctured tyre. I pedal around to see how it handles, but the punctures make riding too difficult and I soon bin that idea.

At the front of the building is a big puddle. After wading through it for about four hundred metres, I realise the road has turned into a billabong. I continue walking until it becomes easier to start swimming. I quietly doggy paddle along, trying to reserve my energy and not alert any crocs.

As I approach another bend, I swim along a treeless path which I assume is the road. My arms are getting tired by this stage and I want to know if I can stand up. I hold my hand up over my head with my finger extended and let myself go under, keeping my eyes open. I start to sink fast, and quickly put both arms out and swim back up to the surface. This scares the shit out of me. My heart is thumping so loudly I can hear it in my ears. I look about for a spot where I can safely take a break and catch my breath again. I swim quietly over to the top of a tree. In the branches are spiders, scorpions and even a snake, all seeking refuge from the floodwaters. I decide I had best look for another tree. Finally, I come across one with no creepy crawlies in it. I wrap my legs around a branch and rest my arms. After about fifteen minutes, I am ready to keep going, so I swim back to the treeless path and continue my way.

By now I have been swimming for over an hour and a half and am starting to think maybe I am just going around in circles. But I stay focused and keep swimming. Then I feel something against my knee. With all my might, I push my arms down into the water, expecting it to be a crocodile, but I realise it is a mound of graded gravel from the side of the road. I carefully stand up. I walk around another big bend and fifteen minutes later, I finally see the road rising out of the water.

Excitement fills my body. I cannot wait to get out of the water. Wow, I think, as I finally put my thongs back on and set off on foot. I circle my arms around above my head to warm them up. I am so thankful to be alive.

About one hundred metres away, a pure black brumby is in the scrub near a small creek. It raises its head up high when it hears my footsteps on the gravel road and snorts. As it trots away, its long mane blows over its broad shoulders and it stops fifty metres further away to look back at me. I have never been into horses, so the option of trying to catch it does not even cross my mind and I just keep on walking, looking back over my shoulder from time to time to make sure it is not going to attack me.

As the afternoon nears its final hour of daylight, a dingo crosses over the road in front of me. I stand still, unsure of whether to continue. I walk cautiously, scanning the bush along the side over the road until I see it again way out in the distance. I'm relieved it isn't hanging around for me either.

By now, I am feeling rather exhausted, but I know I must not stop until I cannot walk any further, so I soldier on. My eyes start playing tricks on me. I am sure the stream I am walking alongside is running uphill.

Soon I reach yet another river. It appears to be on the crest of a hill, and I psych myself up for the crossing. I look for somewhere I can get in and across to the other side. Then I walk upstream for about seventy metres and wade out into the strong current. I am up to my waist in the water, with the money back in my mouth and my thongs once again shoved down the back of my shorts. I lunge myself out into the raging water and yet again swim for my life.

I manage to get across, straight out onto the road, and face a few more of these rivers as the darkness starts to consume the late afternoon sky. Suddenly, the faint sound of a generator catches my attention. I stop walking to double check that my ears are not playing tricks on me. Happiness flushes through my body when I realise the sound must be coming from Ngukurr. Determination and a massive sense of achievement give me a second boost of energy.

Soon, the sound of the generator is drowned out by yet another river. It is too dark by now to even see a couple of metres in front of me, let alone how wide this river is or the bank on the other side. I walk out into the water and listen for the generator. That will be where the road is.

I sit down in the water for a couple of minutes, contemplating my next move. The water feels warmer than the air, so I lie down with only my head bobbing out. It crosses my mind that I could possibly get away with sleeping here for the night. I close my eyes. Suddenly, I hear the water smashing against something, which I hope is just a log. I spring back up, concerned that it could be a croc.

I can still hear the faint noise of the generator in the distance and walk out into the water to determine the direction of the flow. I fear being taken by a crocodile, but think I would rather die trying than just give up. When I have things figured, I head up the riverbank through the scrub for about a hundred metres and once again plunge into the water. This time it is harder. I may as well be wearing a blindfold because I am playing every move by ear. But miraculously I make it across to the other side and climb out into more scrub.

As I catch my breath, I listen carefully for crocs. But all I can hear is the sound of my heartbeat throbbing in my ears. Once my heart rate slows down, I hear the generator again. It is clearer now, with the river behind me.

After stumbling around in the dark for about fifteen minutes, tripping over branches, I eventually come out onto the road. Tears roll down my cheeks as I make my way towards the town, hoping that there are no more rivers to cross. I wonder about Bryce and JohnJon, and whether they are far behind me or still back at the outstation at Phelp River.

Twenty minutes later, I reach the turn-off to Ngukurr. I am only a few hundred metres away from the town centre now. I wonder if the service station is still open and walk eagerly up the road into the light of a streetlamp. A black fella sitting on the veranda out the front of his house notices me appear out of the darkness. He quickly heads inside, looking over his shoulder at me as he shuts his front door. Maybe he thinks I am the devil or a witch doctor, possibly even a Kurdaitcha man. In any case, I could have done with his help.

The town is quiet; it is just on eleven p.m. I set out at nine a.m., so I've been on my feet, so to speak, for fourteen hours.

When I reach the service station, it is closed. Everything is in darkness, except for a couple of streetlights and the public phone box. I am starting to feel cold and hungry, even more than before.

The shop on the other side of the street is also in darkness. I think maybe I could sleep there for the night, under the veranda. Then I can grab something to eat as soon as it opens in the morning. But as I look up the street, I notice the sign on the police station, lit up in the distance.

I eagerly march up and loudly knock a few times on the door. There is no answer, so I try again. This time, I knock harder. Once again there is no answer, so I decide to go around the back, where a light is on in a separate part of the building. I knock on another door but still no answer. I decide to try the handle in case the officer inside has not heard me.

'Knock, knock, knock,' I say as I slowly push the door open.

There are three freshly made beds and they certainly do not look like they are for criminals. Just beyond the beds is a kitchen sink. I am feeling pretty thirsty, so I go in to get a drink. As I make my way into the kitchen, I notice a fridge. Suddenly my need to drink is replaced with the desire for food. I open the fridge door but all that is inside is a jug of cold water. I pull it out and drink till tears roll down my cheeks.

Maybe there is something in the freezer, I think. When I open the door, I find a whole loaf of bread and a packet of butter. I find a knife, separate some slices of bread, and put them on the counter. Then I cut some frozen butter off, spread it as best I can and start wolfing the lot down. I get a few extra slices of bread out from the packet and make some more frozen butter sandwiches for the morning.

Up till now, I still intend trying to sleep down at the shop, but I feel a lot safer in this building, so I lie down on one of the beds and put the bread I ha've prepared on the mattress alongside me. As I close my eyes, I tell myself I must get up around five a.m.

On the dot of five, I wake up and eat the bread, which by now has thawed out. I grab a pillow and a sheet and go down to the shopfront, where I soon drift back to sleep. When daylight breaks, the street becomes lively with people. The police drive past, looking at me. When they come back, I explain about being stranded out between Ngukurr and Numbulwar and tell them that Bryce and his mate are still out there.

'You won't be able to get a car or even a boat out there to rescue them,' I tell them. 'The only way would be by helicopter.'

'We'll give them until this tomorrow morning, and then send a rescue team out to bring them in,' the officer responds.

Later that day around three p.m., in stroll Bryce and JohnJon. Bryce explains how JohnJon checked at each river for my tracks to see if I made it across safely before they kept walking themselves.

The next day, the three of us catch the plane to Numbulwar. While I am there I ask Bryce, whatever happened to his Ford that he had driven out to boarding school in the middle of 1990.

'I'll take you to see it tomorrow,' he says.

The next day, we drive out for a look. His old Ford is a rusted-out wreck on the side of the road, just a chassis without tyres. It has a blown head gasket, Bryce tells me gloomily.

We sit for a while in the vehicle that Bryce has borrowed from the powerhouse, before making a U-turn back to his place. I stay with Bryce for a week. After he has paid for my flight out from Numbulwar and my bus fare from Katherine so I can get back to the station, I call Father to let him know that I should be home in a couple of days' time.

Bryce doesn't collect his Suzuki until a few months later once the wet season has passed and the road is accessible again.

16

Thoughtless Act

I get off the plane in Katherine with a couple of others from Numbulwar, and we all go our separate ways. I am pointed in the direction of the bus depot. Not far away, there are a few tourist shops. I still have a bit of time before I board my bus, so I go window shopping. Bryce has given me $50 food money for my trip back to Meekatharra, but an Akubra hat catches my eye and I just have to have it, no matter if I go without food for the rest of my journey.

I try it on and it is the perfect size. It is light tan, with a three-strand dark brown plate just above the brim, and some small feathers shoved in along the side. The price tag says $40. Surely, I can survive on $10 till I get home. I put my money on the counter with the hat and wait to be served.

The sales assistant picks the hat up to take off the price tag, then passes it back over the counter. 'Try it on for me,' he insists.

I place it on my head, and he steps back.

'Yes, it really does suit you,' he says with a smile. He looks at the price tag and shakes his head. 'You couldn't make it yourself for this price, could you?'

'No,' I agree. 'That's why I can't pass this up. I've always wanted an Akubra.'

After he's rung the price through the register, I walk out feeling as if I have just won the lotto.

'G'day, mate,' a man in his late fifties says, tilting his head at me.

'G'day,' I reply.' And I laugh to myself, thinking that he must think I am from a station around here somewhere.

At the depot, a bus pulls up. I look at the sign on the front windscreen: Port Hedland. It's my bus. I race into the toilet, quickly relieve myself then wash my hands. I can't help looking at myself in the mirror, with the new Akubra on my head.

The bus driver starts putting people's bags in the luggage compartment. I only have a blanket Bryce has given me because all my stuff is still in the Suzuki.

'Do you want me to put that under here?' the driver asks me.

'No, it's okay,' I reply, and I hug the blanket tighter, thinking of Bryce.

I share a seat on the crowded bus with a young guy, about twenty-five years old, I guess.

'I like your hat. I'm Donny,' he says, extending his arm across.

I thank him, introduce myself and shake his hand.

'Where are you off to, mate? Myself, I'm heading to Broome.'

'Cool,' I say. 'Broome is a really nice place. I've seen loads of pictures, but I haven't been there myself. Are you going there on holidays?'

'No, I've been offered a job on Cable Beach doing the camel rides for the tourists, hey,' Donny says.

I tell him I'm on my way home to my father's station, just ninety kilometres out of Meekatharra.

We chat for most of the journey and I tell him about my silly choice of buying the hat rather than keeping all the money for food.

Around seven p.m., the bus pulls up at a roadhouse.

'If any of you want to get something to eat or need the toilet, this is your opportunity,' the bus driver announces as he opens the door.

I get a drink from the tap outside and stretch my legs for a bit. After half an hour, the driver returns to the bus and everyone starts getting back on. Donny is still in the roadhouse when I take my seat near the window, but he soon boards the bus.

'Here you go, mate,' he says, passing me a pie and a bottle of Coke.

'Oh gee, thanks, Donny. That's really thoughtful of you.' I start scoffing the pie like a starving animal.

'Gee, you were hungry, all right. If I'd known you were that hungry, mate, I would've grabbed you a couple of pies.'

'Yeah, I haven't eaten anything since last night back at Numbulwar,' I reply between mouthfuls of pie. 'All I had this morning was a cup of tea before getting on the plane to Katherine.'

During the rest of the journey, I tell Donny about the station and boarding school, while he talks about where he grew up and how he can't wait to start his new job in Broome.

'This is my stop here, Luke,' Donny says, as the bus approaches the Roebuck Plains Roadhouse. It was great to have met you. If I ever manage to get down your way, I'll try and find you.' He holds out his hand, as the other passengers start queuing in the aisle behind him, but Donny makes no attempt to speed things up, saying goodbye to me.

'Goodbye, Donny,' I say. 'I guess the rest of my bus journey will be pretty boring now.'

The following afternoon the bus arrives in Port Hedland. By this stage I have spent most of the $10, so I just walk around the quiet streets thinking this place is like a ghost town. Everything is covered in purple, red, or ochre dust; even in a car yard, all the cars for sale are covered in dust. I run my fingers over the window of one as I walk past and stop briefly to draw a smiley face in the dirt.

How can people live here, I wonder as I make my way back to the depot. My bus isn't leaving for Meekatharra till three p.m. the next day, which means staying overnight. I find an alley, squeeze in between two transportable office buildings, and go to sleep.

I wake early the next day, shove my rug under a bush near the bus depot and go for another walk, this time in the other direction. There are a few people out and about, taking advantage of the morning. I sit in a small alley between some shops for a couple of hours and watch people walk by, then I go looking for something to eat.

The smell of chips cooking fills the air and I follow my nose to a fish and chip shop, which is a converted train carriage. I look at the menu board. Even a minimum serve of chips is more than the coins I have left in my pocket. I scratch my head, trying to work out what to do.

'Excuse me, I only have $2.65 and was wondering if you could sell me the minimum chips. I know you have $3.50 on them,' I plead, displaying the coins in my hand.

'No, we can't do that, sorry,' replies the grumpy old man behind the counter. He looks at me like I'm holding up a crowd, even though there's no one else there. 'Well then, are you going to get something from here or not?'

I look at some chocolates he has displayed behind the glass counter. A Mars bar catches my eye. I ask the grumpy old man how much it is.

He reaches into the cabinet, pulls it out and puts it on the counter. 'That'll be $2,' he says rudely.

I pass the money over and, on my way back to the alley, start nibbling on the Mars bar slowly, holding the wrapper lightly so the chocolate won't melt. Eventually, after nibbling away for over an hour, I come to the end of the chocolate. An old man walks past and smiles so I smile back. Several minutes later, he comes back.

'I haven't seen you around here before, have I?' he asks.

'No, I'm just waiting for my bus, it leaves at three p.m.'

'That's a while to wait yet. I'm Colin.'

He holds out his hand and I quickly stand up so that I am not seen to be disrespectful. I introduce myself and wonder if he might be compassionate enough to buy me something to eat. So I tell Colin about the fish and chip shop and how they wouldn't sell me $2.65 worth of chips. I tell him about how grumpy and rude the man was to me too, and I tell him about the Mars bar.

'Are you still hungry?' Colin asks, a worried look on his face.

'I'm starving,' I tell him, putting on a sad face. 'I had a pie around midday yesterday and nothing since.'

'Right, come on, I'll buy you some lunch.'

We walk back to the fish and chip shop and he asks me what I want.

'Some chips, please,' I reply.

When the grumpy old man comes over to take Colin's order, he gives me a dirty look.

'No,' Colin says, 'you're a growing lad. How does a nice big piece of snapper with a serve of chips sound to you, Luke?'

I just nod.

'Right, go and sit over at that table then.'

I go over to the table and sit down.

'Do you want a drink, Luke?' Colin yells over his shoulder to me.

'Yes, a can of Coke, please,' I yell back gratefully.

Colin waits near the counter until the grumpy old man hands him the order. Colin has not ordered anything for himself; he just sits there asking me questions as I eat.

'You've still got another couple of hours before your bus leaves,' he says. Would you like me to show you some places around Port Hedland while you're here?'

I am starting to feel a bit funny by now, with the way Colin keeps looking at me.

'Yeah, okay, maybe a quick look around, as long as I'm back before the bus leaves,' I say, thinking if I need to, I could easily get away from him if anything goes astray.

I finish my meal and follow Colin to where his car is parked half a block away.

'Have you been out to Pretty Pool before?' he asks as we're putting our seat belts on.

'No, I've only seen what's around here.'

'Okay, I'll take you there. I like that spot and it's not far away.'

On the way, I take close note of all the scenery in case I need to get myself back to the bus depot. When we get to Pretty Pool, there are a few other people there, wading around in the water. Colin turns his car around and we head to another location further along the beach.

He and I sit there, watching the people in the distance. The time passes slowly, but I guess we are out there about an hour. Colin's wearing a pair of silky short shorts and suddenly he starts rubbing his cock through the fabric. I do not pay any attention to him, but out of the corner of my eye, I can see him doing this. Itis becoming clear why he offered me a free meal and a sightseeing adventure.

I start undoing my seatbelt. First, I act like I have an itchy hip and scratch it quietly as I undo the buckle, holding it as it releases so he will not be alerted to what I am doing. Then I pretend that the itch has run from my hip up to my left shoulder. Colin is still looking into the distance and I am sure he has no't noticed me. But by the time I have completely removed my seatbelt and am reaching out towards the door handle as if I am stretching, he turns to me.

'What time did you say your bus leaves?' Colin asks, looking at my hand on the door handle then back at me while still rubbing his cock.

'Three o'clock. We'll have to get going, I think. It must be after two by now.'

Colin looks at his watch. 'You still have a bit of time.'

'Yeah, but I have to confirm my booking and check in.'

Colin starts up his car. He does not say much on the drive back to the bus depot, and I just sit there looking out the passenger window while keeping an eye on him.

'Thanks for the fish and chips, and the Coke and the sightseeing,' I say as we pull up.

'No problem, Luke, I'm glad to have met you.'

I am so happy to be back at the depot, I walk briskly up to the entrance without looking back. I am going that fast I slam into the locked door. I quickly look back at Colin who is looking at me. I go back to his car and tell him the depot is still closed.

'Jump in and I'll take you around to the tourist bay,' he offers.

I jump back in, cautious.

The tourist bay is just around the corner from the depot. Colin drops me off and parks his car some distance away from the front door. I know he cannot see me, so I go over to the partially closed blinds and look out the window. He is outside on the footpath, waiting for me to return. But after twenty minutes he drives off with some other young fella. I wait until the car has turned at the end of the road, and then quickly race around the corner. The bus depot is now open, so I check in, grab my blanket from under the bush across the road and wait in front of the bus out of sight until the door is opened. I am the first to get on. I find my seat and quietly stare out the window, thinking about the poor young bloke who is in the car with Colin now. As the bus fills up, a man in his mid-thirties sits down next to me, in the window seat. I do not say anything for the next several hours, and the guy alongside me sleeps most of the way.

As we approach Mount Newman, he sits up. 'This is my stop,' he says, as the bus pulls up at the service station.

I get to my feet and wait in the aisle while he gets out. Then I sit next to the window and watch him meet up with his family.

No one else gets on the bus, so I tell the driver I will be getting off about forty kilometres this side of Meekatharra. I ask if he can drop me off at the turn-off. Around ten p.m., we leave Mount Newman, and I figure I will be right to have a sleep for the next couple of hours until we reach the turn-off to the station.

Instinctively, I wake up as we are approaching the station turn-off and I peer out into the darkness. The area is definitely starting to look familiar and I am sure we are not much further to the turn-off. Suddenly the bus passes the spot where I had asked the driver to drop me off, but the driver has completely forgotten about me and keeps on going.

I race up to the front and ask him to pull up so I can get off. I thank him and stumble down the steps. The bus doors close behind me, and I run down the road in the darkness, looking for Father, but he is not there. I figure I will light a fire to keep warm while waiting for him. I stay near the fire, hoping that Father will soon arrive but there is no sign of him. Camping out at night has never fazed me, and I know I will be safe from here on, even if it means I might have to walk all the way out to the homestead which is more than forty kilometres away.

I am exhausted by now, so I wrap my blanket around me and lie down really close to the fire. I shut my eyes, only to wake sometime later to the smell of burning cloth. The blanket has caught on fire! I stomp the flames out and sleep the rest of the night a little further away from the fire, and a little colder from the hole in the blanket.

Warm sunshine wakes me at seven a.m. and straight away I start walking towards the homestead. There's plenty of water to drink from puddles on the edge of the road, so I know I will not become dehydrated. But my legs have only just recovered from my long walk in Arnhem Land just over a week earlier. Walking seems to have become a common theme on this journey of helping Bryce get his Suzuki.

By one p.m., I make it to the boundary fence. There are about another fifteen kilometres to go before I am home. I a'm so tired I lie down for a quick snooze. An hour later, I set off again. I walk non-stop, keeping an eye on an arrangement of unusual cumulonimbus cloud formations developing just to the north of me, which grows darker by the minute. As I continue walking, it seems to be keeping in time with me. The top of the cloud looks like grey popcorn stretching a couple of kilometres into the sky.

I am now only about a hundted and fifty metres from the workshop, which is about another fifty metres away from the homestead, when I hear a loud noise coming from the direction of the strange cloud. Suddenly, hailstones are falling around me. I pick one up, brush the dirt off it, put it in my mouth and crunch it between my teeth. Mmm, that's nice, I think, and reach back down to pick up a couple more. I am standing there eating a few more hailstones when the noise picks up and the hail becomes heavier. I run over to the workshop with the rug on my head. The noise from the hail hitting the shed roof is deafening. I yell out at the top of my voice but cannot hear my own voice. For the next forty-five minutes, hailstones the size of golf balls bounce into the centre of the workshop, which is about twelve by twelve metres and open on three sides. When it finally stops, I make my way over to the house.

Father has heard me coming through the front gate. 'Where did you come from?' he asks, looking surprised.

He takes some photos of the damage the hailstorm has caused to the house.

'I just managed to get to the workshop before the heaviest part of the hailstorm hit,' I say, following behind him while he continues taking pictures.

'You should have grabbed the saucepan from the back of the Rodeo and held it over your head to get over here to the homestead,' Father replies. 'I was under the impression that you'd be getting off up at the bitumen road on the station.'

'And I thought you'd come to the turn-off closest to Meekatharra.' I respond.

Rivers of hail are washing down the road, covering every inch of the ground. Around the buildings it is piled nearly thirty centimetres high in parts. The roofing iron on the veranda is all beaten and warped out of shape. Some of the vehicles are also damaged and their windscreens are smashed.

17

Bryce Returns

Several months later, just after the middle of 1992, Father asks Bryce when he is coming back to the station. By this time, Bryce is looking forward to returning and tells us that his mate JohnJon is keen to come with him. An extra set of hands is always welcome, and we are all looking forward to his return.

It is a relief to have Bryce back on the station. I have been working my arse off, and he and JohnJon take a huge load of pressure off me.

JohnJon only stays for a few months. He gets sick of the station life and heads back home to Numbulwar. Bryce and I continue working together and summer is soon on its way once again.

One day, we arrive at the infamous Emerald at around eight in the morning to find it isn't pumping up any water. We can hear water spraying, and when we look down into the well, we can see that the pipeline is losing water about thirty centimetres up from the waterline at the base of the well.

'Fuck pulling this windmill. I hate pulling up pipes from wells,' Bryce says to me crossly, with his face pale.

'Yeah, let's just slide down the pipe with some rubber tube and fencing wire and patch it up,' I suggest. 'That'll fix it, yeah?'

Bryce gets the old tube from behind the driver's seat of the Rodeo. 'It'll take fifteen minutes at the most to do it,' he says. 'Much quicker than pulling the pipes up. There's some old fencing wire on your side of the tray.'

Bryce puts the tube on the tray and cuts a strip of rubber from it. We slide down the pipe one after another, all the way down the well, which is seventy feet deep, till we are at the bottom. The water is not very deep, so we stand in it and patch up the hole in the rusty pipe. Soon we can hear the strain of the windmill as it begins to pump water up the pipeline again.

The walls of this well have been collapsing since it was dug out many, many, years earlier and the last forty feet are now shaped like a pear.

Bryce tries to climb out first, but the pipes are still wet from the early morning condensation. He only makes it twenty feet up before he slides back down, exhausted. Once he is out of the way, I give it a go, but I only get twenty feet too. We attempt this several times each but are unsuccessful until Bryce removes his shorts, which he uses to dry the pipe as he climbs. He reaches the spot where he can have a rest by wedging his legs into one side of the wall of the well and his shoulders into it on the other side, while clamping onto the pipe with his thighs.

Having rested his arms, he is able to climb the rest of the way out. I follow along behind and when I reach the better part of the well, I have a rest too. I wave my arms around a few times and after a couple of minutes break, I climb the rest of the way. It takes at least two hours for us to get out of the well.

'That's the longest fifteen minutes ever,' I say, as I regain my breath.

'But at least we didn't have to pull up all the pipes,' Bryce replies, looking like he's never ever going to do that again.

A few months later, we end up having to pull all the pipes up from Emerald anyhow because the pipe we mended rusted out in another spot. This time there is no suggestion of sliding down the pipe. We just pull out the old pipe and replace it with a new one.

In November 1992, a few months after my seventeenth birthday, I go into Meekatharra with Bryce and JohnJon, and apply for my driver's licence. Even though I have been driving a lot on the station, and drove up to the NT, I have never driven on the bitumen, unless it was on the station. What is more, the theory part of the test has always knocked me down, and I have had to sit for it several times.

I am not good at the multiple-choice questions and often pick the wrong answers. Getting my licence is not as easy for me as it seemed to be for Bryce. All he had to do was drive from the front gate in the work ute and park it in the shed fifty metres away, while the visiting officer watched him from the veranda as he talked to Father. The local police would drop in from time to time to introduce themselves and have a chat with the station owners in the area.

Father tells me to ask for an oral exam when I resit my licence, which means the police officer will explain the questions. This sounds like a great idea, so the next time I go for my licence, I ask for this oral test. The police officer on duty helps me understand and even does a drawing on a sheet of paper so I can see things more clearly. Finally, I pass my theory test. All I need to do now is pass the driving test.

As I walk out of the police station, I nod excitedly at Bryce and walk over to Father's Mazda van. Bryce and JohnJon give me the thumbs up from the other side of the road, where they are sitting under some trees on the lawn outside the swimming pool.

The officer and I jump in the Mazda and put our seat belts on.

'Okay, let's go up this way, turn left here, and left here. Okay, pull up here a second.'

The officer gets out and races over to the house near where we are parked. He pulls some keys out his pocket and goes inside. He is not in there long before he returns with a sandwich in his hand. 'Okay, let's head back to the station,' he says.

As we pull up out the front of the police station, I am sure I have failed but the police officer congratulates me for passing. Inside the station, I pay for my licence. I am so happy that I finally have my licence. Ever since, the first week in December reminds me of the day I ran the officer around to his house to grab a bite to eat.

I drive back out to the station that day, happy as a pig in shit. Father is proud I have finally passed, and he soon starts sending me into Meekatharra whenever we need supplies for the station.

Tough as Father is, it is clear he still cares about me. A few weeks later, he and I set off to Perth. Father has promised me we would make this trip as soon as I have saved up enough money for a car. I really enjoy the times when it is just me and him together.

Father talks about things he used to do when he was younger, after he left home, or about some of the people he met when he was in the police force. One time he tells me about a guy they called Scissors, a homeless guy who was great at sharpening scissors. Maybe he was a former barber. Another story was about one night when he raced off his own father's farm in the dark of night in his VW bug, with his father chasing after him. I was never sure what that was all about, but it sounded dramatic.

Apart from the good stories he likes to share with us, Father is also a fantastic singer. He knows a lot of the great songs from his era, and especially loves those sung by Dean Martin, Chubby Checker, Roger Miller, Jerry Lee Lewis and their ilk. I remember Father blaming me for taking a lot of his cassettes to boarding school and not bringing them back. It is probably true because I enjoyed listening to them too.

When we get to Perth, we head straight to the second-hand car yards at Victoria Park. There are a few raggedy-looking cars that cost a few hundred dollars and among them at McGoo Motors is one I set my sights on. It is a metallic gold Sigma sedan with a black bonnet. The car dealer can tell I have my heart set on it and says for me to take it for a test drive around the block. I decide going around one block is not enough to really get a good feel for a car, so I do two blocks. The only problem is there are not two blocks and, before I know it, I am stuck in busy city traffic. The streets are filled with commuters and workers making their way home after a long day. I fear getting lost as I am forced along with the traffic, but eventually there is a place where I can quickly turn round. Then I must find my way back to the car yard.

As I pull into the car yard driveway, I feel as nervous as hell. Father and Mr McGoo are just about to come looking for me. But all is good and I buy the Sigma. I follow closely behind Father until we are well out of the city. I can barely believe that I now own my first car, and no one can take it away from me.

Back at the station I cannot wait to start going into town on Friday nights with Bryce and Bidjid. Most weeks, we go to Bidjid's friend Vee's place in Meekatharra to smoke dope, listen to music and drink alcohol. Vee is an Aboriginal girl around our age, who Bidjid met at boarding school a couple of years earlier.

In February 1993, Bidjid is pregnant and goes back to Geraldton to live closer to her partner, and in April, Mum returns to the station from South Australia to help Bryce and me, by doing our cooking. It is great to finally get to know her, even though we have had several years of being fed her bullshit about coming over. One thing we did learn is that Mum's promises are like writing in the sand, long forgotten when the wind blows over.

A few months after my eighteenth birthday, Father calls me aside. 'It's time now, Luke,' he says. 'You have your licence and your own wheels. You should go and experience life on your own now, like Bryce and Bidjid have done.'

Father was not always thinking of himself; he just wanted to make us tough for what we had to face in the future.

'Yes, I'm looking forward to it,' I tell him. 'I think I'll head down to Geraldton and see where I end up from there.'

'Well, if you get into any trouble or just can't cope, you can always come back here, you understand?'

'Yes, Father, but I should be all right. Shain has told me that I can stay with him for a little while, if I get stuck, so I'll see what happens when I get there, I guess.'

The next day, I pack my belongings and throw them in my car. Mum and Vonn are both sad and happy for me to be making my way in the world. By now, I a'm living on a Newstart allowance from Centrelink, but also have about $2,000 in my bank account that I've been saving up for this adventure. I do not care where I end up. All I want to do is get well and truly clear from the station. I do not even really care about leaving anyone behind.

'Are you looking forward to going?' Bryce asks.

'Fuck, yeah. I can't wait to hit the highway and get away from all this red dust and the swarms of flies for a bit.'

Everyone comes out to see me off. As I turn on the ignition, tears of sadness but also of excitement roll down my face. I turn my head away so they cannot see. I quickly wipe my face while putting the car in gear and smile at everyone before I take off. I look in the rear-vision mirror as I drive away and a few more tears fall. For a moment, I feel like I am not ready to go away and I almost stop. I wave my hand high out the window and everyone waves back.

'Stay safe, Luke,' Father yells out.

A few seconds later, I can see him and Bryce talking. Dansan and Loui run back into the yard, but Vonn and Mum continue waving until I disappear out of sight, behind a big tree in the creek. Slowly, I increase my speed and, before I know it, half an hour has passed. When I turn onto the highway, I stop on the bitumen for a few seconds and smile, thinking of everyone back at the station waving me off, and it gives me the courage to continue on my way. Then I head straight to the Swagman Roadhouse in Meekatharra to fill up my petrol tank and grab a few nibbles for the journey.

By the time I arrive in Geraldton in 1993, Bidjid has already settled in and is living in a small unit and I move in with her for a while. We start hanging at the nightclubs most nights and spend a lot of time drinking and smoking loads of dope. I meet up with some old school friends and make loads of new ones who are all doing what Bidjid and I are doing, nothing but drinking and smoking weed around the clock, day after day. Shain is the only one of us who really has his head screwed on.

I bump back into Bran in my new circle of friends, although at boarding school I never really got along with him, since he was under the protection of Deano that day at the secret hideaway. This time, Bran is different, and we share loads of common interests and soon he becomes one of my closest friends. We are like Luke and Beau from the *Dukes of Hazard*.

My life now has become daring and adventurous, and I start becoming a little reckless. One day, as I am pulled up at a set of traffic lights behind a guy in a yellow Datsun 120Y, we are waiting for them to turn green and I notice him staring me down in his rear-vision mirror. Like me, he is also on his probationer licence. The next thing, he starts smoking up his tyres in front of me and they are squealing. Smoke billows around the intersection and when the lights turn green, he speeds off like a lunatic. There are a couple of girls in his car and they get him to slow down, so I can catch up to them.

At the next set of lights, I am side by side with him and he yells out the window for me to smoke it up. I am not sure how to do it, I tell him, but he tells me to hold one foot on the brake and hit the accelerator hard with the other. Before I know it, I am on the spot, squealing my tyres, and he joins in.

One of the girls in the back, sitting closest to me, shoots me a look that catches my eye. Soon we are formally introduced: she is Sally.

This is my very first experience of becoming involved with someone so intimately and before long she takes me back to meet her family, who are all true bogans. They are into V8s, chrome wheels and fat mag tyres, and they all have long hair and earrings. I am invited to join them on the weekends at the Geraldton speedway to watch the main attraction, which to them is the burnouts.

Now, I rarely hang out with my original network of friends or see much of Bidjid either and when Sally's family decide to move to Cannington, a suburb just south of Perth's CBD, her father asks me if I would like to come too. To me, this sounds like a great idea, to be finally away from everyone and to start living my own life independently and so I go with them and stay for several months in Perth. I manage to get a couple of months' work in Welshpool, working with Beta as a car detailer, mostly cleaning cars from car yards in the area. But the relationship soon dissolves, so I head back to Geraldton and settle back at Bidjid's place and chill with everyone there again.

Bidjid throws in her flat, and I move to the new place with her. It is better than living in the unit but now it is further away from the night life of the clubbing scene, and we tend to just stay home after dark and play the Super Nintendo.

One day, I am sitting around with Bran and a few of the other fellas in the lounge room, when out of the blue there is someone at the door. Bran, being the closest to it, gets up to answer, while I continue playing Super Nintendo. When he opens the door, I crane my ear to listen in on the conversation.

'Hey, what's up, brus?' Bran asks.

'Oh, I'm sorry. I thought Luke and Bidjid lived here,' a familiar voice says. 'Hey, I know you. Aren't you Bran? Weren't you in Luke's class at boarding school?' he continues.

I quickly make my way to the door.

'Yes, how do you know me?' Bran asks. When he sees my eyes light up, Bran is pretty sure he knows who he's talking too. 'Oh, now I remember you. You're Luke's brother Brendon, aren't you?'

'Yes, I'm Luke's brother, but it's Bryce, not Brendon, but you were pretty close, though, Bran.'

I open the screen door and go out the front to talk to him. 'What are you doing here?' I ask Bryce, as I reach out and shake his hand.

He explains that due to the drought, Father has sent him and Mum away from the station because there is not any money in it any more. 'Father suggested we move to Collie for the time being because the rent's cheap there. So that's where we're heading, and we decided to call past here on our way through to see if you Bidjid wanted to join us,' Bryce says. 'Where is she anyway?'

Just then, Mum appears from around the corner, giving me a big hug, and asks the same question.

I tell them she is living with her friend a few houses up the road from me. 'We had a disagreement and aren't talking now,' I add.

Bryce and I walk up to where Bidjid is staying but before we get to the front door, she races out to greet us.

'Hey, what are you doing here?'

Bryce fills her in, and she comes back down the street with us to see Mum. By the time we get there, Bow has been talking to Mum and made plans in his head to head down south to Collie to see what it is like.

'I'll come for the drive to Collie too, if I'm allowed. I've always wanted to see what it's like down there. If it's okay with you and your mum, that is,' Bran asks.

'What about you, Luke?' Bryce asks.

'Yeah. I have to tie up a few loose ends here first. I can't just up and leave this place. Bidjid only just transferred it to my name. I'll have to give the real estate agent notice, which could take a couple of weeks. I'll come straight down after that. I want to say goodbye to Shain, Peal and a couple of other fellas first too.'

Later that afternoon Bryce, Mum and Bran all set off and when he returns to Geraldton after being away for over a week down in Collie, he cannot wait to tell me all about what it is like. Bran makes Collie sound like the best place on earth.

By late April 1994, encouraged by Bran's high praise of the place, I hand in the rental in Geraldton, and head down to Collie with Bran and his younger brother Mal. I am nearly nineteen years old and, rough as it is, I absolutely fall in love with the place instantly. Although Collie is only a small coal mining town, it has a lot of great attractions, including its swimming holes. Black Diamond soon becomes my favourite place; the water is sky-blue and all the minerals in the water make you feel like you are using shampoo. Your hair feels especially soft and sleek. I have been growing my hair for the past couple of years, and it is long, below my shoulder blades, and nothing has made it feel so smooth in all my life.

As I have been on Centrelink payments for a while, I know I must inform them as soon as possible of the change of address, so I can receive my dole forms. Otherwise, if I do no't hand one in every fortnight, I will be cut off from unemployment benefits, which I have become reliant on basically since leaving boarding school.

I miss my mates back in Geraldton and have never had trouble mixing with in black fellas in my life. Apart from Shain, Peal and Bran, the rest of my mates were Aboriginal. Down south in Collie, it was not the same, and I found it harder to make black fella friends here. I am not sure but I felt as though, because I was not from the area, I was excluded, especially by the younger generation, black fellas in my age group.

Not long after I move to Collie, Centrelink sends me a letter at my new address. I am instructed to attend a CDP (Community Development Program), or my Centrelink payments will be terminated, leaving me with no money.

I am not real sure what to expect when I climb aboard the small commuter bus with the rest of the group, but I soon learn what my duties are, and I feel like I have been selected to do clean-up jobs for a very basic wage. Several of us are Aboriginal, and I feel like the outsider again, like I always do when I am put into a group.

This program runs for a couple of weeks, and during this time I get to know a few people and meet Tesha, an Aboriginal girl. She seems to really like me. Tesha's about eighteen years old and is constantly looking at me smiling and whispering with the other girls she knows.

One of her friends comes up to me and asks if I want to get with Tesha and I kindly refuse her offer because I just do no't find her to be my type. When she realises this, she gets angry and tells her boyfriend, Ethan, who I never knew existed, that I have trying to crack onto her, calling her up at her home and harassing her.

This is all bullshit, of course, but Tesha manages to stir up her boyfriend with the lies and Ethan is furious. I am still blissfully unaware of the stories that Tesha is spreading about me around Collie.

When Friday comes around, a week after we have finished the community educational development program, I finally find out what she has been up to. Bryce, Bran, Mal and I are all keen to see what Collie's nightlife has to offer us. So we jump in the station wagon and head downtown. We pull up in the dark car park across the road from the pub, planning to have a couple of drinks. Before we know it, the car's surrounded by a gang of local black fellas, ranging from about seventeen to thirty-five years old. I am sitting behind Bryce who is in the driver's seat when the gang descends upon us.

'You fucken wait, Luke. I'm going to smash your dog face in,' one of them shouts.

'Why ya been callin my girl, Tesha, up for?' Ethan is cursing me from outside my window.

'Hey, we don't even have the landline on at home. The nearest phone box to our house is more than a fifteen-minute walk. And besides, I don't even like your girlfriend. She's not my type at all.'

My attempt at explanation falls on deaf ears. Ethan believes his girlfriend over me, which I guess is understandable. He does not know me from a bar of soap. All he wants to do is settle this here and now.

'Open the door, ya dog.' Ethan punches at the window a couple of times.

'Fuck this, Bryce,' I say. 'He's going to break the fucken window in a minute.'

'Nah, don't do anything, Luke. They'll go away soon.'

So I stay in the car.

Suddenly, one of Ethan's fellas opens the rear hatch and takes up position, ready to throw an empty 700-ml Jim Beam bottle at my head. I reach for my door handle and open the door quietly.

'Stay in da car den, ya scum dog. Tru ways, I'll drill ya from ere,' yells the fella with the bottle.

By now, Ethan is still right outside the car door, just beside me but looking in the direction of his mate with the bottle ordering him to take the shot. He does not realise I am about to get out of the vehicle. As I push the door, it catches him off guard, and I force the door hard into him. He is launched backwards away from the car. He slides on his feet on the loose gravel and starts to lose his balance. A few of his mates try to catch him but he slides into them, and they all fall to the ground like pins in a bowling alley.

When the bottle-wielder sees me getting out of the car, he comes around for me, his arm extended high above his head, ready to strike. I grab his wrist and squeeze it hard, digging my fingers into his flesh with one hand while I wrestle the bottle from him with the other. I quickly drop it by my foot and kick it under the car. He gets down on his hands and knees to retrieve it, but then notices me stepping back, repositioning my legs, ready to kick him. He decides not to bother with the bottle and starts to get back up, but I punch him in the back of his head, and he falls to the ground like a bag of potatoes.

Ethan is back on his feet by now, and yells at me above the commotion. 'Oi, Luke! Come here, ya dog. I'm gonna smash ya, ya dog face. I'm gonna cave ya head in.' He rips off his T-shirt and throws it at the base of a nearby tree.

'Yeah, whatever you reckon, tosspot,' I respond.

I march over to him, and we both shape up. I allow Ethan to take his best shot first and dodge his fist, then I follow through with a punch straight in his mouth. Ethan loses his footing on the loose gravel and starts to slip backwards. I throw a few extra punches and he falls to the ground. I jump on top of him and punch several shades of piss into him for a few moments as he lies there defenceless, flicking his head from side to side, trying to dodge the blows and crying out for help from his gang.

At the time, I do not realise that the crowd I am surrounded by is Ethan's gang. They come in and rip me off him, then start laying their boots into me. I curl up into a ball with my arms over my head to protect myself from the kicks and blows. Bryce and the others are being held back by other gang members, and cannot help me, but fortunately Bryce yells out 'Police' and with the click of your fingers, the gang disappears into the darkness from where they came.

News spreads very quickly in small country towns, and by next morning everyone in Collie has heard about the fight. Even the mates I have just made are keen to talk to me about it, calling the gang a bunch of cowards.

'Yeah, well, it takes at least thirty local gangsters from Collie here to take me out,' I tell them.

This message is rapidly relayed through the community. After the word is out, I can walk down the streets alone, even though I have never hesitated to do so before, and if any of the gang from that night see me, they always cross the road, only crossing back over when they think it is safe enough. Living in WA, I made many friends, ninety per cent of them being black fellas, like myself. It never crossed my mind once that I would meet black fellas who wanted to fight me over a girl. Especially as I was not the type of person to go out looking for a fight.

I eventually meet a girl from Collie, Natlee, at a party just up the road from where I am staying, and we start going out. Natlee's family are racist but they pretend it is nothing. They have a blue heeler called Killer that they wind up with a black Aboriginal doll that has blonde hair. They say black fellas in Collie often targeted them, so they sic their dog onto any black fella who comes close to their home.

Natlee's family have a scooter that Natlee uses quite a lot. She comes around to Mum's place and picks me up, and we go everywhere around Collie on that scooter. When Natlee's not around, I spend most of the time at home. By now, I am into weed a fair bit, even more than I have been in the past, and cannot drag myself out of bed without picking up my bong and smoking a few rounds. Weed is a major part of my life, and everyone I am associated with in Collie smoke weed except Mum and Natlee's family, who are not into it.

Eventually, while scoring from a dealer, I am introduced to Bratt, a small stocky white fella who has an older brother I have met once or twice. Bratt and I become great friends. Although he smokes just as much as I do, he still gets out and makes the most of every day. Bratt loves free diving for marron in the Collie River. He can stay under for quite a few minutes before returning to the surface with a big fat marron in his hand and a great big smile across his face.

Bratt grows the best outdoor weed I have ever come across. It is purple in colour and has a strong scent; you can almost get wasted just holding it in your hand. Bratt calls it his jacaranda strand. He's been growing and improving it for the past ten years, since he grew attached to weed himself during high school.

Many times, I attempt growing weed but it takes too much work, and I never have the time to be running around carting water.

'How do you get water out to your crop?' I ask Bratt one day.

'I have a supply at my site. I've buried a few wheelie bins together in a line and keep them full of water, so I don't have to cart water with me every time. I've glued sand and vegetation on the lids, so it looks like the ground. No one will ever find them,' he divulges.

As another year passes, and another summer approaches, we know by now Father will be struggling on the station once again. He soon calls to ask if we could come back to help him. If we do not, he will likely lose the station to the bank. So we head back.

Towards the end of November 1995, Father leaves Bryce and me to manage the station while he moves further north with Vonn, Zoann, Dansan and Loui to manage Mulan, an Aboriginal community just south of Halls Creek at the top end of Western Australia. He needs this work to keep up the repayments on the mortgage and fund the station's upkeep.

Mum throws in her trust house in Collie, and she too returns to the station to help. We always stand united whenever it comes to maintaining our family's pride. But in March 1996, Mum gets a call from her sister back in South Australia, Auntie Ivy, with news that their mother is on her deathbed.

I call Father with the news of our grandmother's circumstances. 'She's in hospital,' I explain sadly. 'The doctor said she's not going to make it.'

'Don't believe a word of it, Luke. She's been dying for the past twenty years and she hasn't died yet. Why is this a problem now? You don't even know her.' Father lets out a couple of laughs.

'Yeah, whose fault is that? We know that's what you always say, but this time everyone is going over to say their farewells to her. I haven't seen my grandmother since I left Adelaide when I was nine and I want to see her.'

Father falls silent on the other end of the phone. For a moment, I think he has hung up on me.

'Think about it, Luke. You have a lot of work on the station, and a lot of sheep to care for.'

I relay what Father said on the phone to Mum and Bryce and Mum is fuming.

'Father also says we should think about all the work here, and the sheep.'

Mum was close to her mother. They did no speak much but Mum was always talking about her. I wrote a letter to Granny while I was at boarding school, and Mum said Granny carried that letter everywhere, she went. Granny would pull out the letter I wrote her and kiss it with a big smile on her face, Mum told me. 'LukeLuke' is what Granny used to call me. I do not have many memories of her, but I know deep down, I hurt for her when I heard she was close to death.

'Bullshit,' Mum curses when I tell her what Father has said. Tears stream down her face. 'Your father hasn't allowed you once to go over and see your family back in SA since you left over eleven years ago.' He's a fucking arsehole.'

Mum would often curse Father, never directly to his face, but she did around Bryce, Bidjid and me. She knew we would likely side with her if her views were valid.

'It's okay, Mum, we'll figure things out and head over there as soon as we can.'

Bryce and I both give Mum a hug.

Less than a week later, Mum gets another call from Auntie Ivy. This time it is what we have all feared.

'Shirl, it's Mum. She's left us now,' Auntie Ivy wails on the end of the phone.

'I'm coming over,' Mum replies in a stuttering cry as she hangs up. 'We shouldn't have listened to your father,' she says to us angrily. 'Now your granny has left us, and we never got to say goodbye to her. Especially you boys, she always thought the world of you both.'

'It's okay, Mum, we may have missed out on saying goodbye to Granny, but we won't miss out on going to her funeral, all right,' Bryce says, trying to reassure her. He looks at me with an expression in his eyes that says he's had enough of the station, and that he knows I have too.

'Yes, all right,' Mum sobs.

'Do you want to get away from here?' I ask Bryce outright.

He looks me in the eye. 'Yeah, let's fuck off,' Bryce says. 'We can get Mr Gibbon from Meekatharra to come out here and look after the station until Father gets back from up north.'

Years back, when we first arrived at the station, Mr and Mrs Gibbon used to come to visit us and they have remained good friends. The Gibbons always had a special place in our hearts, as we did in theirs. I really liked Mrs Gibbon the best; she was so kind and would always show appreciation. We know we can count on them in circumstances such as the one we are now facing.

I go outside to look for Mum, while Bryce calls Mr Gibbon. Mum is sitting on the edge of the concrete and we can faintly hear the call between Bryce and Mr Gibbon in the background.

'Mr Gibbon will be here in a couple of days,' Bryce tells us. 'He passed on his condolences to us all and told us to get going and not to worry about the station. "Go, be with your family," he said.'

The following morning, we pack as much stuff as we can into the car and leave for SA. We don't call Father to let him know we are going; we just take off. We know what he would say, something like 'Oh well, the old bat had a good innings, didn't she?' None of us is interested in his shallowness any more, especially at this time of grief.

We make it back to SA in time for Granny's funeral. Although it is a time of deep loss, it is good to see all the family. Some of them I have not met before. But I remember quite a lot of them. The only difference is they have all grown a lot older now. I stay for a week and later return to WA on my own, back to Collie to be with Natlee.

I get a job with a steel company that also makes precast concrete pavers, septic tanks and leach drains. I also do a fair bit of sandblasting, cleaning giant steel pipe connections used by the Worsley Alumina power station. I work hard over the next couple of years and save enough money to buy a house to settle down in with Natlee. It is like my own Moolapool station, and I feel fulfilled. The place has even got a swimming pool.

By 1999, I have been living down in Collie for close to four years, if I include the first time, when I had the job at the steel and precast concreting yard. I worked for the Italian family that owned the business for two and a half years, but things ended on a bad note with them, and now I am unable to find work. Collie is only a small town, and the word spread like wildfire about what supposedly happened.

It is all bullshit, but as I am the Aboriginal person and my employer is not, who are other potential employers going to believe? Certainly not me, that is for sure.

So I enrol in an Aboriginal Studies course and start studying by correspondence through the Edith Cowan University (ECU) in Perth. Because this external program for Aboriginal students requires me to attend the ECU campus every three to six months, I decide it is time to move somewhere closer to Perth. My main aim in doing the course is to become an Aboriginal police liaison officer. I am on an Abstudy payment from Centrelink, which is good because while I am studying, I am under no pressure to find work.

18

Father's Place

As Father is now my closest relative in WA, I call him every couple of months, and we write letters back and forth to each other too. I tell him about my situation, and how I am about to lose my house because I have lost my job. Then Natlee and I break up. I decide to let the bank repossess the property and have only three weeks to vacate the house.

Heartbroken from losing everything, I call Father and he kindly suggests that I stay with him for a bit and help with some jobs around his new place on the outskirts of Perth, roughly sixty-five kilometres north-north-west of the city.

Just before Christmas of 1999, I reunite with Father and Loui, after not seeing either of them for a couple of years. I move to Muchea, where Father has a small fifty-acre property, just out of the small town on the southern edge of the WA wheatbelt. Loui, who has chosen to stay with Father because he is in a better position to keep him on the right path, has a job working at a local tyre shop. He works Monday to Friday, which means we only have the weekends and evenings to hang out. He is only fifteen, turning sixteen in a few months, and races off to work on his pushbike every morning. In the late afternoons, I see him zooming back up the driveway.

Father tells me that the Department of Conservation and Land bought the station and they planned to remove all the windmills and fences. Then they were going to hand it back to the traditional owners, the Yamatji people, and the parents of kids attending the Karalundi Aboriginal mission, less than fifty kilometres away from the station, will be allowed to stay at Moolapool homestead under the new conditions.

Not long after I have moved to Father's new place, in the New Year, Dansan comes down from Darwin for a couple of weeks to catch up with us all. We three brothers hang around together a lot. Loui asks his boss for some holidays, and his boss is kind enough to allow him some time off, even though he has basically only just started.

We go travelling all around Perth and visit just about every beach we can, whenever we get the chance. It i good to see my once-little brothers now grown up into eager young men. I canno believe how smart and tough they have both become.

Just twelve months earlier, things seemed to have gone from bad to worse for Father. It was the year when Vonn and Zoann moved back to Numbulwar, and Dansan also moved away. As everyone slowly abandons him, it seems life will never come good for Father again. Loui is the only one who has remained loyal to him, mainly because he is still too young to leave home and fend for himself.

Then, around the middle of that year, Father meets Suzy, a Chinese lady who works as a nurse in Sydney, New South Wales. She travels to the other side of the continent to the station to look at the wildflowers with a group of other tourists who are interested in seeing these magical blooms on very rare occasions. During her stay at Moolapool, Father and she soon form a bond.

Over the next six months of 2000, Father spends a fair bit of time going back and forth to the station, collecting things, and the rest of his time is shared between his new home and flying to Sydney to see Suzy, who is going through a divorce.

I continue studying and work on a brick building connected to Father's workshop, about a hundred metres away from the main house. Father teaches me a few handyman skills while I am doing this work, which is in exchange for free board. Several months later, when the building is finished, he asks me to move out of the house and into the newly completed apartment. It is fully self-contained, with a kitchen, shower, toilet and laundry, and it is good to have my independence once again, but I miss Suzy's fantastic cooking. She is such a lovely cook and I feel very fortunate whenever I a'm invited up to the house for dinner.

At the end of the year, Father marries Suzy, and Loui stays in the house with Father and his new wife. She is a religious lady and although she never attends church, she worships three Buddhas by leaving offerings of fresh fruit and a small teacup filled with hot water each day.

Dansan comes down from Darwin with his partner Jackie for the wedding, but Jackie leaves the following day, while Dansan stays on for a bit longer with us. It is quite a hot summer, and one weekend, while sitting around the table watching the TV, I suggest we go to Scarborough Beach.

'Yeah, it's too good a day to be sitting around here,' replies Dansan.

Loui gets up. 'I'll go and grab my bathers,' he says, racing out the door in the direction of the house.

Dansan and I start to get our beach things ready but Loui's soon back with a serious look on his face.

'Come on, let's get out of here quickly,' he says.

But before we know it, Father is standing in the doorway.

'Come here, you little prick,' he roars. 'I thought I just told you to clean up your fucken room before going anywhere. Father walks over and slaps Loui hard behind the left ear. At the same time, he cuffs his hand and yanks him out of the room by the ear, like a wild dingo trying to rip flesh from a live animal.

Dansan and I follow them outside. I haven't seen Father go off like this for a few years. Father continues cursing Loui and starts looking around for something to clobber him with.

Between Father and where Dansan and I are standing, there's a brick on the ground. As Father heads towards it, I take a couple of quick strides and put my left foot on top of it. If Father attempts to reach down for it, I wil kick him. I have never done anything like this before, never really stood up to Father. He freezes, practically bent over, and looks up at me while still holding onto Loui's ear. Then he slowly stands, not taking his eyes off me. He looks over at Dansan, who has also taken a few steps closer.

Time stands still for a moment, then Father releases his grip on Loui's ear and turns to him. 'Okay, you can go to the beach, but I want you to promise me you will clean up your room when you get back, okay?'

I use the side of my shoe to kick the brick a few metres away from us all.

'Yes, Father, I promise,' Loui whimpers.

'Okay then, you better get going. It'll be lovely down at the beach right now,' Father responds in a cheerful tone, trying to break the tension in the air.

And we are all in the car and out of there before he changes his mind.

After we get back from the beach, Loui moves up to live with me in the little apartment, and a few days later Dansan goes back to Darwin.

After a few weeks, I manage to get myself a second-hand Commodore and spend countless hours working under the bonnet on the engine. I loved how basic the 202 straight six engine was to work on without all that double overhead cam and fuel injection crap to deal with. Another addition I added to the Commodore was to supply water to the inside of the car. This I did by adding a tube from the windshield washer bottle and attaching a pump to the line. Water was then pumped up through the line into the car. I would only use fresh drinking water in the windshield water container and it would pump fresh water out of the hose whenever I needed it. I also had a twelve-volt camping TV which I put into the dash so wherever I pulled up I could watch what was on TV.

Eighteen months of living with Father and one day I am sitting under the veranda out the front of his house enjoying a cup of tea and smoking cigarettes with him. Suzy and Loui are there also. I am not sure how the conversation started but it struck a nerve deep inside me even though I never let it show.

Suzy must have been arguing with Father and did not give a shit who she hurt in the process. The comment she made got no defence from Father, Loui and I just sat there totally gobsmacked.

I could sense I was being studied and I looked around the table. Suzy was looking back and forth at Loui and me.

'Aboriginal people look like monkeys.' she blurted out, without showing any sign of remorse about her remark.

I looked at her and shook my head from side to side gradually. All I wanted to say was 'Chinese people look like orangutans', but I wasn't there to have a pissing contest with anyone. I just bit my bottom lip and said nothing out of respect for Father and besides that, being spiteful at someone just because they are having a bad hair day just was not my cup of tea.

What got me was that Father turned a deaf ear to that and did not say a single thing to her to pull her up about what she had just said to us.

From then on, I sense Suzy has had enough of me taking up Father's time with things on the farm, and she starts to become more reserved towards me. So, when Loui and I are invited down to the house for dinner one night, I was not at all surprised that Father had something he wanted to talk to me about.

After the meal, Father orders Loui to help with the washing up with Suzy. She clangs around with the pots trying to block out the conversation Father is having with me. It is obvious they do not want Loui to hear what Father is saying.

'I think it's time now, Luke,' Father starts. 'It's been good having you around here, and the work you've done on the little apartment is great, but I think you ought to move on first thing in the morning.'

By now, Suzy's back from the kitchen, and she and Father look at me, trying to gauge my reaction.

'So where do you think you'll go?' Father asks.

'Umm, well, I could take up Shain's offer of a place to stay, so Geraldton, I guess.'

'You two will probably still be friends when you're old and grey,' Father says.

I'm deep in thought about Shain and Geraldton. 'I like Geraldton, it's a nice city, and I think Shain and I will always remain friends,' I muse.

'Yeah, that's nice,' Father says.

By now, Loui is making his way back from around the divider between the kitchen and the open-plan dining/lounge room.

'What about your studies?' Father asks. 'Are you going to continue with them?'

I tell him I plan to. I only have a few more units to go until I have completed the course and then hopefully, I can find a decent job.

'That's good to hear. Just keep focused, Luke. You'll get there in the end.'

As Loui sits back down at the table, Father turns to him. 'Luke is going his own way in the morning, mate. He's going to move to Geraldton and possibly stay with his mate Shain for a while. What do you want to do? Stay here or go with Luke?'

Loui looks at me and then back at Father. 'I want to go with Luke,' he says softly.

I'm not shocked to hear his decision but I'm sure if our father had the opportunity again, he would have never given Loui that choice.

I call Shain later that evening to let him know I'm coming up to Geraldton and ask if it's okay if I can stay and Loui comes too.

'Yes, of course. That'll be awesome. What time do you think you'll be here tomorrow?' Shain asks excitedly.

'We'll get going first thing in the morning, so we should be there around midday.'

'Cool. I'll knock off work as soon as you get here.'

19

Geraldton

It is late in 2001 when Loui and I go to stay with Shain in Geraldton on the Batavia Coast. Shain has a little poodle called Jam, and whenever I take him for a walk down at the beach, people come over to give him a pat. Most of the time, I just float along with Loui by my side. We tend not to contact anyone in the family because they are only negative towards us. I do not speak with Mum or Bryce back in SA either.

By early autumn 2002, after much thought, I decide it is time for Loui and me to move on, before Shain sends us on our way unprepared. I am twenty-six years old and Loui will be eighteen in a few months' time. The nights are becoming colder, though it is still quite warm during the day. We have been at Shain's place for several months now, but things have started to become a bit tense since Shain's partner moved in with him. I have seen this sort of thing in the past, living with Father and Suzy, so I know it is time to make tracks.

I know I can get along with Loui, no matter how tough things get; even if we hate each other's company from time to time, we always find a way to keep the peace between us. After all, we share many common interests, like smoking weed and tobacco, and drinking.

After being in Geraldton for the past few months, I had let my studies go, and eventually I get put back onto the New Start Allowance again and my payments drop down to around $400 a fortnight. It is only just enough to survive on, so life is hard going. And there are barely any opportunities to get a decent job anywhere. Loui is on social security payments too, far less than what I am receiving. His Youth Allowance (YA) is roughly $190 a fortnight.

I cherish my second-hand Commodore above everything else I own, which is not much more than the clothes on my back. So my priority each fortnight is always my Commodore. I fill the petrol tank and then put aside some money, which I only ever use for refuelling, no matter how bad things get. When things get to a point where I am unable to buy any food, I go down to the nearest Salvation Army store and ask them for assistance with food or vouchers, which they provide to people struggling on low incomes.

Loui and I go down to Muchea, just under 350 kilometres from Geraldton, often to catch up with one of our mates there, Rod. We have been good friends with him ever since Loui posted an ad in the local paper to sell his old Cortina. Rod came around with his tow truck to pick it up for his mate, Perky, who had bought it from Loui. We yarned with Rod for over an hour that day. He gave us his number and invited us around to his place, so the following day we got in touch with him. We soon find we share a lot of interests, like working on cars and smoking a little weed here and there.

Rod runs a backyard mechanical workshop from his home and, after we get to know each other a bit more, I start helping him to service cars or fix up some of the wrecks he is working on. It is always good being around Rod, doing something useful, and getting my hands covered in oil and grease. He really appreciates me working on his cars because he knows I will not lose my temper and smash the car up or throw tools around his yard, like some of the other guys he has working for him. One of Rod's workers has a short fuse and steams up over the smallest of things.

Before long, Rod starts recommending me to his friends when they have work to be done on their cars. He often phones and asks when I am coming back to Muchea because he always has loads of work for me to do. He slips me either some weed or cash, depending on what I am running low on.

Sitting around Geraldton broke is devastating. Day after day, I hear a voice inside my head saying, 'Luke, what the heck are you doing with your life? Go back to Muchea. It has more for you than mopping around here.'

On one of our journeys down to Perth, I end up trading in my beloved Commodore at McGoo Motors, the place where I had purchased my very first car back in 1993. Over the years, I often dropped in to see John, the owner, and we wouldd chat about how things were going. From time to time he wouldd ask how my father was. This time when I drop by, I have no intention of getting a new car, but I fall in love with the Barina straightaway. John sees me looking at it from his office window, and when I walk in, convinces me to buy it. He could sell ice to Eskimos. The Barina's a metallic sky blue, and Loui's extremely impressed with it. It is also cheap to run around in; the petrol tank holds just short of forty litres.

On our way back to Geraldton, Loui and I call into Muchea.

Rod is very surprised when we pull up in the Barina. 'What happened to your Commodore, Luke?' he asks. 'I thought you'd never sell that.'

I tell him I needed a cheaper car to get around in and the car dealer convinced me about the trade in.

Rod walks round the vehicle and chuckles quietly. 'You want to stay for a couple of cones? We're just about to take a break.'

'That'd be sweet,' I say, and tell him we'll take half an ounce with us too.

After a few cones, we set off later that evening back to Geraldton. As I drive along, I consider my options. What does Geraldton really have to offer me? Nothing. I decide I want to go back to Muchea to help Rod out working on cars. My mind is made up. I will leave Geraldton and go live out in the bush, closer to Muchea. But for the time being, I keep my plans to myself.

A few weeks later, I'm lying restless on my mattress on the floor, unable to go back to sleep. In the morning, I hear Shain in the kitchen making his breakfast before he sets off for work. Today is the day, I tell myself.

I have just received my allowance after yet another long, struggling, fortnight. Listening to my tummy rumbling for the past couple of days has been hard.

Moving on from Shain's place has nothing to do with him, and I want to leave on a good note because I value our friendship. I spring up out of bed, go out to the kitchen and say good morning.

Shain spins around, startled, holding a cup of coffee in one hand like a shield and a couple of slices of toast on a saucer in the other, like a weapon. 'I didn't hear you walking up the passage,' he exclaims. 'You're bloody lucky I didn't throw my cuppa all over you.'

Shain pulls out a chair and sits down, trying to calm his nerves, while I make myself a coffee.

'I had a shit night's sleep,' he tells me grumpily. 'I'd be still in bed if I didn't have to go to work.' He puts the last piece of toast into his mouth and washes it down with a big gulp of his coffee.

I join him at the table and ask about his plans for the day, if it is going to be a busy one ahead or an easy one.

He puts his empty cup down and stretches his arms out like he's about to be crucified. 'Not sure yet, man,' he yawns. 'I'll find out soon enough when I get to work, I guess.'

He picks up his mobile and quickly checks to see if he has had any missed calls or messages, then springs up out of his chair. 'Well, I better get going. I won't get any bills paid just sitting around here all day.' As he picks up his keys from the TV cabinet, he reminds me to let Jam out.

'No worries,' I say. 'Have a good day.'

By the time I hear Shain's car start, my mind is made up. I am going to get the hell away from Geraldton while I have the money to do so. I just need to run it past Loui. Even though I know he would say yes to just about anything, it is always good to include him in any major decision-making. If anything goes wrong, I will not be the only one to blame.

I decide to wait until Shain has come home from work to tell him that we are leaving. This will give Loui and me enough time to grab a few things from the shops and pack up our belongings without him hovering around like a blue-ass fly.

I walk down the passage to Loui's bedroom door and knock a couple of times. 'Are you awake in there?' I ask through the door.

'Yeah, come in.' Loui is still sitting up in his bed with his blankets over his legs, and he's collecting the resins from the bong. What he's already collected is spread on some paper towel alongside him drying out.

I sit down on the floor alongside, using the wall as a back support. Loui can tell I am about to ask him something.

I lean forward a bit and reposition myself. 'What would you think about us heading out bush and camping somewhere closer to Muchea, not far from Rod 's place? Maybe down near that water treatment place where we used to go rally driving when we lived with Father.'

Loui's ears prick up. 'Yeah, that would be bloody great, hey.'

I can see in his eyes that he has had enough of Geraldton as well, and it looks as if a huge weight has been lifted from his shoulders. Despite him being much younger than me, it is reassuring to know he is keen to make the move too. I find an old envelope to write on and we make a list of what we will need.

'A tent for a start, and some pots to cook in. Maybe we can find some at the Salvo store,' I say, scribbling the items down.

Loui mixes some tobacco with the resin from the bong and carefully packs a cone for himself, making sure not to cram it in too tight. 'Some plates, cups, knives, forks and a couple of spoons,' he adds. He lights the resin and slowly inhales. As he exhales, he warns me not to inhale too hard. 'Otherwise it'll just fall straight through,' he says as he packs another round and hands it to me.

'So, first stop is Kmart, then after that I get some money from my account,' I say, finishing my smoke.

'You know I'm really looking forward to this, hey?' Loui smiles.

'Yeah, so am I.'

Once I've taken $300 out of my account at the ATM, we head up to Kmart.

'Excuse me,' I say to a guy dressed in a Kmart uniform who is just inside the store.

He looks like quite a decent guy, apart from the way he is presented. He is tubby and red-headed, with pimples all over his face. His cheeks are as red as a tomato, and his glasses are like thick Coke bottles. He is wearing oversized, bright-red nylon shoes and his shoelaces are dragging along behind him. His shirt has been buttoned up incorrectly and one of his back pockets is hanging out of his black slacks. The poor fella looks like a fish out of water. He turns around and stares at us like we are headless chooks, until he registers that I am trying to ask him something.

'Err, umm, c-ca-can I h-help y-you?' he stutters.

'Yes, whereabouts is the camping section?' I ask.

He ignores me briefly, as white people often do. Then he darts his head from side to side, as if he is being watched by the Secret Service. His name, Ryan, is displayed on the front of his shirt, on a crookedly placed name tag. When he comes up close to me, his breath is putrid. And when he speaks, it is like he i divulging a secret.

'Ohhh, umm, it...it...it's o-on...on th-the o-other s-side.' Ryan's hands are shaking in time with his stuttering as he points us in the right direction.

'Thanks, Ryan,' I say.

Loui has already taken off and is a few metres down the aisle by the time I catch up with him. We cannot help laughing.

'Ohhh, umm, it...it...it's o-on...on th-the o-other s-side,' Loui cackles.

'Err, umm, c-ca-can I h-help y-you?'

I am sure Ryan can hear our cruel laughter, because when I look back at him his face is even redder than it was before.

In Camping and Outdoors, I pick up a three-man tent.

'This should be perfect. What do you think?' I show Loui the picture on the box.

'Umm, what about this one, though?' he says, holding up a box containing a dome tent.

There is the outline of a fish on the outside near the zipper, with the word 'Silverfish' below. It looks pretty good, and it has got a little veranda out the front too. As I put the other tent back on the shelf, I notice a portable single-burner gas stove.

'Wow, look at this. It takes aerosol cans of gas. This will save heaps of time and we won't have to bother messing around with fires.'

'That's a bloody good little stove,' Loui agrees.

He spots the enamel pannikins, and I pull out the list of things we need from my pocket.

'Yeah, those cups are nice and big,' I say.

We grab them and move along, taking a plate each and an enamel kettle from the shelf. I also grab a twenty-litre water container and a camping sink, and we make our way along the aisle to the cutlery.

'We should have got a trolley,' I say, struggling to keep hold of everything.

The water container slips from my hands and bounces along the floor, loudly crashing into some saucepans. Ryan comes tearing around the corner, looking very annoyed. His glasses are fogging up.

'I-is everything okay here?' he stutters, looking over his shoulder, and again darting his head from side to side.

'Everything is fine,' I say. 'But I don't suppose you could get me a trolley by any chance?'

'N-n-no. I c-ca-can't, I…I'm s-s-sorry.'

Ryan's stutter is really beginning to give me the shits. Our joke has long burnt out, and I cannot wait to get the fuck out of Kmart.

While Loui heads off to fetch a trolley, Ryan hangs around checking the saucepans are not damaged. When Loui gets back, we throw everything into the trolley and go to the nearest register, where, luckily, there is a nice, friendly girl on the checkout.

'That'll be $64.95,' she says pleasantly.

I pass her $70. She smiles at Loui, while handing me my receipt and change. I am sure she can see how red his eyes are.

'That wasn't as much as I expected,' I say. 'Maybe we can go see Lyn and get some weed before we leave.'

We pack everything in the back of the Barina and head to the Salvos to see if they have any cheap pots. Loui's eyes are bloodshot and glassy by now, but when I look in the rear-vision mirror, I discover mine are just as bad.

'They might even have a cheap TV there,' Loui says, pulling down the sun visor and looking at himself in the mirror before putting some Clear Eyes drops in his eyes, followed by whacking on his sunglasses.

I grab the Clear Eyes after he has finished and put a couple of drops into my own eyes before setting off.

At the Salvos, we score a couple of decent-sized saucepans for $2 each. Loui heads over to the electrical items to look for a twelve-volt TV, but we are out of luck.

'Excuse me, do you have any small TVs we could run off a car battery?' I ask the old lady behind the counter.

She looks puzzled and points over to the electrical section. 'Did you have a look over there?' She pulls a recycled plastic bag up from under the counter and flicks it open.

When I tell her yes, we have, she just shrugs and starts running the saucepans through the register.

'That'll be $4.'

I reach into my wallet and give her a $5 note. As she goes to hand me my change, I motion to her to keep it, and just take my receipt.

She suggests I try St Vincent de Paul's for the TV. 'They're just down the road and they have lots more stuff than us, dear.'

On our way to Vinnies, we pass a Cash Converters and decide to look in there first. And there on one of the shelves, is the perfect little twelve-volt TV for only $20.

'How much will you let this go for?' I ask Ben the cashier.

Ben looks at me with disdain, then back at the TV. He cranes his neck around to look at the item number. 'Oh, make it $15 and it's all yours,' he says with a patronising sigh.

'That sounds fair enough. I'll take it.'

I turn around to Loui and use my head to point at Ben. Loui stares at him and shakes his head.

I hand Ben a $20 note. 'Keep the change,' I say. 'I don't want to catch whatever that disrespectful attitude is that you've got.'

Ben puts the money into the till and picks up a cleaning cloth to wipe his hands.

As we walk past the Salvos store on our way back to the Barina, we spot the old lady. I hold up the TV and give her a smile, and she smiles back.

'So you found one then, my dear?' she shouts.

'I think the old lady likes you,' Loui sniggers.

Our shopping all out of the way, I suggest we head to Lyn's place for the weed. Loui nods but I can tell he's still thinking about Ben.

'I can't believe that racist, white, cunt from Cash Converters. What a fucken dickhead.'

'Ahh, don't worry about him,' I say.

But Loui can't contain himself. 'I'd love to run into that fuckwit in a dark alley one night and punch several shades of piss into him.' He clenches his fists together in front of him and grits his teeth.

'Don't worry about him, matey. You'll find the world is full of fucks like him,' I say as we turn into Lyn's driveway. 'Nothing a few cones can't fix.'

I knock quietly on Lyn's door and a few seconds later the lounge-room curtain moves slightly. She opens the door cautiously, sticking her foot behind it as she peers out. When Lyn realises it is us, she quickly steps back and opens it all the way. Lyn always has a huge warm smile on her face whenever she greets us. She gives us both a big hug.

We follow her into her kitchen, sit down at the table and tell her we are leaving Geraldton.

Lyn looks sad, as if she has just heard someone close to her had died. 'I'm going to really miss you both,' she says. 'Especially you, Luke. We've known each other for quite a few years now, and I've always loved listening to your stories of growing up out on that station.'

'Whenever we come back, you'll be the very first person we come to see, all right,' I say, looking at her in a reassuring way.

Some tears start to pool in her eyes, and she wipes them away. 'Bloody smoke, I should have opened the window,' she says.

Lyn gets up and opens the kitchen window. When she sits back down, we smoke a few more rounds until I notice the time on the wall clock.

'Hell's bells…we have to get going,' I say to Loui. 'We still have to pack our stuff up before Shain gets home. I'd rather do it while he's not looking over our shoulder. You know how it is with people that do that, hey?'

Lyn looks at me and smiles sadly. 'I know what you mean but if I ever hear that you guys have come back to Geraldton without dropping in to see me, I'll come after you and knock you out.' Lyn reaches out her arms and pulls us all together tightly.

'We promise,' Loui and I say in unison.

'You better or else.'

She waves us goodbye and as we drive down the street, I beep the horn.

'Gee, that was unexpected,' I say, breaking the silence.

Loui is sitting quietly, tightly clasping the dope we have just bought. 'I really like Lyn. She's a nice chick, isn't she? How did you meet her?' he asks, carefully putting down the weed, and reaching for the tobacco to make himself a rollie.

'Bran introduced me to her. I used to get stuff from her a few years back, when I was hanging around in Geraldton the first time I left the station. You remember Bran? He was that fella who came out to the station looking for me in that stolen mining vehicle and Mum said to Father, "Don't trust him, Neil, he's a liar."'

Loui lights his rollie and inhales deeply. 'Yeah, I sorta remember him. I'm just trying to picture his face. Did he have a tattoo of a scorpion on his arm?'

'Yeah, that was Bran,' I say, as we pull up at Shain's. 'Right, while we still have plenty of daylight left before Shain gets home, let's make a wooden box big enough for that car stereo we scored from that wreck we came across on the side of the road that time. You don't mind if I stick those speakers you took out of your Cortina in it, do you?'

I explain that I'm planning on making a portable music station we can run off the car battery. And I'll put a cigarette lighter socket into it too so we can charge our phones. I still have the dash light from the old Ford Courier ute, so I'll put that in as well, so we have a night light.

'Yeah, that's a bloody good idea,' Loui says.

Out the back, in Shain's shed, I get busy cutting some wood on his saw bench while Loui starts to pack his things. I wire the box all up and put a two-pin plug connection onto a ten-metre cord on the side of the box, and another two-pin plug just under the front grille of the Barina. No one would know it is there unless they knew what they were looking for, and it will be easy to connect the box up when we set up camp for the night.

Loui and I gather up our belongings and get the car packed well before Shain returns. We are all ready to say our goodbyes to him when he pulls up in the driveway and notices the Barina packed to the hilt.

He gets out of his vehicle, walks past the Barina and glances in briefly. 'Are you guys heading off?'

'Yeah, mate,' I start. 'It's been great of you to put us up all this time, but I think it's time we got going. I know things have been a little awkward round here lately.'

'Nah, man. You guys have been bloody awesome, loads of fun. We've done so much shit. I won't ever forget how you emptied that wallet you found on the road that night right in front of everyone without any of us seeing a thing, even though you were standing in front of us in the headlights of the car. I'll be sad to see you go, hey. But you won't be around at shearing time, so how will I know when the time is right?' Shain jokes.

Shain and I used to call weed 'wool', in case anyone might be eavesdropping.

'At least you won't be able to accuse me of fleecing you or pulling the wool over your eyes,' I reply with a laugh.

'So where are heading?' Shain asks. 'Will you stay around here?'

'We're going to head out bush for a while, maybe set up camp down nearer to Perth, around Muchea, to be closer to Bob so we can help him on his jobs.'

'Oh, cool as. Are you going to stay for dinner or are you ready to hit the highway right away?'

'Nah, I think we've worn out our welcome here. We'll be off now. We just wanted to wait for you to get home so we could say goodbye.'

'It hasn't been that bad having you fellas here. It's a wonder you guys were able to put up with me for so long. Not many people can. And Jam is really going to miss you taking him for walks along the beach.'

'Yeah, but I'm sure you'll be happy to get your house back. It's been a long eight months and this last month has almost counted for two.'

We all laugh, and as I walk over to shake Shain's hand, he pulls me towards him in a tight hug. When he finally lets me go, his eyes are all glassy.

'See ya,' I say, trying not to look worried.

'Yeah, goodbye, mate. Take it easy and you better keep in touch, eh.' Shain looks at me like he's struggling to swallow.

Loui goes over and shakes Shain's hand. 'Thanks for letting me stay here with you. I really enjoyed it.'

'Yeah, no worries. You two look after each other now, okay.' Shain steps back a couple of paces so that we can get into the Barina.

I stick the key in the ignition. As I reverse out of his driveway, I turn the headlights on and beep the horn a couple of times. Then, I fling my arm out the window and with my hand above the roof, I wave as we take off down the street. Shain's still looking sad but I know he's also delighted to see the back of us.

'He was about to cry, hey?' I say.

Loui's already rolling himself a cigarette. I can see he's feeling saddened by the two farewells we have had today, but he is trying hard to put his confident face on. I always know when something is upsetting him because he goes quiet and gazes out the window at nothing.

'Yeah, and he nearly made me cry too when he gave you that hug.' Loui lights his rollie then slowly winds the window down, just enough to let the smoke out.

20

Squatters

The drive south towards Perth takes a few hours. Even though I would be happy for Loui to take the wheel out on the open road, I do all the driving because he has not got his licence yet. But he is happy to chop up roadie sessions and share them out between us, so I do not bother asking him if he wants to drive.

'Chopper's choice of who goes first, yeah? So I'll have the first one,' Loui announces as he starts smoking. Then he packs another and passes the bong over to me.

I take it carefully, using my knee to steer while I light up. I inhale the entire contents then blow the smoke out the corner of my mouth towards the window, producing a big mushroom cloud as it curls behind my shoulder.

'Mmm, that's some nice stuff Lyn sold us.'

'It looks like it's been raining here this afternoon,' I say.

We approach a couple of kangaroos standing their ground on the centre of the bitumen road just south of North Badgingarra next to a small puddle of water. They look as if they are trying to play chicken with us. I have no choice but to slow right down to a crawl.

As we slide past them slowly, I could have wound down my window and slapped one of them over the back of the head.

'How come when you don't want them to move when you have them fixed in your sights, they do, but when you want them to move, they just stand there?' Loui asks.

'Yeah, I know, right. It's as if they sense danger,' I say, speeding back up to 110.

By the time we get to the outskirts of Muchea, it is nearly midnight. We pull off the main road and turn down a dirt track that we know from when we were living at Father's new place, not far away. I find a spot, pull off the track and switch off the engine.

'Let's have another sesh before we go to sleep, yeah?' I ask Loui, turning the interior light on and looking in the direction of the glovebox to where the mull bowl is kept.

'Fucken oath.'

Loui reaches into the glovebox and takes out a pair of scissors and the Tupperware container we use for chopping up dope. He opens the tobacco pouch and pulls out a couple of buds. 'Just remember there's a couple of buds still left in the tobacco, so don't roll them in your next rollie, okay?'

'Yeah, I was worried you were going to roll them in a rollie before,' I laugh.

We smoke the session and sit there spinning out, listening to the Perth radio stations that we can pick up on the car radio.

'I've missed these radio stations,' Loui says.

'Me too. They beat that boot-scooting crap they play in Geraldton any day.'

I get out of the car and walk a couple of metres away to take a pee.

'Shit, it's bloody cold out there, Loui,' I say as I jump back in with my teeth chattering. This is soon drowned out by my rumbling tummy.

'We've been so busy with getting everything ready to get on the road, that we didn't bother to eat anything all day,' Loui laughs.

'Yeah, the only thing that really matters to either of us is that we have weed and somewhere warm to sleep,' I add.

Loui shivers and crosses his arms to warm himself up a little as he inhales deeply and yawns. 'I might hit the hay now, Luke. You weren't planning on setting the tent up tonight, were you?'

'Nah, not tonight, mate. Let's sort something out tomorrow.'

'Great idea.' Loui stretches his legs out in front of him and grabs his pillow and rugs up from the floor by his feet. Then he pulls on the lever to drop the seat back. 'Goodnight. Luke.'

'Yeah, goodnight, mate.'

This is going to be an exciting adventure, I know, and we are both ready to make the most of it. I am sure we are doing the right thing. I lie there in the driver's seat, stoned, and look out the window. Every now and then, the full moon breaks through the clouds lighting up the landscape around us. I listen to the radio for a while until it starts to rain heavily. I close my eyes and almost drift into a trance, until Loui starts snoring. I always find it harder to fall asleep when he snores, but I am so tired, and as soon as I close my eyes again, I feel like I am falling down a deep hole as the effects of the dope relax me.

Several hours later, I wake to the sound of Loui getting up and the clicking noise of the car door closing behind him. I lie there for a bit before I sit up, reposition my seat and roll myself a rollie. As I get out of the car to stretch my legs, Loui is returning from where he has popped behind a shrub to go to the toilet. He opens the passenger side door and flicks his rugs into the back, then begins to roll himself a rollie.

'How was your sleep last night?'

'Yeah, it wasn't too bad, but my bloody neck hurts from sleeping crookedly on the headrest, though.' Loui turns his head around in a circular motion.

'Chop up the rest of that stuff, hey?'

'Looks like we might get three each out of this session,' he says as he gently shakes the mull bowl.

'Nice.'

Once we've finished smoking the weed, I grab the portable stove and kettle we got from Kmart, from behind my seat.

'You want a coffee, Loui?'

'Yeah, I'd love one, thanks.

'Me too. Grab the water container out of the back and chuck enough for us both in the kettle here,' I say, as I pass it to him.

'No worries.'

'We'll head into Midland soon and grab a couple of McMuffins from Macca's for breakfast, yeah?' I suggest.

'Mmm, yeah, I could murder a muffin right about now.'

'I have a couple of spare dollars which we can use to get a little treat for us. Then we better do some shopping at Woollies and get some main supplies if we're to make it out here.'

After our coffees, we head to Midland and go straight to McDonald's. I pull up in the drive-through, right in front of the menu board where orders are placed. I already know what I am going to order for us, but it is good to see all the other choices on offer. The smell of sausage, bacon, eggs and cheese coming from the extractor fans on the side of the building fill the air and waft through the Barina.

'Doesn't that smell make your mouth water?' I say.

'Hell, yeah!'

'Welcome to McDonald's. Please place your order when you're ready,' announces a voice through the intercom speaker.

Before Loui has a chance to say anything, I speak into the microphone. 'I'll have two bacon and egg McMuffins, thanks.'

'Do you want any drinks with that?'

'No, thank you.'

'That'll be $4. Please drive along to the next window, thank you.'

I collect the order and pull up in the car park. After we have eaten our tiny McNothings, we go over to the Midland shopping centre to get supplies for a nice big feed of spaghetti for dinner.

'Luke, look! Only $1!' Loui exclaims. He picks up a packet of biscuits from the shelf.

'Oh wow, what a bargain! You could get a whole load of them on your payday,' I reply, walking past quickly so he cannot see the smile on my face.

As I pull up to survey something else on the shelf, I see Loui in my peripheral vision putting the biscuits back on the shelf. We grab some tins of tomatoes, a couple of packets of pasta, some onions and garlic, noodles, coffee, powdered milk, and sugar – enough to see us through for a few days until Loui's Youth Allowance comes in.

'Maybe we can do some jobs for Rod to tide us over until you get paid.'

Loui nods. 'We could always scab some things from the rubbish dump too. He's bought a few things from us from there.'

We can't wait to see Rod again, and decide to go straight to his place. We've only been in Midland a couple of hours and already we have had enough of it. Besides, we are both hanging out for a session of Rod's gear.

I pull up on the nature strip out the front of Rod's house, and he's standing in his driveway talking to someone while looking at their car.

When he sees us, he stops talking and comes over. 'G'day. How are you guys going? Are you passing through again or have you moved back this way now?' Rod asks.

'Nah, we're just going to rough it out in the bush. We got a tent and plenty of supplies to tide us over till Loui's payday,' I reply.

'Oh, great. I have some work for you, Luke, if you want it. You want to stay for a few cones then?' Rod chuckles.

'For sure,' I say, turning to Loui, who i also nodding.

Rod fills me in on what jobs he needs to get out of the way as soon as possible. 'So when do you think you can do those jobs for me, Luke?'

'We'll set up camp this afternoon and then I can come over tomorrow and get into them for you straight away,' I respond eagerly.

'Loui can help you with a couple of the two-man things and earn himself some extra cash, doing the smaller jobs, can't you, Loui?' Rod asks.

'Yeah, I can.'

It is getting late in the afternoon by now, too late to head back to where we intended to make camp. The weather is turning cold too. Dark clouds in the distance are heading our way, and the wind is picking up. So we say goodbye to Rod and head off to find somewhere to pitch our tent for the night. The only place we can think of is near the waterworks.

Once we've set up the tent, I cook a cheap spaghetti meal under the small veranda.

'Cheap spaghetti' is what we call it: browned onions, garlic and a tin of tomatoes with pasta. There is a special knack to it. It is not just tossing it all together in a pot. It is done in a way that it i a quality meal for a very cheap rate.

After we have eaten, we sit in the tent and watch some TV while smoking a bit more weed. Just on sunset, it starts to rain heavily. It rains so hard that I think we are going to get washed away during the night. I can feel the sides of the tent around the base pushing inwards with all the water. With less than a millimetre between us inside the tent and the slosh outside, we are in danger of becoming engulfed in mud, and it is too late to do anything about setting the tent up elsewhere.

When I go out into the pouring rain and darkness for a pee, puddles of water are pooling right outside the tent zipper. The mud is thick and sloppy but luckily, I have left my shoes just within arm's reach sitting under the veranda on the esky with Loui's. I put them on before setting off in the rain.

When I come back a minute later, I put my muddy shoes on the esky again and get back into the tent. While I was outside, the rain came down by the bucketload and drenched me in seconds. By the time I get back into the tent, I am soaking wet and freezing cold.

'Gee, it's really coming down out there,' I say to Loui, quickly ripping off my wet clothes and leaving nothing on but a pair of shorts.

'Bloody hell, Luke, you look like you fell in a river.'

'Brrrr. I feel like I have too, I'm going to jump in bed and go to sleep now, mate. Goodnight.'

'Goodnight, Luke. Gee, you look like you're having an epileptic fit the way you're shivering. Are you sure you're all right?' Loui asks.

'Yeah, I'll be all right in a few minutes. I just need to warm up a little.'

My teeth chatter as I lie in my bed shivering with my head under my blankets. I close my eyes and try to fall asleep but I am still shaking like a leaf, and the rain outside is even heavier than before. After a few minutes, I pop my head back out. I can vaguely make out Loui's silhouette from the LED light on the TV; he has ducked his head under his blankets too. I lie there looking in his direction for a couple of seconds before closing my eyes again and pulling my blankets back up over my head.

During the night, I hear a couple of cars drive by even though we are in an isolated spot. By morning, the rain has cleared, and we scout around for a better campsite. Eventually, we decide on our new base and string a few strands of fencing wire around it from some trees, leaving an opening just large enough to get the Barina through. From the road, our campsite is as good as invisible. Many times, over the period we stay there, people drive straight past us without looking our way even once. We always cover up the Barina's tracks by sweeping over them with some brush and then throwing a dead tree into the opening in the wire.

It soon becomes annoying to have to pack the Barina with all our camping gear every single time we want to go anywhere. We start off folding up the tent and putting it away in its little bag. But as the days pass, we just shove it in the back of the Barina unfolded. After a few weeks, we can't even be bothered taking care of our blankets and all our gear is just crammed into the back of the Barina.

One day, an idea pops into my head. I mention it to Loui straightaway. 'Wouldn't it be good if we had Bob here with us? Then we wouldn't need to pack away our stuff every single time we go anywhere, hey? He could just camp here with us and keep other people away. He'd make a good guard dog. He scares a lot of people off.'

Loui agrees, but doesn't quite sound a hundred per cent, so the following day I ask him about it again. 'What do you think about us going to get Bob tonight?'

'Yeah, maybe we should get really stoned at Rod's first and grab a few drinks on our way back,' he says, but I can see sorrow in his eyes at the idea of taking the dog from Father without asking him first.

Bob is roughly fourteen years old now, and for some time he has been bloody useless at mustering sheep, even though he is a cattle dog/blue heeler mix. Many other dogs on the station have either taken a dingo bait, been put down for killing sheep, or simply been neglected to the point that they have had live out their remaining days on the end of a chain, so Bob is very fortunate to have made it to this ripe old age. Quite often, he got in the way when we were trying to chase sheep through the gates closer to the homestead, and we would wonder why the sheep were just standing there. When we realised it was Bob, we would curse him until he ran away from the gate, and then the sheep would flow through without a problem. Even so, Bob was a bloody good guard dog and these days he is living outside on a chain at Father's place, not too far away from where we are camped.

I know Father cares a lot for Bob, but I am sure it will soon be the firing squad for him, once Father no longer sees him as a useful guard dog. I certainly do not want that end for Bob, and I figure that it makes sense for him to come to live with us.

So that afternoon, after we leave Rod's place stoned to the hilt, we swing by the bottle shop on our way back to our campsite and grab a few long necks of Emu Bitter and a bottle of Passion Pop each. We sit around the huge campfire we have built, drinking till late into the night. Around eleven p.m., after we've worked up enough Dutch courage, we decide it is time.

There is a full moon that night when we go to get good old Bob, so we can see where we are going quite easily without having to use a torch.

We walk up along a man-made water channel to Father's boundary fence. The light on the front veranda is on but it is not long before Father gets up from his seat where he has been having a cigarette, goes inside and switches the light off.

Loui and I crawl through the fence and sneak over to where Bob is curled up fast asleep in a forty-four-gallon drum which has been sliced down the centre to make a kennel. Bob jumps up instantly; he is so happy to see us. We untie him and motion by hand for him to come. Then the three of us race off back to our camp.

The next morning, I get a text message from Father: 'Luke, please explain your actions last night.'

I show Loui the message, feeling worried that Father might come looking for us. But it is too late now to take Bob back. If Father is feeling spiteful at all, he might shoot Bob on the spot and I do not want anything bad to happen to him; I love him too much for that. Loui just shakes his head and stares blankly beyond the screen; he looks like he has just lost everything on a high wager.

    I do not reply to Father's text. Sometimes I feel sorry for hurting him that way, but I do no know what I could say to explain myself. I am sure any word from me might make matters worse, so I say nothing. I know I have done my father wrong, but the truth is, I was simply too scared to ask him if I could have Bob. My hunch is that more than likely he wouldd have refused me, but I will never know.

Living in the bush is mostly fun, apart from the freezing nights and all the rain. It is not at all like back on the station where we fixed fences and windmills or mustered sheep for a living. But those past days of living on the land have given us the strength to survive in any situation, no matter how tough it is. Once again, our way of life is basic; we are eating practically nothing, as we often did growing up on the station, just a few years earlier. But the upside of living rough is we do not have any bills or rent to pay, which leaves us with more money in our pockets to do whatever we want.

    Back on the station, Father would often send me out to fix things. Most times I would be allowed to take Dansan or Loui with me, and we'd work as a team. I would pack a small, makeshift esky, usually just a cardboard box, with some black tea leaves, a packet of noodles or two and an onion. We would take some .22 bullets for the rifle to shoot a kangaroo for dinner when needed. Often, we survived alone, living off the land for up to a week or more, in some of the harshest conditions and most isolated parts of Australia.

    Once you left the homestead, there was no way of communicating with anyone, so it always paid to be smart. When things broke, you needed to be a great problem solver – and many problems could arise when you were out bush. You could easily die in that environment if you made the wrong move.

21
Bob

It's great having Bob at our camp. He scouts around a bit to familiarise himself with the campsite and, once he knows his new surroundings, hangs around close by our tent unless he wants to go to the toilet. He has been well trained in this regard. When he was a pup, if I caught him doing his business nearby, I wou;d yell at him and tell him to sit. After a few months of that, the only place you would see Bob squatting would be more than a hundred metres away, tucked behind a bush trying to stay out of sight.

Bob does not even need to be tied up; he seems to know what is expected of him. After a few weeks, though, he is starting to look a bit thin, so I take a walk along the fence line until I come across a trail that some roos have made to get between the two sides of the fence. I make a snare out of some wire, which I have cut from a section of the fence further up the line, and I set it up on the centre of the path. Then I grab a load of dead branches and put them each side of the path to make a passage, so the roos have no other option to get to the other side.

This works well and by the next morning we have a nice big kangaroo in the snare. I drag it back to our camp and cut it up for good old Bob. He hooks into it until he cannot eat any more.

The kangaroo lasts nearly a week before I need to reset the snare. The kangaroos that I am snaring for Bob are referred to as euros. They are dark brown with a woolly type of fur and are also known as the common wallaroo. Loui and I never eat any of the meat from them because they remind us too much of the roos back out on the station.

They were always sweaty and smelt funny, and their meat was much darker than the more popular big reds. What is more, the euros often have worms in their stomach cavity.

Now that we have Bob with us, it is easier for Loui and me to get away. We spend a lot more time at Rod's place, smoking cones, working on cars, or doing other jobs for him. Loui usually rearranges Rod's storage of engines, gearboxes, tyres and other car parts in his sheds, or gives me a hand lifting gearboxes or diffs and the like into the vehicles I am fixing.

One time, I tile Rod's bathroom and toilet for him. I had picked this skill up when I was staying at Father's place after I left Collie about eighteen months earlier. Rod is surprised that Loui and I are so good at so many different sorts of jobs, and I really respect him for giving us the opportunity to use our skills, even though I walk in on him one time and overhear him saying to someone, 'Yeah, I got the boongs out the back working for me today.'

A few weeks later, when we're sitting around the bong table, I confront him about it. 'I know you've been telling your friends that you've got some boongs working for you and laughing about Loui and me behind our backs,' I start. 'I'd just like to say we'd never say that you're a fat lazy white cunt or a fucken racist white prick to disrespect you in any way, Rod, and I'd appreciate it if you didn't disrespect us.'

Everyone is silent while I am speaking and Rod's face drops.

'I'm sorry, Luke, I wasn't thinking. I apologise. I know you two guys are nothing like the rest of them who hang around the city doing nothing,' he says.

'I understand you may feel that way,' I reply, 'but the number of useless white people out there whacking up speed, and spaced out off their heads, far outweighs the odd Aboriginal you might see sitting around.'

'Yeah, I know. I just wasn't thinking clearly.'

Rod packs a huge cone and passes me the bong, doing his best to salvage our friendship. Once I've smoked it, I calm down.

Rod passes me the rest of the bag, just over half an ounce, and stands up. 'Well, I've had enough. I'm going to have a lie down. You take that with you, Luke, okay. I promise there'll be no more running you down, and if I hear any of you guys here disrespecting you or Loui, you'll be fucken sorry.' Rod looks around at the others, who just nod.

As he's about to go into his house, Rod turns round. 'Luke, come back tomorrow, okay?'

'Yeah, no worries,' I say. 'We're going to get going now ourselves.'

And Loui and I get up and say see ya to the rest of the fellas.

The next day Rod is so happy when we turn up that he invites us inside his house and asks if we want a coffee, which he has never done before, and we take him up on his offer.

'Sit down, you guys.' Rod gestures towards the kitchen table as he goes out to the shed and returns with the bong.

Rage is on the TV and all the top forty songs are playing on a countdown to the number one for the week. It is amazing to see this program in colour, having become used to our little black and white TV.

I have always been forgiving to people who have wronged me. No matter how hard or often I get sand thrown in my eyes, it always washes out in the end with a few quiet tears. And it was no different this time with Rod. All is soon back to normal. If anything, Rod now favours Loui and me over his other workers. He starts calling them a bunch of useless fucken cunts, and whenever they come to join us at the bong table, he sends them back to work after having a go at them for not finishing the job. We can see that Bob's other workers now hate us, but they are not game enough to speak up like I did.

From then on, Rod flicks us cash. Sometimes he even pays us in green. After a week of helping Rod out, we end up with a good stock and Loui and I decide to take a break. We reckon we can stay at our camp for a week or so, head up to Meekatharra for a few days, or go down to Collie for some different scenery and see my mate Anthony Snapman, who preferred to be called Snappy, and take him some weed.

After a few weeks of snaring kangaroos for Bob, he starts to pack on a bit of body and begins to look healthy, even more so than he was back at Father's place. We are able to fatten ourselves up a bit too, mainly on junk food as it does not require any messing around cooking. Pizzas, chicken and chips, or McDonald's are our main choices. We drink a fair bit of alcohol too, but never become a public nuisance. That sort of behaviour is just not our thing; we just get our booze and head back to camp.

Since having Bob guarding our belongings, we now find ourselves heading into the city a bit more for the nightlife on Friday or Saturday nights. It is good to be amid the action, even if we are just doing laps around the streets in the Barina. On one occasion, while refuelling at a servo in the Upper Swan, we notice a couple of signs we have never really paid much attention to.

One advertises free coffee for drivers; the other, in the male toilet, says they provide free hot showers. It i's impossible for the staff to know which occupant the driver of the vehicle is. We take advantage of this fully. The foam cups of coffee at the servo always have us craving more, so we start bringing in our enamel pannikins which hold 600 ml.

After not having had one for a couple of weeks, the showers are even more enticing.

'Arrr, isn't this great?' I ask Loui in the next shower cubicle.

'You're not wrong, Luke.'

Those nice hot showers always bring some heat back into our chilled bones as well as washing away the stink of our body odour.

We stay in the showers until the hot water runs cold. Sometimes a truckie is hanging around, waiting for the showers to become free, but we hightail it before he can accuse us of using all the hot water and tell the manager.

We make sure we rotate who goes in first for the free coffee in case we are confronted by one of the staff, but we never are. Even so, we always pull up out the front in a spot where the staff cannot see who is driving.

We soon become regulars at the servo, until a couple of months later, they decide to rearrange the whole set-up and have the bathroom renovated so they can monitor what is going on.

One time, I get my toothbrush and toothpaste and head to the toilet to brush my teeth while Loui grabs his cup and goes into the servo. We get back to the Barina around the same time, and I grab my cup and head in to get it filled. The person behind the counter looks at me then looks out the front to see which car I have just got out of. I fill up my cup with a double hit of instant coffee and an extra serving of sugar and grab a couple of the little packets of Arnott's biscuits that are also on offer.

Loui is sitting in the passenger seat sipping his coffee and smoking a rollie when I return a few minutes later. I roll one for myself and we sit there watching people come and go.

'Hold on a second. I almost forgot. I was meant to get us some more tobacco.'

I race back into the servo just as a busload of tourists pull up. I manage to beat the crowd and I go straight over to the counter.

'Can I get a fifty-gram packet of Champion Ruby, thanks? Oh, and a packet of Tally-Ho papers,' I ask.

The servo attendant gets the first packet he sees out of the smokes cabinet.

'No, not that one. The biggest packet, please,' I explain, signing with my hands.

'That'll be $27, thank you,' the guy says, running the payment through the till.

By this time, there are over thirty people from the bus queued behind me, waiting to be served.

I pull out a $50 note and hand it to the attendant. He looks at it, holds it up in front of his eyes, then flicks it a couple of times, stretching it out from all corners.

'What's wrong?' I ask.

'We've had reports of counterfeit notes circulating around here,' he snarls.

Being intimidated in front of all these people is just bullshit. I have encountered it so often in my life, but this time it wears thin. So, when the attendant finally puts the note in the till and passes me my change, I hold up the notes and, one by one, stretch them and flick them before I put them in my wallet.

Then I turn to the crowd behind me. 'Apparently counterfeit notes are being circulated. I suggest you check your change from this servo before leaving, hey?'

I still have a cheeky smirk on my face when I get back to the Barina and tell Loui all about it.

'What a fucken toss pot,' Loui says, shaking his head.

I start the Barina up and we head off back to camp. Bob comes snooping around as soon as we pull up. I reach into the back seat and pull out a half-eaten chicken pack.

'Here, Bob. Look what I saved for you,' I say, patting him on the back of his thick furry neck.

Bob eats the chook slowly as he tends to do with these takeaway feeds. It is like he too is trying to savour the flavour. Meanwhile, Loui goes to get some wood for the campfire, and I set off down the fence to set another snare. By the time I get back, Loui has the fire going and I warm myself up.

'Let's have a few cones, then cook something for dinner before it gets too dark,' I say.

And without any hesitation, we jump into the tent, chop up a session, get wasted and watch the cartoons on the ABC.

22

Bush Humpy

After hanging around our camp for a few days, Loui and I decide we might be able to make some quick money out of the stuff we got from helping Rod out. We take off up to Meekatharra, a good seven hours' drive. When we get there, we pull up at the shop for supplies. We need more coffee, sugar and milk, and something for dinner, maybe noodles. Back outside with our shopping, we stop on the footpath in front of the liquor store. Loui is holding the bag of groceries, banging it onto the side of his leg. Back and forth, it crashes. Maybe he has forgotten what is in it.

'Hey, be careful, you don't want to burst the sugar bag open or crumble up all the noodles,' I say, glaring at him.

I open my wallet to count how much money I have left. 'We have $80, how about we get a bottle of Passion Pop each and a bottle of Father O'Leary to share?'

I wait for Loui's answer.

'Yeah, okay. Who cares if we run out of food? We've managed to survive this far, and I'm sure someone will buy from us sooner or later, hey?'

In the liquor store, the shop assistants watch as we make our way over to the fridge section where the bottles of Passion Pop are kept.

'These are the same price as back down in Midland, aren't they?'

Loui nods, so we grab one each then go in search of Father O'Leary.

One of the shop assistants is pretending to clean the nearby shelves and comes over to us. 'Is there anything, that you two fellas are looking for?' he says. His name is Dennis. He's an older man, balding on top of his head and with a neatly trimmed beard, kind of like Abraham Lincoln's.

'Do you sell Father O'Leary here, Dennis?'

'We do, yes. Follow me.'

'Yeah, that's it,' I say when I spot it.

'How many bottles are you after?' Dennis asks with a dirty look on his face, as he takes a bottle down and passes it to me.

'Just the one thanks, Dennis.'

Dennis walks ahead of us, looking back every now and then, as Loui and I follow him to the counter.

'Do you have any ID on you?' Dennis asks Loui.

Loui reaches into his wallet and pulls out an expired driver's licence of mine, which to date has worked well for him in the nightclubs of Perth. He passes it to Dennis.

'Yeah, here. Sorry, it's expired. I lost my wallet and I'm waiting on a new licence to be sent out.'

Dennis looks at it for a couple of seconds then passes it back to Loui. 'You might want to get that sorted out real soon then, okay.'

Back outside, we make our plans for the day.

'Let's find somewhere to set up camp first,' I say.

We drive out to the main water tank, on top of the highest hill, just north of Meekatharra. The local people hang out here some nights.

I spot a small thicket of bush. 'Over there, see, we can camp on the other side of that, hey?'

'Yeah, maybe we can find a big enough tree that we can stick the tent under,' Loui suggests.

We head down the hill in the direction of the thicket and drive along the highway until we reach a track just beyond a floodway sign. I pull off the highway, drive along the dirt track for about six hundred metres and park in front of a tallish mulga tree to get some shade. We can see some semis in the distance, but I am sure the drivers cannot see us.

'Let's chop up a session,' I say, as we open our bottles of Passion

Pop. 'After, we can set up the tent under this mulga tree here. It looks like it will fit if we break away a couple of those lower branches, hey?'

Loui reaches into the glovebox. 'You can chop up this time. I'm always chopping up.'

He puts his drink on the bonnet and starts snapping off mulga branches and piling them around the base of the tree we're about to use. When he's done, he comes around to my side of the Barina to see how I'm going with the mix.

'I might go gather a few more of those branches while you do that.'

'Yeah, let's make a humpy,' I say. 'It looks like you've already started.'

Loui takes another swig of his Passion Pop, then opens the back of the Barina to get the tent out. He sets it up under the mulga in the space he's just cleared for it. 'What do you think?' he asks.

'Oh yeah, that's perfect. Let's have this session now.'

'By the time word has got around Meeka, I bet we'll have smoked all this stuff,' Loui laughs.

'Yeah, and loads of people will be chasing us by then, hey? That'll be just our luck.'

I grab some more branches and start weaving them together. Loui fills his empty Passion Pop bottle with half of the Father O'Leary.

'The rest is yours,' he says.

Loui ventures off and Bob tags along behind him, until a flock of galahs roosting in the nearby mulgas swoops down towards the ground before regaining elevation, vigorously flapping their wings. Loui claps his hands loudly a few times. It sounds like someone is taking potshots at the galahs with a shotgun. They scatter but soon reunite as a group.

Bob races past Loui after them, looking like he is trying to become airborne himself, taking lengthy strides with his head held high. He yelps a few times in excitement but after fifty metres, he is exhausted, and makes a beeline back to Loui.

After I have rolled myself a smoke, I join Loui dragging branches back and we start making the humpy. It takes a couple of hours until we are happy with our construction. It is massive, big enough to conceal the whole tent. We then extend it on one side, so we have somewhere to park the Barina. Now our campsite is completely unnoticeable from the highway.

We camp outside Meekatharra for a couple of days and then head into town to see if we can make any dope sales. It is not much more than half an ounce Rod has given us, but we are hoping to make enough to fund our trip and keep our mull bowl filled. Considering it is Friday and just after midday, we are sure we can find some buyers.

Loui runs into a couple of young black fellas and asks them if they know Ty and to pass on the word if anyone is looking for weed to flag us down.

Not long after, a Toyota Land Cruiser pulls up across the road from us, and a black fella gets out. He looks at Loui like he is trying to figure out if he knows him or not. 'Loui, is that you?'

Loui looks across at the black fella but says nothing.

'It's me! Ty.'

Loui and I look at each other. We haven't set eyes on Ty since 1990.

'Ty! Isn't that Edvard's son?'

'I think it is,' Loui says.

Ty waits for a semi to pass then races across the road.

'Ty, how the bloody hell have you been?' Loui exclaims.

Ty holds onto Loui's hand as if it's keeping him from falling over. 'I'm really good, eh. I'm working for the CDP.' Ty suddenly realises who I am. 'Aye, Luke, I hardly recognised you bro. I never seen you before with a beard, eh. How ya been?'

We shake hands, while Ty tries to get his breath back.

'What are you doing for CDP?' I ask him.

'Oh, I was just working on them there garden beds at that Centrelink office up ere, and I been just come down this way to get myself some lunch from that there takeaway shop you two were just in. Perfect timing, eh?' Ty smiles.

'Yeah, we were hoping to catch up with you,' Loui says.

Ty came from Meekatharra, so we have been kind of hoping we would run into him there.

'Yeah, I been hear it from my cousin brother earlier part, eh, em been tell'em me yesterday, that he was sure he'd been seen Loui in town, eh, so I been come down this way ere tu-dai for some lunch for myself to look, maybe I see you maybe not. Next ting I bin caught a sight of Loui ere as he'd been come out of that there takeaway place over there.' Ty has an enormous smile on his face all the while. 'So, what you two been doing here anyways?' he asks. 'I heard you been moved to da city now, true? I could hardly imagine you mob living in da city now. And ya dad, em right, aye?'

'Yeah, Father's good. And we're not in the city, city, more like on the outskirts of the smaller towns thirty kilometrres from the city. We're just camping around now. Just Luke and me, out near Muchea. We just wanted to come up here to visit. We have some nice dope for sale if you're interested. Really top-quality stuff from Perth.'

'Oh, sweet! I'll grab some from you brus for sure. I can't get it now, though. Come down ere to the Commercial tonight, eh?' He indicates the pub behind him with his thumb over his shoulder. 'I have to get back now, though, okay. My boss he been tell'em me to be real quick an will be expecting me back by now.' Ty speeds off in the direction of the takeaway shop.

'Okay, we'll be there tonight,' we shout to him.

Ty must just grab a pie or something from a pie warmer and a can of Coke because before very long, he darts back across the road and hops in his work car. 'See both of yaz late'az tonight, right? Commercial, eh.' He reverses the vehicle.

'Yeah, okay.'

He flings his arm out the window and gives us the thumbs up.

'Let's grab a few drinks to get us in the mood,' I say.

At the liquor store, Dennis is on shift again but he seems a little more agitated this time. Loui and I ignore his sour face and walk straight past him and over to the fridge. I pull out a six-pack of vodka and lime UDLs.

'Grab a couple of bottles of beer, Loui.'

We go straight to the counter and wait for Dennis to return from his tour of the store. It is clear he has been keeping an eye on us.

'I hope we have enough to sell,' Loui says as we hop back into the Barina. 'I think we're running really low.'

'We might have to tell Ty we sold it all,' I reply. 'I don't want to run out of greens up here. It's too expensive to buy up this way.'

On our way back to our humpy, just out of Meekatharra, we meet the owner of the station we are camped on. He is driving around on the track to our camp when he pulls up alongside us and winds his window down. He motions for me to do the same.

'Hello, fellas, I'm the owner of the station here. Phil Pickle's the name.'

I am glad he does not recognise either of us. It was not long since we went to his homestead with our father to collect a few old Lister engines for the station.

Mr Pickle's eyes scour over our belongings that are stacked messily in the Barina.

'Oh, hello, Mr Pickle. I'm Luke and this here is Loui, my younger brother.'

'I don't mind you guys camping out here as long as you clean up after yourselves,' Mr Pickle says. 'Also, I just wanted to point out that there are dingo baits in the area to control any dogs straying out of town. They're constantly killing my livestock.'

'That's no good,' I reply, shaking my head sympathetically. 'People need to control their dogs a—'

Mr Pickle cuts in before I have a chance to finish my sentence. 'Yeah, well, I've seen your dog wandering around near the highway just up this track and was a bit concerned for it. I suggest that you keep him tied up otherwise he could end up taking up a bait.'

Bob is now approaching us on the track from our camp.

I am quick to respond. 'He knows what they are, and he avoids them. Also, he won't go near your livestock or kill any of them, he's not like that.'

Loui waves Bob around to his side of the car and opens the back door for him to clambers up into the back of the car.

'No worries, fellas, it's all good. Stay as long as you want to, okay?'

'Thank you, Mr Pickle,' Loui and I say together.

Mr Pickle does a U-turn and heads back towards his homestead while Loui and I continue our way back to the camp, waving to him as he drives away.

Back at our camp, I look in the bag of dope. Loui is right. We don't have much left at all to sell.

'We can sell one to Ty, but stuff selling any to anyone else. Otherwise, we'll have to start buying some ourselves in a day or two.'

Loui and I look at each other and let out a snickering laugh.

'We can still go out tonight, though,' Loui says. 'Maybe Ty can shout us a few beers for old times' sake.'

Later, we drive back into town and grab two packets of crumpets, some butter and some noodles. That evening we head to the Commercial Hotel as we previously arranged with Ty. It is packed with drinkers but there is no sign of Ty. Loui and I grab a couple of drinks and talk to some other guys while we wait. After a while, a group of fellas walks in and Ty is with them.

'Hey, look who just walked in,' Loui says, looking over at Ty.

Somehow Ty has heard Loui over the noise in the crowded bar. 'Eh, you made it then?' he shouts. He reaches out and gives us each a handshake like those gangster-style types: a bit of a shake, soul brother monkey grip, and a closed fist punch, then he introduces us to his friends.

'Yeah, we thought you might have got your days mixed up and weren't going to show up tonight,' Loui says.

'Nah, I got hassled by the missus. She wasn't going to let me out tonight, but I said fuck this, eh, I'm gonna see Loui and Luke and av a charge with them two at the pub.'

'Yeah, you got to show them who's the boss, you can't have them controlling you, can you?' Loui replies. 'You only got one life, hey, Ty?'

'Aye d's two brutha boys ere and me, we go way back, aye?' Ty explains to his friends.

Loui and I nod and smile at them. They all follow through with the same style handshake.

Ty and his mates head over to the counter to order some drinks.

'You two right for a charge or wot? It's my shout, I just got my CDP pay today,' Ty says. 'Dhoo pints ob Emu Bitter oh kay?'

'Yes thanks, Ty,' Loui and I reply.

Ty orders our beers.

'You want that stuff then?' I ask.

Ty nods without saying anything.

'It's the last we have, so you better be quick,' Loui explains.

'So, where it den aye, Loui?' Ty has a hungry look in his eyes.

'Yeah, it's right here,' Loui replies, reaching into his pocket.

'Mmm yea, dis iz sweed aye, lez go outside. I have a ssh'moke.' Ty taps his friends on the shoulders, mustering them to follow us outside.

We smoke it all between us, then go back inside for a few more beers before closing time. Ty is spending a lot of money, and we are all getting quite pissed.

'Last calls,' shouts the barman.

Suddenly the bar is packed with people wanting to order their last drinks and takeaways.

'We're going to head back to the camp now, okay,' I say to Ty. 'If you want to come out, you still remember where we told you to find us?'

'Yea, ya jus off da road yea, on da right jus pas tha furs grid, aye?'

'No, look for the first floodway sign. There's a dirt track on the left of it. Just follow that. We'll go and get the fire cranking, so you can find us,' Loui explains as we finish off our drinks.

We take off to have a few cones before the others arrive.

'Shit, there's bugger all here,' I say, passing the weed to Loui. 'We smoked it all besides this last small bud.'

'Gee, let's smoke it quick before they come then.' Loui chops it up and we have a smoke in the darkness.

After a while, we hear a vehicle slowing down on the highway as it approaches the floodway sign. Then it turns off.

'Don't show them where we are just yet,' Loui says as we quickly finish what is left in the mull bowl.

Ty and his mates drive straight past our camp, continuing for another couple of hundred metres, before they realise there are no fresh tyre tracks on the track. They do a U-turn over a couple of fallen trees in their path. We can hear the branches being crushed as they head back in our direction. They are talking loudly, loose from intoxication.

Then one of them yells out, his speech slurred. 'Aye, ere look! Follow this track ere to the right!'

They turn and follow the track around the wing of the humpy to where Loui and I are hollering and doing star jumps and striking our cigarette lighters, acting as though we had been trying to alert them the whole time that they were scouting around looking for us.

Ty and his mates get out. They're all holding beers.

'Ya want a nudda charge or wot?' Ty offers, while taking a huge gulp from the can he has in his hand.

'Yeah, thanks, we forgot to get some before we left,' I say as Ty hands me the beer. 'Cheers!'

'Wod about you, Loui?'

'I'd love one.'

'Where's ya fire?' Ty asks Loui.

'It's gone out but there are some logs over there, so we can make another one.' Loui drags a few branches over and piles them onto the embers.

Ty and his mates stay for about an hour and then one of them says they better get going. By this time, the fire is cranking high.

Ty looks at his mobile to see the time. 'Any more ssh'moke?' he asks.

'Yeah, only resins, though.'

Loui scrapes the bong and scores a few cones. He passes the bong around, but one fella falls short of getting one, so Loui improvises and thumb screws straight tobacco into the cones and hands it to the last fella. Without hesitation, he ignites it and smokes it straight down, holding it in for a few brief seconds, before coughing his guts up. Loui tells me what's going on and we have a chuckle.

'You're going to get it from your missus when you get home,' another one of Ty's mates says.

Ty shakes his head. 'Yeah, well, I better get gowen den. Maybe I see ya before ya's head back ta tha city, aye?' He gives us the stylish gangster handshake again.

His mates follow suit, and they all get in the vehicle.

'Yeah, we'll be back,' Loui tells him. 'We had a lot of fun up here.'

After they leave, at the expense of Ty's mate, Loui and I burst into laughter, and keep laughing until tears stream down our faces and our stomachs cramp.

The next day, we hunt around town with the last bit of money we have left to score a deal for ourselves. I ask around to find out where Vee is living, and we go to see if she can help us out. We are told to come back later that evening because she has some stuff coming up from Geraldton. So we go to the shop and get another packet of crumpets each, our meals for the next few days until Loui's Centrelink pay comes through.

When we return later that evening, we manage to score. On our way back to camp, a police car which has been patrolling the area starts following us. Fortunately, we are driving parallel to each other and there is a block of land between us. I swing off at the intersection and head away from them, but they also swing in our direction. When I notice they are speeding up a bit, I take the turn-off at the next intersection and go faster to try to leave them behind. The cops do not have their flashing lights or siren on, and soon I am starting to lose them. A couple of black fellas on foot see us losing the patrol car and stop, allowing me to swing onto the gravel track beside the townhouses on the outskirts of town.

By this time, I have switched off my lights and am avoiding using the brake. I just put on the high-beam lights manually from time to time so we can see where we are going. With no taillights, we are almost invisible. We play a little cat and mouse, but the police are too far behind us to catch up without alerting us that they are actually chasing us. As we speed off up the dirt track towards the water tanks, it is hard for them to figure out where we have gone. At the top of the hill, I pull up using the handbrake. The Barina screams to a stop. Back down towards the town, the police are still searching for us on the dirt tracks behind the townhouses.

'I knew they were trying to catch us,' I exclaim.

'Yeah, that was a real good idea. I'm going to turn my lights off too if they ever chase me,' Loui laughs.

'Better throw it all in the bowl in case they follow our tracks,' I say.

We catch our breath first. Then we go through the weed like Cyclone Tracy hitting Darwin, leaving nothing but the remnants behind. It has been more of a rush running from the cops than we had from the crappy weed we got in Meekatharra.

'Now we have nothing left but the resins and some crumpets until Wednesday.'

'Yeah, six crumpets each,' Loui replies. 'That's two a day.'

'Better not light the fire tonight. We don't want them finding us and taking the only thing we have left,' I say wearily.

'No, we sure don't.'

The next few days are hard for us, so we just stay out at the camp and conserve our energy. On the morning Loui's pay is due, we go around Meekatharra and say goodbye to people we know. We fill the Barina up and are glad to be on our way back to Muchea.

'If we get there in good time, let's go straight around to Rod's and get a decent bag of weed,' Loui says.

I don't need any convincing.

23

Rod's Jobs

We get back to Muchea around eight that evening. Rod is sitting outside with a few of his workers when we pull up.

'Who's that there?' he asks, as we walk up his driveway in the darkness.

'Just us.'

'Oh, I was just asking if anyone had seen you lately, Rod says. 'What have you guys been up to for the past week or so?'

I tell him we've been up to Meekatharra to do some fencing on a station up there for someone we know and have only just got back. I always tell Rod we are busy doing stuff like that, because then it sounds like we are not just a pair of lazy black fellas. I have heard that term too many times in the past, and I do not like it, even though we do tend to laziness when we feel fucked, just like anyone else, black or white.

'I got a Land Cruiser there I'd like you to replace the rear diff in if you want to make yourselves some extra money or something,' Rod says, taking a swig from his can of Woodstock.

Rod often offers us work. He makes a lot of his money by wheeling and dealing in cars and weed. If you can make a dollar from it, Rod is into it. He is a good friend of mine to this day, and even though we have not seen each other in twenty-plus years, and that chapter of my life is well behind me, I still value his friendship and we keep in touch.

'Yeah, we'll come over first thing in the morning and do it for you,' I say.

I look at the can of Woodstock. The condensation is running down the side of the can and onto the table.

'Grab yourself one from the fridge if you like,' Rod offers.

Loui goes over to the fridge and returns with a can for each for us.

'Cheers,' I say as I crack the can.

'So where are you setting up camp now?' Rod asks.

'Umm, not sure yet.'

'Have you looked at that shed out on Robinson Road I told you about yet?'

'No, but we'll check it out. Where is it exactly?'

'Not far from here,' Rod replies.

One of Rod's workers cuts him off before he can tell us much more about the shed and says he has got to get going.

'Yeah, we might get a bit of weed from you and hit the road too,' I say. 'I'm stuffed from the long drive.'

Rod reaches into the top pocket of his flannelette shirt and passes me some dope.

'No problem, fellas. I'll see you tomorrow.'

'For sure, Rod.'

The next morning, after spending the night back at our former campsite, we take off to the servo to grab a free coffee each and have a nice hot shower. We really need to wash off all the dirt and grime from camping out at Meekatharra.

When we arrive at his place to do the Land Cruiser for him, Rod asks if I have come alone, having seen me walking up his driveway by myself.

'No, Loui's in the Barina. He's just rolling himself a cigarette.'

'Morning, Loui. You've come to help your brother with the diff replacement?' Rod asks.

'Yeah, I figured we could get it done quicker if there were two of us on the job.'

Over the next few days, we help Bob out, working solidly, until we decide to take another break.

'We have to go down to Collie now,' I say at the end of our last job.

'Okay. What are you doing down there?' Rod asks.

'I promised a mate down there that we'd help him with things for a couple of days. He has a marron farm.'

Rod looks surprised at how many people we know around WA. 'So when do you think you'll be back up this way again? Some of my friends have specifically requested you to do some work for them.'

'We'll only be down there a couple of days, mate.'

Sometimes, Loui and I just go for a drive and camp around Collie, maybe spending a bit of time with my mate Snappy who lives on a marron farm about thirty kilometres away from his grandparents.

Snappy smokes dope too, and we like to take a session out to him and sit around his place for a few days getting stoned out of our heads. His mum brings him supplies from town; often it is pizza singles. We eat, smoke, drink, sleep, and repeat. He is always mucking around building stuff, and he is always keen to show me his new inventions.

He likes messing about with small electric motors he finds inside broken DVD players or other electronic items. After seeing the ones I used to make, he starts making mullamatics, which use electric motors taken from broken cassette players and attached to the inside of the lid of a plastic jar. You put a few chopping blades inside the jar, then fill it with marijuana and screw the lid back on. Then you connect the motor and turn the power on. It saves a lot of time, compared to manually chopping up weed. He is really proud of them.

One time, Snappy cooks me a nice big freshwater crayfish, also known as a marron. He slices it from the tip of its head to the end of its tail, then puts the two halves shell down on the barbecue with garlic and butter over the top. It is so nice and I often think about how he has done it.

A few years earlier, Snappy pranged his panel van when he lost control of the vehicle and wrapped it around a tree. His throttle foot was squashed, and the boot he was wearing at the time was embedded in the mangled mess of the floor pan next to the accelerator. He was lucky to escape but kept the vehicle out the front of his place.

After a while, he got himself another panel van. Slowly he removed the salvageable parts from the wreck he had on blocks and put them onto this more recent panel van. For some reason, this became a big job for him. He was always messing around with it, and he really liked his project car, but he hardly ever drove it. I think he was still too nervous to drive but he never said that to anyone. What it meant, though, was that about ninety-nine per cent of the time, Snappy was home, which was good for us because we could always count on him being there.

We really enjoy getting outdoors with Snappy. He loves playing cricket or kicking the football around, and he is always keen to go camping at Wellington Dam, no matter what time of the year. From the first week in January to the first week in February, during the marron season, this huge water catchment reservoir is usually packed out with campsites.

24

Stormy Night

A few days later, we head back to Muchea. It is starting to get colder as the weeks go by. The night we get back, there is a big storm, with strong winds and heavy rain. We go to see Rod and have a few cones with him and the other guys who we have gotten to know quite well over the past eighteen months at his workshop.

Once again, Rod mentions the large abandoned shed a few kilometres away, down a deserted road. It is owned by the Royal Australian Air Force.

'You should go check out that shed,' he says. 'There's also a small run-down house out there that you could squat in.'

'Whereabouts is it?' I ask for not the first time.

'Just head down the road here and look for a few white lette boxes on the right-hand side of the road. Then turn up the dirt road and follow it for about two kilometres. You'll know you're on the right track because there's a sharp right turn about a kilometre along. It then turns sharply left a few hundred metres further on. Just continue along the track, and you'll see the shed out in an opening on the right.'

Now we have the exact location, we decide to set off straight after the session with Rod and the others. The wind has been blowing hard all afternoon with heavy downpours, and it is still blowing a gale as we drive down the bitumen road after leaving Rod's place. We swerve past small branches that have fallen from the trees along the nature strip. Eventually, we find the road Rod has told us about.

'This is it, I'm sure of it. What do you think?' I ask Loui.

He unbuckles his seatbelt and slides himself on his seat to peer through the fogged-up windscreen. 'Yeah, he said there were a few white letter boxes in a row all together where we needed to turn off.' Loui uses his fingers like a squeegee to wipe some condensation off the windscreen.

We're both happy to have come across the right place, and I pull off the bitumen onto the dirt track cautiously, dodging more branches. By now, the rain has become even heavier, and it is hard to see the road in the gloom. We drive slowly along on the track, our eyes scanning through the darkness for the shed.

We are just about to turn back when we spot it, exactly where Rod has said it would be. We turn off the dirt road and drive through an open farm gate all the way up to the shed. Two big sliding doors are lying on the ground, one in front of one entrance. It looks like hooligans have used it to get their cars up onto the concrete pad in the shed to do burnouts.

We manage to get the Barina into the shed and bunker in, not daring to step outside, fearful the winds will rock us from side to side like a couple of rag dolls. Hay swirls around inside the shed, covering the window in fine loose chaff. It is pitch-dark outside and there is not a single sign of life.

'This could be a good place for us to stay,' I say.

Loui and I sleep in the Barina inside the shed that night while the storm blows around us. At times, it feels as though we are sleeping on a ship that is drifting around in rough seas.

In the morning, we take a good look around. The shed is about twelve by nine metres, with a pitched roof about three metres high. Six poles, about three metres apart, hold up the main roof rafters, which are evenly spaced inside the structure.

The storm has abated now, and after a coffee and a poke around outside, we notice some ruins not far away. We jump in the Barina and drive down for a closer look. All the while, I am on the lookout for some materials I could use to enclose the shed. Luckily, there are plenty of long lengths of timber and corrugated iron lying around that I can salvage; enough to put up some room dividers.

I start carting some lengths of timber back by hand and set about making a kitchen area by tying a few pieces of timber to the support poles using fencing wire which I removed from the fence. I leave enough space for a doorway to a future lounge area, and another doorway to a future passage, to a future shower area.

As I am busy constructing, a vehicle comes through the open gate and up to the shed. I walk out to see what they want, but they just keep driving, doing a full loop around the shed and back out the gate. I go over and shut the gate, straight after they have left to stop anyone else just popping in.

A barbed wire fence runs parallel to one side of the shed, about twenty metres away. I strip enough wire off to make a five-strand fence from this fence to the shed, then drag an old farm gate over from the ruins of the shed, to make a second gate, between the shed and the existing fence line. I also remove some posts from further up and dig them in to make a new fence. This should stop anyone from driving around the shed.

Next, I salvage an old, smashed-up Metters stovetop that is lying outside on the ground. I wire it back up and put it on an air conditioner box which is the right size. Then I wire a piece of steel below the stovetop for the fire to sit on and stick a few rims inside it. I finish by putting another sheet of steel on top so we can cook things on it like toasted sandwiches or pizzas.

Later, I find a piece of flue from the ruins, which completes the stove. Over the next few months, we are safe to stay there, as long as we remain under the radar. And because we can now cook a lot of our meals ourselves, the stove also keeps us warm on cold days and nights.

I string a few lights around which run off the car battery and put the TV in the kitchen so we can sit in the warmth and watch our favourite programs. An old table and a couple of chairs which we find down at one of the ruins go straight into the kitchen area I have made, which makes mealtimes a whole lot more comfortable.

RAAF aeroplanes are constantly flying overhead so we try to stay out of sight as much as possible, to avoid attracting attention. But one day, a few weeks later, when I have finished lining the shed, Loui and I are sitting in the kitchen watching TV, when we hear a vehicle pull up. We peek out and see it is an RAAF patrol vehicle. I motion to Loui to turn the TV off, and we sit there not saying a word.

'RAAF police,' an officer yells out. The guy walks around to where the Barina is parked in the shed. 'Hello… RAAF police here. Is anyone in there?'

He is so close to walking in and finding us just sitting there but we stay quiet. We know what he will say, and we do not feel like leaving.

Bob, who has been asleep under the table, lifts his head up. I put my index finger up to my lips. Bob looks at me for a couple of seconds, then lies back down and closes his eyes again. We hear a car door open and shut, the engine starts, and we hear the vehicle turn around and head back out onto the track.

Now that we have a place to settle for the time being, we arrange for our Centrelink forms to be delivered to our new address. I go down to the turn-off where the letter boxes are and check further along the road in both directions. When I feel happy about our location, I come up with a number for us. Back at the shed, I find an old rectangle-shaped thirty-litre water container. I cut a slit in the front to take letters, and a larger opening in the back so we can collect them. I write Lot 87 onto the container, take it down to the turn-off, sit it alongside the other letter boxes, and put a brick inside to stop it blowing away. This simple, yet very effective letter box solution, standing among the other letter boxes on Robinson Road, serves its purpose, until we eventually leave.

The following day, we head straight into Midland to sort out things with Centrelink so we can get our fortnightly forms posted to us. I also change the details on my driver's licence.

A few days later, I pull the car up next to the letter boxes and Loui jumps out to check if we have got anything.

His face is beaming as he leans over and pulls out a pile of letters. 'There's quite a few here,' he says, getting back into the car. He shuffles through them, pulling out the ones addressed to him and handing the rest to me.

'These all look like they're from Centrelink. I'll have a look at them when we get back to the shed,' I say, shoving my mail on the dash above the instrument panel.

Loui opens his mail as we head back to the shed. 'Yay, I got my Centrelink form,' he yells in excitement. He holds it up so I can see it.

At least it is not a major form, I think. Every six weeks, Centrelink requires jobseekers to supply the names and contact details of six businesses you've applied to for work. Staff at Centrelink are known to call up the contacts you have listed to check if you have been looking for work.

When we get back to the shed, I go through my mail. Loui breaks up some small twigs and shoves his torn envelopes under them in the fireplace below the stove top. When the fire catches, he shoves a couple of larger pieces of wood in and sits with his back to me, warming his hands.

'I got my new licence,' I say, 'with the new address on it.' I tap Loui on the shoulder and hold it up like I have won first prize in a competition.

Loui spins around, as though a spider has just landed on his shoulder. 'You scared the shit out of me,' he laughs.

'I guess this will help keep track of the speeding fines I always seem to be getting,' I say, removing my old licence from my wallet and slipping my new one in.

It feels good getting mail again, like receiving a free newspaper. The new mailbox set-up works well, and we even start getting junk mail – catalogues from Coles, Woolworths and Kmart, and discount vouchers for deals with McDonald's and Eagle Boys pizzas. The letters from Centrelink, though, only have the same old shit in them every time.

Have you looked for work in the past fourteen days? List two businesses and phone numbers you have contacted in the past fourteen days while looking for work.

The forms are quite basic but if you don't return them by the due date, you do not get paid until you have submitted them.

After three months of living out at the shed, Tristan, a fella a couple of months younger than Loui, who we have got to know from helping Rod out, asks if he can join us.

'Yeah, that'll be cool,' we agree.

Tristan is also on a Centrelink income but I am sure we will manage.

One day, Tristan finds an abandoned wreck. He throws a battery he got from Rod in it, and after tinkering around and putting a couple of litres of petrol in the tank, he gets it running. It always stalls, though; then he has to mess around with it again. Tristan loves his wreck, but after he has been staying with us for about four weeks, one day it stalls out in the open down by the gate where he has been hooning back and forth along the dirt road. That is how the RAAF police finally catch us out.

A RAAF patrol vehicle pulls up, and four officers get out.

Tristan is still messing around with his wreck. The officers approach him to get his details.

'Hello,' one of them begins. 'We're RAAF police, based not far from here at the Pearce base. You probably know where I'm talking about.'

'Mmmm, yeah. I know where that is.' Tristan nods a couple of times briefly.

The officers all introduce themselves.

'I'm David Spearson, and these officers are Jim Reed, Justin Turner and Gary Franklin. This is RAAF property. Are you aware you are trespassing on private property?' Franklin asks.

'Err, I don't know,' Tristian gloomily replies.

'What's your full name, buddy? And what's your address and date of birth?' Franklin sternly demands.

Tristan looks up, grabs a rag he has been using to dry inside the distributor cap and starts to clean the oil from his hands. He picks up the rollie that he left on the air cleaner cover. 'Tristan Jon Sole. My date of birth is 13 January 1985. I live here with those two guys.' He points in our direction, as he puts the rollie between his lips and lights up.

'Officer Reed and I will head down to the shed to grab those two fellas' details,' Officer Spearson says as they set off on foot towards us.

'I may as well take the patrol car down to the shed. You'll be all right to finish getting what you need here from Tristan, won't you, Officer Turner?' Franklin asks.

'Yeah, no worries. I'll meet you there shortly.'

Turner gets into the vehicle and follows Spearson and Reed, who are now over halfway down to the shed, where Loui and I are waiting. Bob strolls out from the shed, catches a glimpse of the officers, and suddenly goes running off towards them. They stop still in their tracks and raise their arms high fearing they will be bitten.

'Oi, Bob. Come'ear.' Loui quickly calls him back.

'Hello, are you living here?' Spearson asks.

'Yes, there's three of us living out here,' I reply.

The officers introduce themselves to me and ask for my full name, date of birth and address.

'I'm Luke Pomery and my date of birth is 25 May 1975. We have no fixed address, and we're squatting here. Loui also lives here, and we are brothers. And I don't have a middle name. Tristan is also staying with us.'

'Yes, I gathered that. Oh, no middle name, hey? That's unusual. Nearly everyone has one these days,' Spearson replies as he looks back and forth at Loui and me, trying to look for a resemblance in our features, while jotting down my details in his notebook.

The officers walk around the fence and through the gate. I follow them to see where they are going but Loui stays back to wait for the officer who is about to pull up any second. When Turner pulls up, he goes over to Loui, his notepad in hand, and it is the same rigmarole, all over again.

'Loui Pomery, my date of birth is the twenty-second of the eighth, 1984.'

Turner writes down his details and then asks, 'So what's in here,' as he heads towards the front door.

'Oh, this is the dining room,' I hear Loui reply as they disappear inside.

I follow the other officers around to the other side of the shed, where the Barina is parked.

'None of this was here when I came out here a few months ago,' Spearson says to Reed.

'No, the last time I came out here, there was just a run-down shed that cows used to get out of the weather.'

Reed stops walking and takes down the registration details from the Barina's number plate.

'Did you do all this work here?' he asks.

'Yes,' I tell him. 'I wanted it to be just like a home for us, because we're homeless, you know.'

'Well, you certainly have managed to do that. I might want to live out here myself,' he jokes.

He catches up with Spearson, who's just finishing up writing down some details. Next thing, Turner appears from behind the tarp with Loui beside him. He holds it open for Reed and Spearson to enter and I follow behind them.

'The tarp's just a cheap way to close off this section from the open air,' I explain.

Spearson continues writing in his notebook.

'What's in there?' Reed asks, walking over to another tarped-off area.

Turner holds back the tarp to reveal our showering facilities. 'They catch water from the gutter on this side of the shed in this old oil drum, then boil water on the stove and add it to get the right temperature,' Turner tells him. 'The whole set-up's operated by two windscreen wiper motors that run off the car battery. The water's pumped through that hose into the shower head.'

Reed is speechless.

'And you should see the rest of the shed. It's amazing. They even have lighting and a TV. And there's a front door and veranda that you haven't seen yet because you came around the other way.'

Spearson and Reed follow behind Turner as he gives them a tour. Franklin joins in along the way, as do Loui and Tristan, and we all make our way from room to room.

'It's very nicely set out, Luke,' Turner says, as they take in our bedrooms. 'I like your floor plan. It's nice and easy. Wow, you've even fixed up the old Metters stove that's been lying around here for years.'

Reed walks over and starts rubbing his hands together. I'm sure it's to warm them, but it looks like he's just thought of some evil plan to get rid of us permanently.

'Yeah, we had one out on the station where we grew up,' I explain. 'They're really good to cook on. I had to wire this one back together because the top had been smashed up. The bottom part is an old air-conditioner casing which just happened to be a perfect fit.'

Reed studies it closely.

'Where does all the power come from?' Franklin asks. 'There's no electricity connected out here.'

I explain how it is all twelve-volt and that I have put a plug on the front of the Barina. 'The battery provides enough for one or two lights, but if we're not careful we can get caught out and all life is drained out of the car. A few times now, we've had to push start it.'

Loui nods in agreement, looking at Bob, who's scratching his neck with his back leg. Earlier that morning, he has eaten a rotten chunk of a kangaroo I snared for him almost a week ago and he has been doing some rotten farts all day. Sure enough, the room suddenly fills with putrid gas.

'Errr, what's that rotten smell?' Reed gags.

The officers all look around the kitchen area. We all look at Bob.

'My dog has been eating some rotten meat,' I explain.

Loui, Tristan, and I all laugh, as the officers quickly make their way outside.

'You can't stay here,' Spearson says when we join them for some fresh air. 'You'll have to move out within forty-eight hours, okay.' He hands me a notice to vacate the property.

I look at it, pretend that I'm reading it and shove it in my back pocket.

'If you're still here in two days' time, we'll have you arrested for trespassing, do you all understand?'

The officers get back into the vehicle. Reed's in the driver's seat. He turns the key and starts the engine.

'It's forty-eight hours, okay, guys?' comes Spearson's voice.

'Yes,' we all reply, and they drive off.

'Well, at least we got to stay here for four months, hey?' I say, turning to Loui and Tristan.

We go back inside the shed, and Loui and I start packing our things up into the Barina. Tristan avoids me because he can tell I am pissed off at him. I feel like dropping him off at Rod's and have nothing more to do with him, but he has become the third leg of our tripod, and we have come to rely on him for our survival.

Once everything is packed up, we take off straightaway in case the RAAF police change their minds and come back to arrest us.

25

Take Two

We soon find another place to stay, but once again it is short-lived, thanks to Tristan. The old run-down house with a couple of sheds we come across not far from the rubbish dump has been abandoned for some time, judging by the old glass milk bottles and ring-pull soda cans that are scattered around; my guess is since the 1980s. This place is further out of town, but we soon find ourselves at the dump in the early evenings, looking for petrol and anything we can sell to Rod.

Meanwhile, Tristan manages to find his way into a locked shed used by dump workers as a kitchen store, but there is no food, or even any tea or coffee. There is a car, though, and Tristan decides to take it.

'I wouldn't,' I say. I don't mind taking petrol but a whole car is just going to attract unwanted attention. And none of us need that.

'Look at this,' Loui says one time, holding up a tobacco pipe he has found on a shelf.

'Oh, cool, just what I always wanted,' I say.

'No, Luke, it's mine, but I don't mind sharing it with you.'

We start using the pipe straight away because it means any tobacco we have is not going to be wasted at the end of the rollie.

Loui and I know Tristan cannot stop thinking about the car in the shed, and even though he knows I do not want him to touch it, that does not stop him.

Late one afternoon when Loui and I are out at our new camp, I am cooking a small damper made with the last of our flour, when Tristan comes back from the rubbish dump. He has been on a mission to find petrol for the Barina.

'Did you find any fuel?' I ask him, noticing the flushed look on his face.

Tristan sits down and packs a pipe of tobacco. 'No, but I got that car out of the shed,' he says.' I pushed it down the hill and it nearly started but then it got to the fence and got tangled up there.'

'Fucken hell, you were going to get petrol, not to steal that car,' I growl.

'Where's the car now?' Loui asks him.

'It's next to the main road before you turn off to the dump.'

'What, so everyone who drives past can see it there?' I ask.

'Yeah, I guess,' Tristan replies.

'For fuck's sake, we can't fucken leave it there, can we, you fucken dickhead. We'll have to try and move it right now. Come on, let's do it before anyone sees it there.'

I'm furious and give Tristan a dirty look. Loui's fuming too, and I can tell he just wants to knock Tristan out, then and there.

For the next couple of hours, we try to free the car. By early evening it still has not budged, so we end up having to leave it there.

Two days later, early in the morning, we are all still asleep when a vehicle pulls up, and two white guys get out. One of them is waving a shotgun around at Bob, who has run over to them. The hairs on his back are standing on end, and he lets out some savage-sounding barks followed by a few deep snarls. The guy with the shotgun works at the rubbish dump, and the other guy must be his friend because I have not seen him before.

Suddenly, the dump guy has the shotgun barrel pointed at Bob. 'Hold onto that fucken dog,' he demands.

Loui quickly gets between the gunman and Bob. 'Bob, come here,' Loui calls him in his deep voice.

Bob walks over to Loui; he knows he's in trouble. The hairs on his back droop but are still ruffled up. Loui gets a hold of him.

Then the gunman starts waving his shotgun at me. 'Whose fucken idea was it to fucken take that car?'

I look round at Tristan. 'It was his idea,' I reply. 'I told him we didn't want him to touch it, but he went to the dump on his own.'

The gunman turns to Tristan. 'I know your parents, you little prick. They're really nice people and they'd be ashamed to hear how far you've stooped,' he says sternly. 'I would've expected more from someone like you. But then again, on the other hand, what can anyone expect when you're hanging around thieving coons?'

The guy points his shotgun at Tristan's kneecaps. It looks like he's deciding whether to fire off a round to scare the shit out of him. Then he tells us to get our stuff and fuck off, adding that if we ever come back, we will be sorry.

We grab all our belongings and pile them into the Barina.

'Now fuck off, and don't fucken come back here ever again, I'm warning you.'

'Don't worry, you won't see us again,' I say.

Our nerves are pretty shot by now, and I am bloody glad to get away from those two guys. But my anger is still raging.

'I told you not to touch that fucken car, you fucken dickhead,' I shout at Tristan.

He just looks out the window and doesn't say a thing.

'Now where can we go?' I ask Loui. 'Just as well you got paid today, otherwise, we'd be totally fucked.'

'Maybe back down to Collie or something,' he replies. 'Perhaps we can go out to Snappy's place?'

'Nah, he wouldn't like it if we just roll up with someone he doesn't know. We'll have to camp out in the bush again for a while. At least I know a lot of places down that way that haven't got mad gunmen running around to move us on.'

I look into the rear-vision mirror, but Tristan is still failing to make eye contact with me. If we didn't have him with us, we'd still be living at the RAAF shed, I think, and not be struggling like we have been since he joined us. Even when Tristan gets paid, he blows his cash all in one day on a small packet of tobacco, a carton of UDLs and a bag of dope. If we were lucky, he would buy some takeaway food. By the end of the day, the carton would be finished and so would three-quarters of the dope and the tobacco, and we would have no food. He had done it every time, and now it is really shitting me off.

I glance over at Loui. 'At least we could catch up with my other mate down there, Bratt, who I've told you about before. He grows some really nice weed.'

'Is he the one who grows those purple buds?'

'Yeah, that's him.'

I look in the rear-vision mirror once again, and Tristan makes eye contact with me for the first time in about an hour.

'Can you pack me a pipe?' I ask Loui.

'There isn't much tobacco left, but yeah.'

When we arrive at Collie, we drive straight around to Bratt's place. He comes out onto his veranda to see who has pulled up in his driveway. A big smile spreads across his face, and his eyes are beaming.

'Luke, how the fuck have you been, man? It's been a couple of years now, hasn't it?'

I open the car door and get out. 'Yeah, mate, it has.'

Bratt looks at the others.

'This is my brother Loui and Tristan, a friend of ours.'

'How are you guys doing? Do you want to come in for some cones?' Bratt asks. 'I only have leaf and tip on me at the moment, but that you can have that for nothing, Luke, if you're interested. And if I know you, you don't knock anything back. I haven't got anything for sale now, though, just some personal stuff from last season. Maybe in a few weeks' time, around mid-September, I'll have something that will definitely be worth buying, if you're still around.'

'Yeah, I'll take some of that off your hands,' I say as we follow Bratt into his house and sit down around the kitchen table.

'Do any of you want a coffee?' Bratt asks.

I tell him we would, and that we all drink ours the same way, with a heaped teaspoon of coffee, one sugar and some milk.

'Where's Miley?' I ask.

'Oh, she went to Bunbury with her mum. A sale on at Target or something. Anyway, it's good that she's not here, otherwise she'd probably tell you to piss off, especially you, Luke,' Bratt laughs as he fills the kettle up.

Bratt grabs four cups from a cupboard above the kettle, which by now is making a noise like heavy rain on a tin roof. From a cupboard below the sink, he pulls out a mull bowl that has a bag of dope in it and slides it across the table to me.

'I don't smoke it mixed with tobacco,' he reminds me. 'So just pack me some bud straight from the bag into the cone. But you're more than welcome to add some to your own mix if you like, hey. Use the bowl to chop up into.'

Tristan leans forward as I pull a couple of decent-sized nuggets from the bag, and Loui's eyes light up when he sees the purple tinge.

'I see you still have that purple jacaranda strand,' I say, holding a bud up to my nose and inhaling the scent deep into my lungs.

'Yeah, it's been my best season ever this year.' Bratt hands us our coffee. 'Your brother and I have done loads of things together around here, haven't we, mate? He's a really good guy to know,' Bratt pats me on the shoulder as he sits down next to me.

'This guy is really good at diving,' I add. 'We used to go diving in the Collie River quite a lot, didn't we?'

'Yeah, we've done our fair share of fishing for marron for sure,' Bratt responds.

Bratt's gaze settles on Loui. 'So, Loui, you must be the one with all the good looks, hey? I've met your older brother Bryce, and your sister Bidjid once or twice, many years ago now and they certainly weren't that crash hot. Then there's Luke. Let's face it, he certainly didn't end up with anything special, did he?' Bratt laughs and slaps me on the shoulder once again, this time a little harder. 'Nah, I was only joking, mate.'

'I wouldn't say that,' Loui says, and a burst of laughter fills the room.

'So what are you doing hanging around with these black fellas for, Tristan?' Bratt asks.

'These two blokes are really awesome, and they know lots of places and people around the whole state that I would have never had the chance to see or meet, such as yourself, Bratt, and this lovely town,' Tristan replies, looking around at us all.

After we have passed the bong around a few times, we are all stoned out of our minds. Bratt pulls open the cupboard nearest to him, takes out about four ounces of leaf and tip, and gives it to me.

'This is for you guys to take. You'll find a lot of nice tips in amongst this,' Bratt says as he hands me the bag. His eyes are blazing red like hot coals, and he has a huge grin on his face.

'Oh wow, thanks a lot, man. This will help us out heaps, hey. Cheers.'

'Where are you fellas off to now?' Bratt asks.

'I'm going to take Loui and Tristan down to show them the river. I might even jump in and have a wash, depending on how the water is.'

Loui rolls the bag of weed over and looks closely at the contents. 'That looks like it's all from the top of the plant,' he says.

Bratt just nods and we all head outside.

'Thanks for the cuppa and the session, and most of all the leaf and tip, mate,' I say, patting the bag that I have tucked up under my jumper.

'Really good to meet you, Bratt,' Loui says.

'Yeah, same ere, and thanks for the coffee. It was one of the best I've had in a very long time,' Tristan adds.

'Make sure you drop in again, you guys.'

I promise Bratt we will and say that if he is going down to the Collie pub on Friday night, maybe we will catch up with him again there.

'Yeah, for sure.'

'No worries, mate. We'll be there around nine.'

26

River Rat

Spring has arrived and the weather is starting to heat up. We pull up at the Collie River and sit for a while, watching families enjoying themselves in the water. Some kids are on the sand at the river's edge, building sandcastles; others splash around in the shallow water, their parents and older siblings wading in beyond.

'Wow, this reminds me of the Moolapool pool back on the station,' Loui says.

'Yeah, there are a few good swimming spots around Collie. I'll show you to them while we're here,' I respond.

Tristan kicks off his shoes and socks and wades out up to his thighs. He stands there with his cigarette hanging out his mouth.

'I might go through the bag of weed Bratt gave us and pull out some of those small buds to do a mix,' Loui says.

'Yeah, get enough for a few cones each, okay?'

A lady walking her dog passes just by where we ae parked. She catches a glimpse of Loui looking through the bag of dope in the front of the Barina but pretends she has not seen anything. When I walk over to the car, Loui is in the driver's seat sorting out the small buds from the leaf.

'Gee, that lady with her dog just saw what you were doing,' I say to Loui quietly. 'You should leave that now. No, pass it here,' I demand, feeling quite annoyed at him.

Loui discreetly passes me the bag. I walk off into the bushes several metres away and hide it under a small shrub.

'Go and hide the bong and mull container now,' I say, when I get back.

Tristan returns from the river and starts to roll himself another cigarette. 'What's going on with the mix?' he asks. 'I thought you were going to chop up a sesh.'

'A lady spotted us, and I think she's called the cops. We'll give it twenty minutes just in case,' I reply, looking each way up the track for police.

No more than five minutes pass before a couple of police cars head towards where we are parked. The cops all get out of their vehicles and crowd around in front of me as I lean back on the driver's side door.

'Hello, guys. I'm Sergeant Gary Dickerson, and these officers are Constables Harry Maze, Tim Mutton and Frank Gaston.

I tell him our first names.

'Well, lads, we've been told by a member of the public that you may have some cannabis in your possession. Is that true?' Dickerson asks.

'No, we don't have anything,' I calmly answer.

'Okay then, if you have nothing to hide, you won't mind if we have a quick look.'

With his fingertip, Dickerson indicates to the other officers to begin searching the Barina.

'Nah, it's all good.' I step away from the car and stand closer to Dickerson.

'Thank you, Luke,' Maze says, happy he's now got easy access to the driver's side.

'Nah, that's perfectly all right, officer.'

'Do you have the registration papers for this vehicle?' Dickerson asks, pulling out his notebook.

'Yes, they're just in the glovebox. Can you grab them for us please, Loui?'

'Can you please pass me those registration papers in the glovebox, officer?' Loui asks Mutton, who is in the passenger seat by now.

Mutton opens the glovebox. 'Here you go.'

Dickerson starts writing down the rego details and then asks us all for our personal details. 'Pomery?' Dickerson ponders. 'Now that name rings a bell. Did you use to live in Collie by any chance?'

He stands back a little to get a better look at me.

'Yes, from the end of 1994 for about six months. Then I went back to my dad's station out near Meekatharra for a while but lived here again from April 1996 to the end of 1999. I used to work at Collie Steel, and sometimes I'd go out in the work truck and do sandblasting jobs on site.'

'Yes, now I remember you. Didn't you apply for your truck licence? You aced your theory test, and even the practical. I was impressed, but I took a point off for not using your indicators, even though you had, because I had seen you hooning around Collie quite often not indicating, as I explained at the time. Do you remember that?'

'Yes, I was as nervous as hell that day. So, you became a sergeant, hey?' I reply.

'Yes, indeed, I did. It hasn't been easy, but I'm enjoying it. Now I can tell my constables what to do.'

Just then, the lady with the dog comes back. She gawks at me with a 'ha' look on her face, so I raise my top lip at her and show my teeth. She turns her head away. Dickerson still has his head down taking notes, when Mutton pulls out a hose that we use for the bong from under the front passenger seat.

'What's this?' he asks me as he passes the hose to Sergeant Dickerson.

'Ha, yeah, just a pipe from the air cleaner on the car. It fell off the other day when I shut the bonnet, and I couldn't figure out where it belongs.'

Dickerson holds the hose up to his nose and inhales. He passes it to me with a doubtful look on his face. By now, Gaston has returned.

'Nothing at all, sergeant, no evidence of cannabis or any paraphernalia at all.' He turns his gaze towards me and studies the hose which I now have in my hand.

Mutton and Gaston look very annoyed, but they have nothing on us. Maze continues to search frantically but soon realises it is useless.

'I'm extremely sorry for ruining your afternoon, boys,' the sergeant apologises. 'I hope you can enjoy the rest of this lovely day.'

'No worries, sergeant, you were only doing your job. I'd never stand in the way of you protecting the community.'

27

Bibbulmun Track

After the cops leave, we quickly gather our possessions from their temporary hidey holes and move on.

We pitch the tent a few metres off to the side of the Bibbulmun Track, a hiking trail that runs from Kalamunda, east of Perth, to Albany in the south. I used to explore round here often on my own, when I lived in Collie a few years earlier, and have never seen or heard of anyone using it. A derelict, unused, track like this is an ideal spot for us to set up camp.

A few days later, though, it seems a hiker must have come across our site when we are in town and reported it to the police. Friday night comes around, and we shove Bob into the tent and zip it up before heading into town to meet up with Bratt as organised a few days earlier.

Around nine p.m., I pull up in a car park. On one side is the shopping complex, on the other side is a train line, and beyond that a little bit further, is another road where the pubs are.

There are four pubs in Collie within a two-hundred-metre strip of the main street. It is a big coal mining town, catering for lots of miners who come to the pubs for after-work drinks, counter meals and budget accommodation.

This night, there are a lot of people out the front of the pubs, and they are rather rowdy. A police car is patrolling the side of street where the shopping centre is. At the exact moment the cops pass us, someone in the crowd beyond sets off an explosion. It makes a huge noise. The brake lights on the cop car instantly burn up and the car swings around.

Tristan races across the train track and joins the crowd out the front of one of the pubs, while Loui and I quickly jump over the train line fence and make our way, as fast as we can, across the tracks. The cops still cannot see us as they come into the car park, so we continue at a steady pace through the nature strip until, out of the blue, the cops pull up and shine a spotlight directly onto us.

'You two!' an officer yells. It sounds like Mutton from the other day.

As we turn around, all three officers crane their necks in our direction. 'Come here, you two,' they demand. The officers get out of the car.

I can hear Gaston in the background saying, 'It's the same guys from the river a few days back. I can't see the third one, though.'

'Yeah, I'm going to get them this time for making me look like a fool in front of the sarge the other day,' Mutton replies.

Loui and I cross the train tracks and head over to the fence line.

Mutton has revenge written all over his face. Gaston and Maze shine their torches around in the dark, looking for Tristan.

'I said come here,' Mutton demands angrily again, this time pointing at the ground with his torch.

'Okay, hold on a second. Come on, Loui, let's walk around the fence. We don't want to get busted for jumping it, do we?' I say loud enough for Mutton to hear.

'No,' Loui replies, a big smile on his face.

This short, forty-metre walk gives us an opportunity to talk between ourselves for a moment. It takes us less than a minute or two, but for Mutton it must feel like ten or fifteen minutes.

As we are approaching him, I can see he is really annoyed with us now, which gives me satisfaction. 'Leave this up to me, and don't say anything,' I instruct Loui.

'Mutton's pretty cranky with us, hey.'

'Where's the third guy gone?' Mutton asks as Gaston and Maze shine their torches over towards the Barina.

They are waving them around like Star Wars light sabres.

'Yes, where is that other fella that was with you the other day…the white lad, Tristan?' Mutton demands. He takes a step closer, as if he can't quite see our faces.

'Umm, he went to see his friend outside the pub,' I say.

And we all turn our heads to see if Tristan is among the crowd that is still hanging around.

'Which one you let off an explosive?' Mutton demands, turning the blinding torch beam onto our faces.

'That wasn't us,' I say. 'You just happened to be driving past when someone from the pub did it. We don't have any explosives.'

Mutton waits for Loui to say something, but Loui just looks him in the eye. Eventually, Mutton drops the beam of light towards his shoes. 'If I hear any reports of you lot being involved with explosives, I'll come down on you like a ton of bricks and make your lives a living nightmare.'

'Yeah, well, we only came down here to have a quiet drink and catch up with some old friends.'

From the police car, the radio starts transmitting. 'R17. There has been a report of an alarm that has been activated on Rowlands Road in the industrial area. Please attend immediately, do you copy?'

It is Dickinson on the other end.

Gaston walks over to respond to the call and informs the sergeant what they are up to. He explains about the loud explosion and how it came from our direction when we drove by and how they thought it best to investigate.

'Yeah, yeah, we've had those reports come in and the pub owner from the Collie Hotel has banned the person for the night and sent him home. I think you should leave them alone now. That's an order. There are much more pressing matters to attend to than wasting any more valuable police time and resources on those guys, Gaston,' replies Dickerson with annoyance on the two-way.

'Roger that, sergeant.' Gaston nervously puts the receiver down and updates Mutton on the sergeant's orders. Then he rubs below his nostrils a couple of times with his index finger and looks at me. 'Okay, guys, we have to head off now,' he says. 'Have a good night and don't drink too much. We'll be patrolling this area all night.'

Loui and I walk back around the fence and cross over the tracks. We are almost halfway across the gravel parklands when the cops pull up next to where I've parked the Barina. The spotlight from the patrol car is shining all over it. The officers get out and point their torches through the windows. Loui and I just look on in wonder before spinning around.

'Oi, what the fuck are you cunts up to now?' I yell at the top of my voice.

A couple of torches shine in our direction. Loui and I sprint towards the cops and jump straight over the fence, knowing this will really shit them off. We race towards them as if we are going to tackle them all to the ground.

'What are you doing now?' I demand, trying to catch my breath.

'We're just checking that your car is secure,' Mutton replies from the other side of the Barina, shining the torch over the roof straight into my face.

'Well, it is fucken secure, and even if it wasn't, I don't need you checking my car out. I thought you had sergeant's orders to leave us alone.'

'The driver's door was unlocked,' Mutton argues back. 'So I just locked it for you. How about being a little more grateful?'

The cops make their way back to the patrol car and Mutton sits in the front, shining his torch on his lap and making a few more notes. Loui checks the passenger side of the Barina while I go round to the driver's side and the hatch to make sure they're still locked.

'By the way,' Mutton calls out, 'your vehicle is unregistered.'

'No, it bloody isn't, it still has another week on it, then I get two weeks on the road after the expiry date and another two weeks off the road before I must reregister it. So technically I still have three weeks on the road before I can no longer drive it. Don't tell me how the law works because I already know.'

Mutton winds up his window, and the police car reverses and takes off. Loui and I wait at the back of the Barina until they have sped away down the street.

'Come on, Loui. Let's go and see where Tristan is, the fucken asshole.'

'He's probably spending all the money on himself,' Loui replies.

'That cunt fucken owes us a few drinks.'

We find Tristan at the bar, chatting up a barmaid three times his age and manoeuvre our way through the crowd over to him.

'We'll have whatever he's just ordered for himself. The drinks are all on Tristan tonight,' I say to the barmaid.

She looks at Tristan and smiles, then turns to Loui. 'Do you have any ID on you, sweetie?' she asks, raising her eyebrows.

Loui reaches into his wallet and pulls out some ID.

The barmaid looks at it and passes it back. 'Sorry, honey, by law I have to ask anyone who looks younger than eighteen, it's my job, I do hope you understand. My name is Christine, by the way.'

'Do you want to check mine, Christine?' I ask and flash my licence in front of her face.

'Nah, you're all right, my darling.' She grabs two empty glasses and fills them with Emu Bitter from the tap. 'That'll be $9, thank you, cutie pie.'

Tristan pushes a $20 note her way, sits down on the closest stool and spins around to face us. 'What took you two so long…and what happened with the police?' he asks. 'Did they end up coming back for us?' He takes a long swig of his beer and looks back and forth at Loui and me, waiting for one of us to answer.

'Yeah, they came back and asked where you were. I said you were catching up with a friend outside the pub.'

We fill him in on what happened.

'Fucken cops, that's why I took off. I couldn't be bothered talking to them cunts, hey,' he says. 'All I really wanted was to have a nice cold beer and have a good night out.' Tristan raises his glass and finishes off his beer.

When Christine reappears, he flings three fingers up high to catch her attention. 'Three more thanks, Christine,' he says, pushing his empty glass towards her side of the counter with his free hand.

I'm scouring the crowd in the bar when I notice Bratt on the other side of the island-shaped counter. He is swaying to and fro like he is trying to balance on one foot in a rubber dingy during a massive swell. His face is glowing red, and he has not noticed us come in.

'Look who's over there, Loui.'

We finish our dregs and place our glasses on the counter. Then I grab our two fresh beers off the bar and pass one to Loui.

'You coming over to see Bratt, Tristan, or are you too busy here?' I ask, while pointing across the room with my thumb at Bratt.

'Yeah, I wonder if he's brought some dope with him.'

'Bratt always has dope on him.'

When I'm standing alongside Bratt, I stick him in the ribs with my index finger. 'Give us everything you got, or I'll have your guts for garters,' I growl.

Bratt spins around to see who it is. 'Hey, look who's here…it's Luke and his merry men,' he laughs. 'Glad you guys finally made it. I started drinking around lunchtime with Miley, then we had an argument about me coming out here tonight to catch up with you. Arrr, I'm so fucken trashed, hey. Do you want a joint with me?' Bratt slurs while hanging off my shoulder.

'Does your famous jacaranda weed only come from Collie? That's a yes, in layman's terms, mate,' I say, trying to confuse him a little.

'Who's the best one of you three to roll a joint?' Bratt asks, as he pulls out a bag of weed from his shirt pocket.

'That'll be me,' I say.

He hands me the bag. 'Yeah, Luke of course. He rolls rollies as if they come straight from a factory.'

I roll the joint and shove the bag back in Bratt's shirt pocket. When I pass him the joint, he sticks it behind his ear and tilts his head sideways, like he's trying to drain water out of his ear.

'Come on, let's go out the front and smoke this then.' Bratt sways into the person behind him.

'Hey, be careful, you fucken cocksucker,' says the guy who has just lost half his drink down the back of Bratt's shirt.

'Ewww, I'm sorry, Cliffy. You want to come out for a puff of the old magic dragon with us, bro?' Bratt reaches back and pulls his wet shirt free from his shoulder blades.

'Nah, I'm right, Bratt. And my name's not fucken Cliffy, ya drunken rodeo clown, it's Cliff, and I'm not ya bro, either. And by the way, cockhead, you owe me another beer.'

'Yeah, yeah, yeah, all right, Cliffy.'

Bratt turns away, but Cliff shoves him hard in the back. He almost trips into someone standing alongside, but fortunately Loui and I quickly grab a hold of him.

'Oi, watch out, you fucken dickhead,' I snarl at Cliff.

Cliff looks down his nose at me. 'Fuck off, ya black coon,' he growls.

A bouncer glances over in our direction, aware the tension is building around us. He strides over. 'Is everything all right here, Bratt? Do you know these Aboriginals?' the bouncer asks.

'Yes, it's just perfectly perfect. Absolutely spot on. These Aboriginals, as you put it, Tim, are my bloody mates, all right,' Bratt huffs.

'Okay, Bratt, that's enough,' Tim replies.

Bratt hiccups. It looks like he's only moments away from throwing up everywhere. Tim steps back a little out of Bratt's firing line and looks back and forth at Loui and me. It is a look I have seen many times. He is just looking for any excuse to throw us out of the pub for the remainder of the night.

'Yeah, we're Bratt's friends. I've known Bratt for the past seven years. We'll just take him outside now, so he can get a bit of fresh air,' I say to break his concentration.

'That sounds like a great idea.' the bouncer says, heading over to the door to hold it open for us.

'Cliff is a fucken idiot, Luke, don't worry about him,' Bratt mumbles as we help him through the bar. 'Even when we were at school together, no one liked him, and certainly no one likes him now.'

Just as we step onto the footpath, a police car drives past slowly. Mutton cranes his neck, looking straight at us.

'Did you see that cop again, Loui?'

'Yeah, he really doesn't like you, Luke, eh?'

'Nah, it's because they don't like it when you make them look like idiots and can prove them wrong.'

'He's the new cuntstable, Cuntstable Hogget!' Bratt slurs. 'He's been in everyone's face here since his transfer from Perth, a couple of months ago.' Bratt hawks up a huge pile of phlegm and aims it in the direction of the police car. But as he goes to fire it in their direction, he doesn't give it enough oomph and it falls short on the ground in front of him.

'Where's Tristan?' Loui suddenly asks. 'I thought he was right behind us.'

'The cheeky little fucker is probably trying to fuck Christine in the disabled toilets by now.'

'I saw him heading back to the bar when the bouncer came over,' Bratt slurs.

'Ha, well, I'd be guessing that he's in the toilet right now with his cock buried up to his balls in Christine's pussy,' Loui says.

We all break out into laughter. But unlike Tristan, Loui and I aren't that interested in wasting our money on girls, just for the sake of a one-night stand. We're much too preoccupied with feeding our addictions, which for us, always come first.

By this stage, a few others are outside, all smoking joints.

'Hey, Bratt, how the fuck are ya, dude? You look like you're fucken hammered,' one of them says, as he staggers towards Bratt and clings to his shoulder.

'That is an understatement, and, for your information, I'm not a dude, dude…a dude is a camel's dick, ya faggot.'

They both nearly end up falling flat on their backs, but fortunately for them, the pub wall keeps them upright until they regain their footing.

'Where's my fucken lighter?' Bratt asks, fumbling around in his pockets. 'It's always the bloody case, when you're looking for something, it's in the last pocket that you look in, isn't it?' he says, when he finally finds it. He pulls the joint out from behind his ear.

'Yeah, you never have enough pockets until you want to find something, then suddenly it's like you have a shitload of 'em,' I agree.

Bratt, Loui, and I are passing around the joint when Bratt starts up again.

'Quit your bloody leaning all over me? I'm not a fucken bandit here, to hold you up, all right,' he says as he gives the guy a hard shove away from his space.

He almost falls face first on the footpath in front of Bratt but one of his mates manages to catch him in the nick of time.

We pass the joint back and forth among us, until the guys who are hanging around realise we will not be passing it to them and head up to the next pub.

'Last drinks,' a voice hollers from inside the pub.

'Shit, we've been out here for ages. Let's get back inside quick.' Bratt peers through the window at the crowded bar, then makes his way back in.

Just then, Tristan appears out of the crowd. He looks like he has been in a fight. His face is glowing, his hair is all ruffled up and his shirt is stretched out of place.

'What happened to you?' I ask.

A smile spreads across his face, and he turns his head towards Christine, who is behind the counter. Christine smiles back at him and resumes pulling beers.

'Oh, I see,' I say, shaking my head.

We are among the last to leave. The streets are quiet, but we take the back way to our campsite out on the Bibbulmun Track. We all squeeze into the tent and, after a session and a rollie, fall straight to sleep.

Next morning, we shove Bob back into the tent, jump into the Barina and set off into Collie again. Red Rooster is just opening when we pull into town. We each order a quarter chicken and chip pack at the drive-through and head to a picnic table by the river to eat our meals. We end up hanging around the river for most of the day because we do not have enough fuel to be just driving around.

Late in the afternoon, we drive back to our campsite and light the fire to cook dinner. Just on dusk, a vehicle comes quietly down the track towards our camp. It is the police again. They switch the spotlights on, and Sergeant Dickerson and Constable Mutton get out of the car. The sergeant gives Mutton the nod to take control of the situation.

'You can't camp here. You have to leave right now,' he shouts like a hyped-up chihuahua barking at a screen door. 'This is a walking trail.'

'Well, whe–'

But before I can ask where we can legally camp, Mutton interrupts. 'I've told you already. You must go, now!'

He is starting to give me the shits.

'Yeah, you already said that. There's no need to be rude. I was jus–'

He cuts me off again, so I decide to address the sergeant.

'Is there anywhere around here where you suggest that we camp?'

As I am speaking, Mutton tries to cut me off again. 'We'll issue you with a fine if you don't leave immediately.'

I look him straight in the eye. 'I wasn't talking to you, constable, I was talking to the sergeant here. He's a lot wiser than you and he's been around for way longer. He also would know a lot of places where we can camp. You, on the other hand, are only a young officer with no compassion, and not the faintest idea.' I raise my eyebrows at him, then turn back to the sergeant.

'You better go and sit in the car, constable,' Dickerson says. 'Start filling out the report. I'll have this one from here.'

Mutton looks like a sulky school kid, but he does as he is ordered.

'Please accept my sincere apologies. Hogget, err um, err ha ha, sorry, I mean, Mutton, can get carried away at times. He's still only new to the force.'

By now, Mutton's sitting in the car with the interior light on, so that he can see what he is writing.

'Nah, it's okay, sergeant. He's had it in for us since he saw us down at the river the other day.'

We all laugh. Mutton realises he is the butt of a joke and glares at me.

'There are a couple of places I recommend,' Dickerson says. ' One is out near Wellington Dam, where you'll be well away from running into Mutton again. Stay on the road, instead of pulling off into the parking area at the dam, then keep driving to the top of the next hill. There's an old unused gravel pit up there on the right where you can camp for as long as you like. There's also a place just the other side of the river, if you want to be closer to Collie, but I don't think Mutton will leave you be.'

'Thank you, sergeant. That was all I was trying to ask from the start, but Mutton just yipped in, like a whinging dog. I don't know how you put up with him.'

'Yeah, I don't know either. But I have no choice. Constable Mutton has been posted here from headquarters in Perth. Unfortunately, I have to follow orders like everyone else in the force. Anyway,' he smiled, almost pissing himself with laughter, 'I better get babyface back. It's getting close to his bedtime.'

Dickerson opens the car door and puts one foot up into the floor well. 'You have till ten a.m. tomorrow morning to move on from here, okay, lads?'

He starts the vehicle up. The tyres spin on the spot, until they manage to get some traction.

'It must be time for some bloody cones,' I say as the car does a three-point turn and drives away, leaving us in dark of the evening sky.

We enjoy a nice big session in the Barina, and by the time we have finished smoking the last cone, it is like we are sitting in a hotbox. The smoke was that dense, we could cut through it with a machete.

28

Lost Campsite

Regretfully, we pack up our belongings once again and head out to the site past Wellington Dam and set up camp in the gravel pit alongside the road. It looks like it has no't been used in years, so we know we will be okay there. The only problem is, by the time we get there, we have run out of petrol and it is a while to my payday.

'Okay, dig deep into your pockets,' I say. 'I have $1.70. What about you two?' I place the coins on the bonnet and start searching through the Barina.

Loui and Tristan come up with a few more coins.

'Arrgh, $4.55. It's fuck all. At least we can get a couple of litres, though. If we can get back to Collie, I think Bratt will run us back out here,' I say. 'But that's roughly forty kilometres away.'

In the back of my mind, I know it is close to an eight-hour walk, based on my past experiences of averaging five kilometres per hour.

'Someone might feel sorry for us and give a lift,' Loui replies.

'I highly doubt that. The only people around here who'd help us would be Bratt or Snappy. But there is a servo at the end of Henty Road.'

The petrol station is about fifteen kilometres down a long steep descent. The only problem is, I am the only one who knows how to get there because there are a few different roads you can take. Heading downhill will not be so bad but heading back up will be tedious.

'What if we walk back to Wellington Dam, and see if someone there can take us to Collie?' Loui suggests. 'At least we can refill our water bottles. And if there's no one to help, then I reckon we should just head down to that servo. I'll come with you, Luke. Tristan can stay here with Bob and mind the stuff.'

Loui gets the big water container. 'There's bugger all water here,' he says, 'only about 1.5 litres left, so I'll share it out for us.'

Loui pours it equally into three Coke bottles so we can have one each. Once that is done, I grab the jerrycan and Loui and I start walking towards Collie. A couple of vehicles cruise straight past, as if we are invisible. No one stops for us. They all just keep their foot to the floor and speed past.

Once we are out on the bitumen, we try hitching a ride as we make our way towards Wellington Dam. After failing to flag down a lift from the side of the road, I give standing in the middle a go. But drivers just dodge me. I even try lying down, covering myself in dust so it looks like I have been in a bad car accident. Still, there is not even a drop in revs as cars keep roaring by.

'This is not going to work, is it? We're going to have to walk all the way,' I say, glumly.

'Yeah, let's just keep moving,' Loui replies.

'I'm fucken sick of Tristan,' I say, a few hundred metres on. 'He's fucked up things for us everywhere we've taken him.'

'Yeah, he was fun at the start, but he's very possessive about anything he buys, and he never gets any food either.'

I know we should no't have said yes to him coming along with us, but when he asked, all I thought about was his contribution and how much he would be chucking in. Then, once he joined us, I could not leave him. He was like a wounded soldier that I felt responsible for.

'I thought he might liven things up and make it easier for us, but you're right, he's very stingy. I asked him for some tobacco the other day and he gave me the smallest pinch. I looked him in the eye, as if to say, "Is that it?", but he just closed the packet and went on doing whatever he was doing.'

We reach Wellington Dam, hoping someone there will offer us a ride.

But everyone we approach just turns away and gets on with their business.

We fill up our water bottles and decide we better head back to our camp up the hill because it is getting late. So, after a five-minute break, we set off. It has taken us about an hour to walk to the dam but that was downhill. Now our energy is really flagging as we make our way up the steady incline.

After about an hour, we are sure the campsite is close but none of the landscape looks familiar. We keep on walking for about another half an hour.

'We must have walked past it,' I say to Loui.

'Yeah, I think you might be right.'

'We should turn back then.'

Our anxiety gets the better of us at this point, and before long, we are tossing our empty water bottles into the bush to lighten our load. We are almost back at Wellington Dam when we realise that once again, we have gone too far, so we turn around and head back up the hill again. By the time we have done this a few times, the sun is disappearing below the treeline and we are absolutely stuffed.

Finally, we give up. We can barely move our legs, so we decide to walk into the bush off the side of the bitumen and sleep the night under the stars.

Then, lo and behold, we walk straight into our camp. Tristan and Bob are both fast asleep and the tent smells strongly of dope. Tristan stirs, then sits up when he realises we are back.

'How did you guys go?' he asks.

'Nah, no good. No one wanted to help us, everyone just avoided us, fucken racist white fucks,' I say.

That night, we make plans to go in the opposite direction in the morning. There is a service station down that way I have seen before.

Just after ten a.m., after I have had an extra-long sleep to let our bones recover, Loui and I take off once again. Fortunately, it is downhill and after a few hours, we are getting close to the servo.

As we pass a house, I tap Loui in the ribs. By this time, we are walking along like a couple of zombies, and our mouths are parched. 'Look, there's a man sitting in the window of that house. He might be able to help us,' I say, hopefully.

'Yeah, I can see him. Why don't you go and ask him for a lift?'

'Okay, he's looking at us now. Just wait here for me.'

I walk along the veranda and knock three times on the front door, then step to one side and look slyly through the window. The man is no longer sitting in the spot he was before. I cannot hear him either. As I start walking back to Loui, the front door suddenly opens, and the man peers out at me from behind the half-closed door.

'Hello, can I help you?' he asks, looking at me wearily.

'Yes, I hope so. We've run out of petrol just up the hill and I'm wondering if you'd be so kind as to give us a lift to the nearest service station, please.'

'That's no problem. Just wait out the front. I'll put some shoes on and get my car keys.' He closes his front door.

'Well, what did he say?' Loui asks, as the front door opens and the man comes out.

'He's going to give us a lift,' I reply happily.

The man reverses his car out of the driveway and pulls up alongside us.

'Thank you so much for this,' I say. 'My name's Luke, by the way, and this is my brother, Loui.'

'Nice to meet you, young fellas. I'm Geoff.'

'Do many people ask you for help?' Loui asks, making conversation.

It is so good not to be walking.

'Yes, you wouldn't believe how many people run out of fuel along this road. One morning I went to the servo up here to get the morning paper, it was about nine a.m., and I passed a woman sitting in her car right about here.' Geoff points out the location as we go past. 'She was still sitting there when I was on my way back home and I never thought any more about it. Later, I had to post a letter, so I went back down to the servo and the lady was still sitting there. So I pulled up alongside her and wound down my window to see if she was all right.

'What was wrong with her?' I ask.

'Well, I asked her if she was all right and she replied, "Yes, I'm all right, but my car has run out of petrol." I said, "The servo's only a couple of hundred metres down the road there, why didn't you just walk there? I would've only taken you ten minutes to get there and back." Then she points downwards and says, "I would walk if I could, but I was in an accident and both my legs were crushed. They had to be amputated." I was so embarrassed that I hadn't offered to help her sooner.'

'Gee, that's so sad, Geoff,' I say, feeling sorry for the lady.

'I told her not to worry and I did a U-turn and raced straight back home to grab a jerrycan. Then as I got near to her, I pulled up and told her I'd be back in a minute. "Don't worry," she laughed, "I won't be running off anywhere in a hurry." When I got back with some petrol for her, I suggested she pull into the service station. I followed her in my car and filled her petrol tank up for her. I gave her my phone number and told her to keep in touch. That was three years ago, and she still calls me to see how I am going. She is the most compassionate woman I've ever met.'

'You must have felt silly when she told you about her legs,' I say as I unbuckle my seatbelt.

I take the jerrycan and put in the $4.55 worth of petrol in then go inside and pay. Then I jump back into Geoff's car.

'Where did you say your car ran out of petrol? Geoff asks.

'Just up the road here, about five to ten kilometres, pretty much at the top of the hill.'

'Okay, I'll run you fellas back there. It's too far for you to walk now. It'll be dark by the time you get there. Maybe one day you can pass on the favour.'

Geoff takes us all the way to where we parked the Barina.

'Thank you so, so much, Geoff. It's been really good of you,' I say as I get out of his vehicle.

'No problem at all, glad to help you both.' Geoff extends his hand. 'Promise me you boys make it out of here safely, okay.'

'No worries. We'll be heading out of here straight away, thanks to you.'

Geoff waves to Loui, turns his car round and heads back down the hill.

When we reach our tent, Tristan is sitting in the Barina and Bob isn't anywhere to be seen.

Tristan looks up when he hears our footsteps in the gravel. 'Did you get any fuel?' he asks, jumping out of the Barina. 'I wasn't expecting you back for a couple more hours.'

'Yeah, a guy kindly gave us a lift to the servo and dropped us back up here.'

I look through the back window. Bob is asleep on the bench seat, I tap on the window a couple of times and wave my hand at him.

'I got some bad news, Luke,' Tristan starts with a worried look on his face. 'The battery in the Barina is flat. I was only watching the TV.'

I could have wrung his neck there and then; I was that ropeable. My nostrils instantly grew wider and to Tristan and Loui it would have looked like I was chewing on a mouthful of sand.

'For fuck's sake, you know how quickly that flattens the battery. I hope we can get enough traction on this loose gravel to roll start it.'

It takes us a few attempts, but finally the engine kicks over. We throw the tent in the back and take off back to Collie to camp down at the river for the night.

The next day is my payday. As soon as I am up, I tell Loui and Tristan I am sick of camping out. It is taking up too much energy. I have lost so much weight already and we will starve to death if we do not do something soon.

They just nod.

'I'm thinking of going to Adelaide, hey. I've had enough,' I tell them, hoping Tristan will decide he is going to stay in WA.

'Cool, I've always wanted to go to Adelaide,' Tristan says. 'It's funny, till I met you two, the furthest I'd ever been from home was just the other side of Perth once with my dad.'

'I haven't been to SA since I was about nine,' Loui says. 'It'd be great to see Bryce and Mum.'

'Okay then, it's decided. Let's leave all this struggling behind us.'

We shove all our belongings into the Barina, head into Collie, fill up with a full tank of petrol and set off.

29

Adelaide

On 10 September 2002, we roll into Adelaide at about three p.m. after a thirty-hour non-stop drive, fuelled by sheer determination.

A few weeks passed since arriving in Adelaide and I was now eager to get my own place once again. This time it was going to be in Adelaide and I was excited about it. After speaking with Loui about the idea, we went in search of a cheap rental.

We ended up finding one in Davoren Park, twenty kilometres further out from Mum's place. Loui stayed with me for a couple of months. We lived in a semi-detached house alongside our friendly neighbour Keith, who we got to know quite quickly after he had practically invited us around to his place for some beers on the first night we got there.

It was good to sit down with Keith, listening to his yarns and getting pissed. Before long we were all feeling the effects of alcohol and some dope he had also supplied, when several objects on his mantelpiece caught Loui's eye. After quietly studying them for a few minutes, curiosity got the better of him.

'What are those things, Keith?'

'Arr, well, have either of you guys heard of trinitrotoluene before?' Keith asked as he stood up and staggered between the couches, catching his knee on the edge of the coffee table in the centre of the small lounge room. 'Fucks me off when that happens,' he slurred.

Soon he had one of the items in his hand and passed it to Loui on his way back to his seat. 'Can you answer the question now, Loui?'

'Is it dynamite?' Loui answered.

'Yeah, more commonly known as TNT.' Keith rejoiced in his sluggish voice, as if he had an evil plan.

Loui held onto the TNT, studying it more intently. 'What sort of damage can this one do?' he asked as Keith extended his open hand, taking back the TNT.

'This one is only capable of blowing a couple of bricks away, but that one up the end there can take down a small building like a house or office,' Keith replied as he got up and picked up an empty can of beer from the coffee table. He walked out to his kitchen and filled up the empty can with water and returned.

'You want to see something?'

'Yeah,' we both replied as we followed him out the front.

On the porch, we stood out like roos in a flat. Either side of us we could see multiple houses, all duplexes like our own and as it was a warm night there must have been close to thirty people all sitting out the fronts of their houses. Keith struck his lighter and ignited the fuse. It sparked like a sparkler as he hovered over the top of the beer can. As he let it go, it caught the side of the can and bounced off to the side and exploded.

BANG!

It was so loud, it sounded like a shotgun going off. The neighbours who had been chattering in the background automatically fell silent as they craned their heads in our direction.

Loui and I quickly made our way back inside. Keith lagged along behind even failing to close the door as he came in. Disappointed in his failure, he walked straight up to the mantelpiece and grabbed another stick of TNT. He stood there for a couple of seconds muttering to it with his back to us.

'Ya coming?' he grunted, as he spun round and suddenly…just for a brief moment…he appeared to be dazed and confused about his surroundings. He had to do a double take to get his bearings as he frowned back and forth at Loui and me. When he came too, he nearly knocked Loui's beer out of his hand with the second stick of TNT he now clasped firmly in a clenched fist as he staggered by.

Because of his careless behaviour or possibly that he was just too out of it to comprehend what was right from wrong any more, we just assumed everyone in this area must be into this sort of stuff, so we just went along with him.

Keith lit the second TNT stick even before he got out the front doorway. Now swaying above the can, he lets go and scores. It was loud but more muffled this time and we inspected he damage to the can under the porch light.

We stood for a split second before realising a police vehicle was approaching. It would have been around nine p.m. because it was dark and the spotlight on top of the patrol car lit up our yard next door, creating shadows from the small melaleuca trees which moved with the patrol car. This would have been confusing to see if anyone was actually running away from the front yard. The patrol pulled into Keith's driveway, while we stayed out the front on the porch so the officers would not enter his property.

'Good evening, fellas, this is Constable Ian Taylor, and I am Constable Dean Phillips. Who resides at this premises?' Phillips continued.

'That'll be me, officer,' Keith slurred.

'We live right next door,' I added.

Phillips took down all Keith's details while Taylor shone his torch around the front area looking for anything that would lead them to the dynamite.

'The reason for the call-out is that we have had reports of explosions coming from this property. Can you shed some light on this for us?' Taylor asked.

Keith was speechless and started mumbling and in the back of my mind all I could think about was us all getting into trouble. Something had to be said before they wanted to go into his house and look around, so I jumped in quick.

'That's why we're all out the front here. It's the second time now that someone has let explosions go off out the front of Keith's door, and every time we come out, the person races off and we lose sight of them.'

'Did you happen to see what they were wearing?' Phillips asked.

'Yes, the person I saw would have been about my height and I'm five foot nine. He was slim build with a fair complexion and had a goatee. He was wearing a black hoodie and black tracksuit pants that had two white pinstripes down the outer side of each leg. He also wore a black baseball cap with the letters UCLA in bold white text across the front, and white sneakers, possibly a pair of Michael Jordan's,' I added, knowing that I'd described over three-quarters of the population from the northern parts of Adelaide.

Loui and Keith confirmed my story, and the officers just took notes.

'We best do a sweep of the area ASAP, Ian,.' Phillips instructs while closing his notebook. 'If you hear any more explosions tonight, please report this straight away to the Elizabeth police station, otherwise the perpetrators will continue to get away with this kind of stuff until someone gets seriously hurt.'

'No problems there,' Keith slurred.

Both officers returned to the patrol vehicle and were soon on their way on a wild goose chase.

'Your quick wit saved me, Luke, thank you. If those cunts had of came inside and found the other sticks, I would have been carted away for sure. I would have never thought of blaming the explosions on someone else either, so golden stars all round for you, mate. Anyway fellas, that's enough excitement for one day, so I'm going to turn in now for some beauty sleep,' Keith slurred as he picked up the empty cans from the coffee table.

'Yeah, no worries, mate,' I replied as Loui and I stood up, shook Keith's free hand and let him be.

Epilogue

It was so good to spend time with my family in South Australia again, after nearly seven years of not seeing them. Mum had her own place in Adelaide at Para Hills, about twenty kilometres north of the CBD. Bryce was living there with her. Nothing much had changed in Adelaide since the last time I was there, apart from everyone growing older. Many faces were familiar to me, but I still had to try hard to remember who some of them belonged to. But they were all so happy to see me and Loui. Septembers have been kind to me ever since.

Loui stayed until Dansan came down from Darwin to visit. We went straight to Mum's place and it was the first time since 1995 that all us brothers had been together. Eventually, when Dansan headed back to Darwin a week later, Loui chose to go with him. He stayed with Dansan for a while before joining the rest of his family out at Numbulwar.

After Loui went north, I threw in my rental and moved back in with Mum at Para Hills. About a year later, I got a job with a brain injuries service, assisting a client on weekends when his regular care worker was unavailable. This work involved meeting the guy at the sobering up unit and then heading down to the Adelaide markets to find a café where he could have some breakfast. After he'd finished, I'd give him his daily ration of tobacco, and he'd be on his way.

It was good being able to help this guy, and after a couple of months I was offered a casual position. I really enjoyed this work. Helping people gave me a great sense of satisfaction, and the Indigenous clients often requested my assistance. This wasn't because I was gullible or let them run wild; they just respected me as a black fella who was trying his hardest to support them.

Around the middle of 2003, I was offered a full-time position at the unit and became a member of the permanent staff. For the first time in my life, I was earning a half-decent income, and it felt like I was slowly moving forward.

After two and a half years, I applied for another job, wanting to do more than just offering clients a place to sober up. I got work at Nunkuwarrin Yunti in Adelaide's CBD, and took up two positions there. One was with a homeless team. A nurse and I would drive around the Adelaide CBD and surrounding parklands looking for clients. We did basic medical checks and sent any severe cases to hospital for further assistance. The other position was also outreach, in the clean needle program. I checked clients' injecting sites, educated them about needle use, provided clean needles in exchange for their used ones, and referred them to the nurse for further check-ups if needed.

A couple of years after I moved back to SA, Bob passed away. I dug him a grave out the back of Mum's house in Para Hills and placed photos of everyone in the family around him, propped up in the soil. Then I gently lowered him into the hole while tears ran down my face onto his snout.

I asked Mum to find her Slim Dusty CD, the one with the song 'Leave Him in the Long Yard' on it. I opened a can of beer, placed it alongside Bob in the grave with him and pressed 'play'. As the song started, I cracked another beer for myself and held it up. I closed my eyes, said goodbye and took a big swig. When the song finished, I sadly buried my four-legged friend. 'I will see you on the bus when it stops to pick me up for the adventure beyond this lifetime,' I said.

In June 2007, my position at Nunkuwarrin Yunti was terminated. The reasons given were breaching the contract I had signed with them and misuse of the internet. The truth was I had told someone from another organisation to fuck off, and they reported me to our CEO. It was something I could have avoided, and I only have myself to blame.

After that mishap, I decided to study nursing and enrolled at the University of South Australia. I was still eager to help people and knew that a certificate would expand my horizons and help me secure work in the future.

In September 2007, I was getting ready to head into university to finish off my week of studies, when I realised I couldn't see anything out of my right eye. I gave classes a miss for the day and went straight to the optometrist instead.

They ran a couple of basic eye tests but couldn't find anything wrong, so the optometrist suggested I see a neurologist at the Lyell McEwin Hospital. I called straightaway and made an appointment. A week later I went in for an MRI (magnetic resonance imaging).

'There is something there, for sure,' the specialist told me. 'We'll forward this on to our neurologist. He'll take a proper look at it.'

A week later, I went to see the neurologist. He looked over the results, read the notes to himself and suggested another MRI in six months' time. 'It looks like you could have multiple sclerosis, but we won't know for certain until the second MRI.'

'Will I get my sight back?' I asked, concerned.

'More than likely, but you'll always have cloudy vision in that eye, I'm afraid.'

Walking out the room, I felt like I'd been kicked in the guts, alone and defenceless. I put my nursing degree on hold and researched as much about MS as I could. I went to the library and took out every book they had there about it, and I read whatever I could find on the internet.

During my research, and looking into what might have given me MS, I stumbled upon some stuff online regarding the Hep B vaccine. I had only just finished the treatment three months before I lost my vision and wondered was it connected somehow. It did say the vaccine could give you up to thirty per cent chance of getting MS but since then, nothing suggests this is the case. Either way, I refuse injections because I was doing fine beforehand and now, I have MS. Whether there is a connection or not I'm not a professional to say for sure, but I do have the right to decide what I put into my body.

In March 2008, I returned for my second MRI. A few weeks later, I went back to see the neurologist.

'The results of this MRI have confirmed what I expected,' he said bluntly.

I stared blankly at him.

'There are treatments which can help MS sufferers from relapsing,' he said, turning back to face his computer. But almost instantly spinning back round for my answer.

I shook my head. 'No, from what I can tell, there's no cure and the treatments only make sufferers more reliant on the medical system. Maybe one day when there is a cure, I'll ask for help.'

The neurologist was furious. He spun round in his chair to face his computer.

'Get out of my room,' he said. 'I have no time for people like you, I'm too busy, I have the whole of the northern suburbs to see. Please leave right now.'

I made my way to the counter to sort things out with the admin staff, and then walked out the front door, never to return to his surgery.

After my diagnosis, Mum moved in to help me out until I got on my feet. I had fallen into a pit of sorrow, and she tried her hardest to stay positive for me.

I had started to think that my life was as good as over, but at the beginning of 2010, I met Tamane, a truly magnificent woman who had her head screwed on properly. It wasn't long before I knew she was the person I intended to spend the rest of my days with. Tamane helped me not take life for granted, as I had done before and after being diagnosed with MS.

These days, I still get shooting pains in my head from time to time; it feels like someone is driving a skewer deep into my temples. But I don't give in. As I like to say, 'I have MS, MS doesn't have me.'

Soon Tamane and I brought into our lives our much-loved daughter, Summer. I do all I can to make the most of every day with them both, although occasionally I find myself snapping at them. I really regret this nasty streak. It always feels as if Father is striking out from inside me.

I have kept in contact with Shain. He has always been there for me, ever since we met that day at boarding school back in 1988. Even though we bump shoulders sometimes, as friends often do, we have never taken our friendship for granted. He is now co-owner, with his partner Louise, of a jewellery business in Geraldton. When I told him I wanted him to make wedding rings for Tamane and me, he was ecstatic and got straight into it. He kept us updated on the progress of the rings by sending photos every step of the way.

I married Tamane and Summer was honoured to be our flower girl. She showered us with petal confetti that we made from flowers in our garden. We were over the moon with happiness.

After twenty years, my good friend Rod and I still stay in touch, calling each other once or twice a year. I know, even today, I could count on him for help if I ever got stuck on the side of the road in his part of WA.

I lost contact with Snappy and Bran, but if I ever end up in WA again, I will try to find them, as well as others I know over there. And I will take my family to see all those places that are special to me.

Father happily gets on with his life in Western Australia with his wife Suzy. I hear from him a couple of times a year, mainly for birthdays and other festive occasions. He has showed me how much I mean to him by dropping everything for everyone else and travelling the entire nation from one side to the other for them.

He practically drove pasts my front door a couple of years ago when his old mum passed away and he came over from WA for that. He was the one who suggested that he drop off some old newspaper his mum saved for me for my twenty-first but then later – much, much later – I found out he'd been and gone. What more can I say?

I would call Mum on the mobile usually once a month until recently when I tried her number was disconnected. It must have been a sign because the very next day I received a text from Bryce informing me Mum was in hospital. I called and spoke to her and she was happy to be in hospital and said she would get all the care she needed.

Later, I spoke with the staff and gave them my number and to contact me ASAP if Mums condition worsened.

With this information and it being the last weekend of the school holidays, I took my wife and daughter to the Flinders Ranges, Mum's country. A few long hours later, we were in Hawker, the place Mum was born. We drove out another fifty kilometres to where we chose to stay for the next two nights, at a little western-style stone building called the Brachina Hut.

We travelled all through Brachina Gorge and saw loads of nice places and the animals were all living in harmony. It was like a garden of Eden. On the second day we went to Wilpena Pound via Ikara National Park and that was special to feel like you're flying through the mountains. That night, the wind howled like I had never heard it even though there was bugger all wind. By the time we got into Hawker that morning, we were all looking forward to going back home to the Adelaide Hills.

The whole forty-eight hours we'd been in the Flinders I had no reception on my mobile but when I picked it up again, it was sad news,

Mum passed away on 17 October 2022 and lives on in all her children's eyes. She meant the world to me and always will.

Bryce still works as a cleaner in a cheese factory in Victoria, and is happily married to his loving wife Keke. They have a couple of kids, who they cherish.

My sister Bidjid and I don't speak and the last time it was the same as every other time, with Bidjid threatening to kill everyone as per normal. She lives with her partner Herman in Victoria, so I was informed by Mum.

Vonn, Zoann and Loui all live out at Numbulwar. I don't hear from them at all but, from what Dansan has told me, Zoann works at the Numbulwar shop and Loui lives out on his mother's homeland.

Dansan is living in Darwin and he has been in and out of the men's shelters for several years and struggles with mental illness.

Tristan moved back to WA and I have never seen or heard from him again. He did go back to Rod's place, according to Rod, so I guess he is happily reunited with his old crew.

In 2016, I took up studies and completed Certificate 3 in Conservation and Land Management at the end of 2018, then I continued to do the Diploma in the same field, which I have had to place on hold at the end of January 2021 due to gaining employment with the federal government, an opportunity for which I am thoroughly thankful. After a ten-month full-time contract working for Services Australia, I was offered a casual position, as was everyone else in my group of twenty workmates. I turned down the casual employment as I wanted to gain full-time permanent work.

I walked out happy knowing I made the right choice for my future and was waiting to gain full-time work elsewhere. It was not until recently that I found out my former team leader was giving me a bad reference stating that she would not employ me again. I was not happy about this because I did everything they wanted me to do.

My Diploma fizzled out as TafeSA no longer provide that unit, so I guess that was a waste of my time, but wasn't everything?

What will be my next adventure, I wonder.

About the Author

Luke Pomery is the third-oldest child in his family of six siblings. He was born in the Barossa Valley at a small country town called Angaston in South Australia. His Aboriginal heritage comes from his mother's side of the family, which are the Adnyamathanha peoples (from the Flinders Ranges area in South Australia). He identifies himself as a black fella, even though his father is a white man.

Growing up in the country for most of his life, he spent the first few years out at the Barossa Valley, then briefly stayed in the state capital, Adelaide, before moving out to Monarto South in the Adelaide Hills. He also had extended stays at Numbulwar, a small remote Aboriginal community located in East Arnhem Land on the Western coastline of the Gulf of Carpentaria. Late December of 1984, he and his siblings moved to Western Australia to help run the recently purchased family sheep station. He returned to South Australia in the spring of 2002.

He now lives in the Adelaide Hills. He believes his upbringing has made him practical and resourceful – if it is man-made, he can probably fix it. He describes himself as a placid person, but he won't stand back to be walked over. Others may say he is a humble man who doesn't ask for much in return.

This story reflects his own view of his life, even though other family members may recall it differently. He strongly believes that if they want to share their version of their own experiences, they should do so.

www.ingramcontent.com/pod-product-compliance
Lightning Source LLC
Chambersburg PA
CBHW021054080526
44587CB00010B/249